The New Atrium

The McGraw-Hill Building Types Series

Wells
Gentle Architecture (1981)

Watson & Labs
Climatic Design (1982)

Dickinson
Adding On: An Artful Guide to Affordable Residential Additions (1985)

Dibner & Dibner-Dunlap
Building Additions Design Manual (1985)

Barr & Broudy
Designing to Sell: The Art of Retail Store Planning and Design (1986)

Bednar
The New Atrium (1986)

Dickinson
The Small House: An Artful Guide to Affordable Residential Design (1986)

Talcott, Hepler, and Wallach
The Home Planners' Guide to Residential Design (1986)

Wakabayashi
Earthquake-Resistant Building Design (1986)

Taranath
Structural Analysis and Design of Tall Buildings (1987)

The New Atrium

Michael J. Bednar, AIA

School of Architecture, University of Virginia

MCGRAW-HILL BOOK COMPANY

New York   St. Louis   San Francisco   Auckland   Bogotá
Hamburg   Johannesburg   London   Madrid
Mexico   Montreal   New Delhi   Panama
Paris   São Paulo   Singapore
Sydney   Tokyo   Toronto

To my father, Peter Bednar
(1916–1980)

Library of Congress Cataloging in Publication Data

Bednar, Michael J.
    The new atrium.
    (McGraw-Hill building types series)
    Includes index.
    1. Atrium buildings — United States — Case studies.
2. Atriums — United States. I. Title. II. Series.
NA4160.B43 1986   720   85-12733
ISBN 0-07-004275-6

1234567890   HAL/HAL   898765

ISBN 0-07-004275-6

*The editors for this book were Joan Zseleczky and Jim Bessent,
the designer was Naomi Auerbach, and the production
supervisor was Teresa F. Leaden. It was set in Auriga
by Progressive Typographers, Inc.*

Printed and bound by Halliday Lithograph.

Contents

5 Design Development   101

II Design Studies

Acknowledgments

The study upon which *The New Atrium* was based and the writing of the book itself could not have been accomplished without the opportunities available at the University of Virginia School of Architecture. A major portion of the research was undertaken during the fall of 1981 while I was a Sesquicentennial Associate at the Center for Advanced Study. The availability of resources at the university's Fiske Kimball Fine Arts Library has supported my work throughout. Comments and support by my colleagues at the School of Architecture have been invaluable, particularly the encouragement and help of Richard Guy Wilson. In addition, the opportunity to test many of the ideas contained herein with students provided the impetus needed to clarify them. Special thanks go to Joan Baxter for her patient translation of scribbles into manuscript and to Janet Cutright for her efficiency in carrying out the demanding requirement for correspondence. James Pandula deserves special gratitude for his efforts in producing many of the precise drawings throughout the book.

Nor would this book have been possible without the willing support and cooperation of the architects whose work appears in it. They provided the information about their buildings, the necessary drawings (many of them in finished form), and many of the photographs. To these architects, and to the staffs in their firms, goes a special acknowledgment of gratitude. Since it comes from the architects themselves, no explicit source has been given for information regarding the projects in the text. These architectural firms include the following:

Anderson Notter Finegold Inc.
Arthur Cotton Moore/Associates
Arvid Elness Architects
Beran & Shelmire Architects
Breger Terjesen Associates
Cannon Design
Cope/Linder Associates
Graham Gund Associates
H2L2 Architects/Planners
Hellmuth, Obata & Kassabaum
Holle, Lin & Shogren, Architects
Hugh Stubbins & Associates
I. M. Pei & Partners

John Andrews International
John Burgee Architects with Philip Johnson
John Carl Warnecke & Associates
John Portman & Associates
John Sharratt Associates
Kevin Roche John Dinkeloo & Associates
Kohn Pedersen Fox Associates
Leo A. Daly Planners/Architects/Engineers
Lockwood, Andrews & Newnam, Architects
Louis I. Kahn Archives
Marshall D. Meyers, Architect
Mitchell/Giurgola Architects
Morris/Aubry Architects
Murphy/Jahn Architects
Office of the California State Architect
Rowe Holmes Barnett Architects, Inc.
Skidmore, Owings & Merrill — Chicago, Washington, New York,
    San Francisco
Swanke Hayden Connell Architects
The Architects Collaborative
College of Architecture and Urban Planning, University of Wash-
    ington
Thompson, Ventulett Stainback & Associates
Welton Beckett Associates

Sources for photographs, drawings, and other data are given in photograph credits in legends and in notes at the ends of chapters. They
are many and include publishers, archives, research organizations,
building owners, governmental agencies, libraries, and individuals.
In particular, I must acknowledge the contribution of the many pho-
tographers whose work as represented herein has set a high standard
of visual quality. Other sources deserving special mention are Dr.
Vladimir Bazjanac, Donald Watson, Eureka Laboratories, and Rolf
Jensen Associates. And certainly the book would not have been possible without the encouragement of the McGraw-Hill organization (Jim
Bessent and Naomi Auerbach in particular) and my supportive editor
Joan Zseleczky.

The completion of *The New Atrium* was supported by a grant from
the National Endowment for the Arts in Washington, D.C., a federal
agency.

Ultimately, any errors of fact or omissions of acknowledgment are
the author's. Hopefully they are few in number. The evaluations and
analyses of given buildings are also solely those of the author, who in
all cases has endeavored to be fair and truthful.

Michael J. Bednar

Introduction

The atrium, which is a particular form of courtyard, was the social center of the ancient Greek and Roman house. Throughout architectural history, the courtyard building form has been widely used for monasteries, missions, castles, palazzos, and grand palaces. In the 19th century, the development of iron and glass technology created a new possibility for courtyards. Now they could be covered, creating an interior space protected from the climate but still enjoying the light and view of the open sky. The new atrium was born and began to develop as a unique building form with a wide range of design possibilities.

In the latter part of the 19th century, the atrium enjoyed popularity along with other glass-roofed building forms: arcades, conservatories, exhibition halls, and railroad stations. Some notable examples of atria were built, such as the Bradbury Building in Los Angeles, Brown Palace in Denver, Wanamaker's in Philadelphia, the Gardner Museum in Boston, and the Pension and Post Office buildings in Washington, D.C. In this century, the atrium has been only sporadically utilized in design until the last twenty years. Now, the atrium building is undergoing a resurgence. Scarcely a month goes by that a new atrium building is not planned, constructed, or published. Since 1959, an atrium building has won a National AIA Honor Award for design in eighteen out of twenty-five years. And this list does not include the John Portman designed hotels or the many atrium office buildings.

The new atrium is a centroidal, interior, daylit space which organizes a building. By being centroidal, it serves as a place of orientation for the rooms which surround it, thereby bringing spatial coherence to the building. The primary distinction between the new atrium and the Roman atrium is its interiorness, i.e., its lack of openness to the sky. This definition for the new atrium is similar to the definition for court given in the *Random House Dictionary of the English Language:* "a high interior usually having a glass roof and surrounded by several stories of galleries or the like." The dictionary definition for atrium, on the other hand, refers to the central space of a Roman house. There has been confusion regarding this terminology for some time. However, the recent commonly accepted meaning for the term *atrium* relates to the kinds of enclosed, daylit, centroidal spaces presented in this book. Of course, it is difficult to consider the atrium apart from its parent building, hence the term *atrium building.*

Why is the atrium space concept now enjoying a resurgence after a half century of sporadic utilization? That was the question which initially prompted this three-year study. The factors are many and depend in part upon the particular case in point. However, some general reasons can be stated.

Atrium buildings have proven to be very useful in carrying out certain urban design strategies. As public places they add immeasurably to the repertoire of available urban space types. The plaza atrium extends the use of public plazas by protecting them from the climate and coherently relating complexes of buildings. Atria in retail developments provide safe, comfortable areas for shopping, with user amenities intended to give shopping a recreational air. Certain historic buildings have been renovated and adapted for reuse by employing atria to link them to new additions or to give them a new interior image. The urban scene has been greatly enriched by atria because of the many ways in which they contribute to sensitive and innovative urban redevelopment.

Economics is always a factor when speaking of atria. In some cases it does cost more to build an atrium building. There is more roof area, usually with expensive skylights and the need for fire and smoke control systems. The footprint is larger, requiring more land. On the other hand, the exterior surface-to-floor-area ratio is lower, and vertical servicing is more efficient. The offsetting economic arguments usually revolve around the marketability of an atrium scheme, i.e., its attraction to office tenants, shoppers, hotel guests, or apartment dwellers. In office buildings the frontage on an atrium brings a higher rental rate. In commercial centers atria provide occasions for public gathering, events, and exhibitions, thereby attracting shoppers. In hotels atrium spaces lend drama and excitement to travel and conventions, thereby increasing occupancy rates. The economics are somewhat intangible and complex, but the results are being demonstrated daily in the marketplace.

Energy consciousness is certainly another factor which has economic overtones. Skylighted atria bring in daylight which is useful in offsetting electrical lighting costs in office and commercial buildings. Many atria are used as heat sinks, places to dump rejected and unneeded heat. They are also often used as return air plenums. The future is certain to bring efforts at more active use of atria as passive energy sources, places for heat storage and ventilation chambers. Many experiments in these uses are already underway.

The technology for making large-scale atrium spaces more feasible has advanced considerably in recent years. Glazing materials and systems are more sophisticated and reliable, making skylight leaks, maintenance, and potential glass breakage less a problem. Sprinkler systems and water screens have been developed to permit sophisticated fire and smoke control. Air handling equipment and techniques have been refined to minimize stratification and condensation. Observation elevator cars in exposed hoistways are now widely used to provide a dynamic spatial experience.

In terms of client needs, atria often provide the necessary catalytic common space which causes organizations and institutions to become more cohesive. Communication is eased through frequent visual contact and informal meetings; the users get to know each other. Sometimes, the atrium floor provides a requisite program space which functionally bonds the plan together. If the outside environment is negative or threatening, the creation of a controlled positive indoor environment with an atrium can be a significant motivating factor for its creation. Buildings with atria usually have more efficient and coherent circulation with excellent orientation. The presence of art, water, and plants all bathed in abundant daylight establishes a pleasant ambience.

Perhaps the most compelling aspect of the atrium concept is its holistic nature, its capacity to control and shape many aspects of a building's design simultaneously. As a spatial concept, its power and clarity are unequivocal; the presence of an atrium creates inherent spatial order in a building. There are, however, other secondary attributes. By generating a strong spatial identity and image, the atrium imbues a building with marketing potential. It can bring social and functional cohesiveness to an institution. The potential for an atrium to bring daylight into the center of a large building is well known, and its energy conservation potential is undergoing exploration. Perhaps the greatest benefit is the capacity of atria to bring spatial orientation, drama, and excitement to architecture. Atrium buildings are indeed memorable.

The present volume is an effort to analyze and document the development of the atrium building from its inception to the present. It is organized as Part I — Analysis and Part II — Design Studies, the latter presenting examples from the past two decades through drawings, photographs, and written evaluations. (Since Part I is largely based upon the analysis of buildings in Part II and continually refers to them as examples, the reader may find it beneficial to become familiar with Part II of the book first.) The emphasis throughout is upon large-scale commercial and institutional atrium buildings which satisfy a variety of programs within varied contexts. The intention of the book is to analyze a prevalent architectural phenomenon, to reveal design principles, and to give technical aid to practicing architects and engineers.

Underlying the study of atria is an attitude toward architectural design which is analytical and methodological. Design is viewed as much more than problem solving. It is seen as a means for maintaining historical continuity while dealing with contemporary issues through the consistent formulation, development, and expression of spatial concepts. The atrium plan is seen as one of a series of architectural concepts which needs to be understood by the well-intentioned architect.

The future of atrium buildings seems to be assured. The fire hazard problems which thwarted its development at the turn of the century have been solved. There certainly is a collective cultural renewal of interest in architectural space, its complexity, aura, and meaning. Moreover, the economic arguments of energy savings, marketability, and construction savings favor this concept. The atrium will continue to have a role in the overall strategy for urban renewal of city cores as a transitional space between the public and private realms. As a semipublic space, it is unique in that it can have both internal and external spatial relationships. Many additional exciting atrium buildings are now under design or construction, with many more promised in the future. The continued design exploration and evolution of this building form will surely contribute significantly to the richness of our architectural future.

Michael J. Bednar

The
New
Atrium

1 Historical Development

2 Urban Design

3 Design Analysis

PART I Analysis

4 Energy Performance

5 Design Development

1 Historical Development

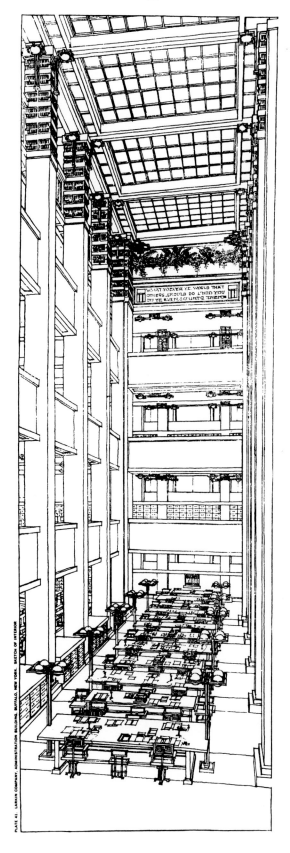

PLATE 41. LARKIN COMPANY, ADMINISTRATION BUILDING, BUFFALO, NEW YORK. SKETCH OF INTERIOR

OVERLEAF: *Atrium rendering, Larkin Building, Buffalo, New York. (Architect: Frank Lloyd Wright. Rendering: Copyright © The Frank Lloyd Wright Memorial Foundation, 1963)*

Recent developments in atrium design are best understood in the context of a historical perspective. The atrium building as a spatial type did not truly emerge until the nineteenth century. However, its antecedents are evident in architecture since the beginning of recorded history.

ORIGINS IN ANTIQUITY

With the emergence of urban settlements, the courtyard concept, which had evolved from the encampments of nomadic peoples, was brought into the individual dwelling, thus creating the atrium house form. There are many examples of atrium plan dwellings which were built in nonurban locations or villages for cultural and climatic reasons. However, the true atrium plan as a prevalent house form is best seen in the early cities. For it is the conditions of urbanism — the lack of privacy, limited land area, and limited exposure to communal space — along with the general need for climatic control, which made the atrium plan a logical form. The atrium plan addressed these conditions while providing positive amenities: a source of natural light and air, protection against the wind, a private outdoor space, a heat sink in the winter, and a place of shade for coolness in the summer.

Although the general conditions of urbanism can be considered as one basis for the development of the atrium plan, climatic control is an equally important determinant. For many centuries and continuing to the present day, the atrium house has been the predominant form in cities with hot-dry, temperate, and/or warm-humid climates.[1] In hot-dry climates with modest summer temperatures (north Africa), shallow atria, one story high, serve as collectors of cool night air and a source of shade in the daytime. In regions with higher summer temperatures (southern Spain), atria with deeper cross sections are utilized for the same reasons but with greater efficiency. In temperate climates with moderate to severe winter seasons (Rome), shallow atria serve both as passive solar collectors and as wind shelters. In warm-humid climates, shallow atria serve to generate wind-induced ventilation, which is necessary for cooling effects.

In his well-known book *House Form and Culture* Amos Rapoport suggests another fundamental rationale for the courtyard house.[2] These houses, used in cultures which are both populous and hierarchic, serve the individual need to get away while still remaining within the familiar territory of the family. The rooms surrounding the courtyard provide this separation of domains, and the courtyard provides the communal precinct. Thus courtyard houses can be found in Greece, Rome, India, Latin America, China, and many Islamic countries.

The earliest example of the courtyard house known to us from archaeological exploration was found at Ur on the Euphrates River in Mesopotamia.[3] It dates from the third millennium B.C. The floor plan (Figure 1-1) clearly shows the influence of the centrally placed courtyard. All rooms are organized around it and open onto it. The hall or passage from the street enters the courtyard at one corner. All of the rooms on the second floor also overlook the courtyard.

Between the fifth and second centuries B.C., the Greeks enlarged and developed the courtyard house. The house plan shown (Figure 1-2) is from Olynthos near Thessalonika, a city destroyed in 348 B.C.[4] A short hall leads directly from the street to the courtyard, which is

FIGURE 1-1 Plan of house at Ur, Mesopotamia: (1) Entrance Hall, (2) Staircase, (3) Washroom, (4) Kitchen, (5) Storeroom, (6) Courtyard. (Source: E. Camesasca, *History of the House*, Putnam, New York, 1971, p. 32 — redrawn)

FIGURE 1-2 Ancient Greek house plan: (1) Main Hall, (2) Courtyard, (3) Secondary Entrance, (4–8) Public Rooms, (9) Staircase. (Source: E. Camesasca, *History of the House*, Putnam, New York, 1971, p. 46 — redrawn)

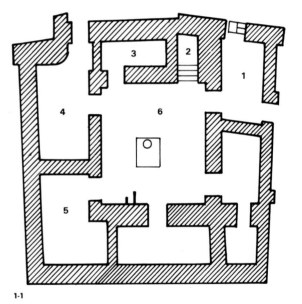

1-1

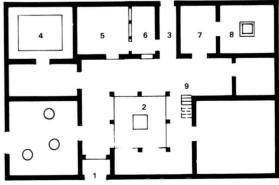

1-2

FIGURE 1-3 Roman house plan at Herculaneum: (1) Main Entry, (2) Shops, (3) Atrium, (4) Living Room, (5) Peristyle Courtyard. (Source: E. Camesasca, *History of the House,* Putnam, New York, 1971, p. 53 — redrawn)

FIGURE 1-4 Plan of basilica atrium, San Ambrogio, Milan. (Source: R. Sturgis, *A Dictionary of Architecture and Building,* vol. I, Macmillan, New York, 1901, p. 50 — redrawn)

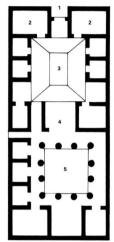

1-3

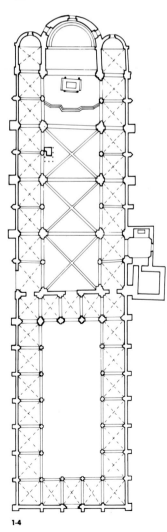

1-4

surrounded by columns forming a peristyle. This peristyle forms a defined circulation zone around the courtyard with the rooms of the house opening onto it. The courtyard space, which is open to the sky, has been formalized as a communal space through the use of the peristyle. The rooms of the house relate to it only indirectly due to the intervening circulation zone.

The classical concept of the atrium is evident in the houses of Rome dating from the third century B.C. The Romans may have actually borrowed the atrium concept from the Etruscans, who used it in the sixth and fifth centuries B.C. Vitruvius, in fact, refers to the atrium as Tuscan in origin.[5] The generic term used by Vitruvius to refer to enclosed courts is *cavaedium.* The atrium itself was that court nearest the entrance. In Chapter III, Book VI, Vitruvius actually defines five different kinds of *cavaedia* (atria):[6]

Tuscan The roof, supported by girders and crossbeams running the full width of the atrium, slopes toward the opening *(compluvium)* in the center such that rainwater can be collected in a cistern.

Corinthian Same construction as the Tuscan except the roof is supported on columns all around the roof opening forming a peristyle.

Tetrastyle The roof girders are supported by four columns, one at each atrium corner.

Displuviate The roof slopes away from the atrium roof opening, throwing the rainwater off the sides. Being high, the roof opening brings in more light to the dining rooms.

Testudinate Used in a two-story house with short spans. The atrium has no roof opening and is used as a sitting room.

Vitruvius also sets forth the plan proportions of an atrium according to three classes:

1. Length to width: 5 to 3
2. Length to width: 3 to 2
3. Length to width: $\sqrt{2W^2}$ to W

The height up to the girders should be one-fourth less than the plan width. Vitruvius then gives proportions for the surrounding rooms, or alae, based upon the atrium length, beginning with 30 to 40 feet and continuing on up to 80 to 100 feet. The dimensions given are certainly quite generous for residences.

In the completely developed Roman house as found in Pompeii and Herculaneum, the Tuscan atrium was joined with the Greek peristyle in the same plan (Figure 1-3).[7] The atrium was at the front of the house, joined to the street by a vestibule. It was the focus of the public part of the house, surrounded by rooms used as shops or offices. In the rear of the house was the peristyle court, the focus of the private or familial part of the house. The living room joined the atrium to the peristyle. At the extreme rear of the house was the dining room, the most important room, on the axis of the peristyle court. This two-part house plan allowed more luxury and privacy. It continued to be used as the traditional house plan in Rome until the third century A.D.

From these origins one can garner a general definition of the Roman atrium. It is the primary space in a plan to which all secondary spaces are related such that they have direct visual and physical access. The atrium, being surrounded by rooms and/or walls, receives its light and air through an opening in the roof and then distributes it to the surrounding rooms. The atrium is a communal space in a building which serves to relate the rooms of that building to each other through their common relationship to the atrium.

In the subsequent period of architectural history extending until the eleventh century, the term *atrium* was used to refer to the space in front of the entrance to a Christian basilica.[8] This space was defined by covered ambulatories—as in a cloister. An excellent example still exists at the church of San Ambrogio (1077–1093) in Milan (Figure 1-4).

The application of the term *atrium* to a space which by present-day definitions would be considered a cloister begins the historical confusion that exists regarding the atrium per se. *The Penguin Dictionary of Architecture* defines a cloister as ''a quadrangle surrounded by roofed or vaulted passages connecting the monastic church with the domestic parts of the monastery.''[9] From our understanding of the nature of the Roman atrium it seems incorrect to refer to this ecclesiastical forecourt as an atrium rather than a cloister.

COURTYARD FORMS

The differences between a Roman atrium and a court (courtyard or *cortile*) are more difficult to determine. *Court* is a very general term which has been applied to many kinds of open-air spaces surrounded or defined by building elements. There exist courts in medieval castles, Italian pallazzos, beaux arts government buildings, college dormitories, and houses from many parts of the world, including English manors. The primary purpose of a courtyard in most buildings is to bring light and air to the rooms which surround it. A secondary purpose is to provide a protected or private outdoor room which can be used in conjunction with the building's interior spaces.

The distinction between a Roman atrium and a court is in the degree of relationship between this space and the surrounding rooms. Physical and visual access to a court from the surrounding rooms is restricted. There exist exterior walls with windows and few doors. Circulation takes place within the building, not around the courtyard. A good example is the plan for Le Grand Commun at Versailles by Mansart (Figure 1-5).[10]

This apparent distinction between the Roman atrium and the court becomes further blurred in the case of the Italian pallazzo of the sixteenth century. The Pallazzo Farnese in Rome, designed by Sangallo the Younger in 1513 and completed by Michelangelo in 1531, will serve as a good example (Figure 1-6). In this spatial type, the cortile (the Italian term for court) is completely surrounded by the spaces of the pallazzo, thus forming a highly defined court. However, the circulation has been placed in arcades surrounding the cortile on all sides, on the first two building levels. (In the nineteenth century the arcades on the second level were enclosed.) Thus the relationship between rooms and cortile has been changed through this mediating circulation zone. On the ground level, the circulation across and around the courtyard is quite free, with many entries to the rooms. On the upper levels, the need to use the galleries for circulation brings a constant vitality to the cortile.

The pallazzo spatial type with its cortile continued to serve as a formal model for many buildings in Europe and the United States into

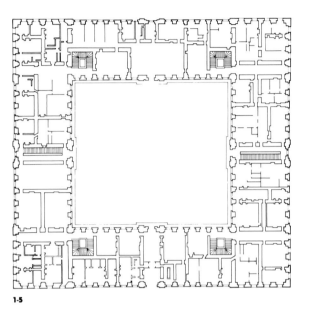

FIGURE 1-5 Plan, Le Gran Commun at Versailles by J. H. Mansart. (Source: H. Mansart, P. Bourget, G. Cattavi, *Jules Hardouin Mansart*, Vincent Freal, Paris, 1956, Pl. LXXIX—redrawn)

FIGURE 1-6 Ground floor plan, Pallazzo Farnese, Rome, Italy. (Source: P. Portoghesi, *Rome of the Renaissance*, Phaidon, London, 1972, p. 200—redrawn)

1-5

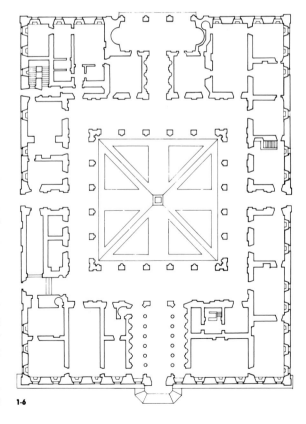

1-6

FIGURE 1-7 Interior view, Galleria Vittorio
Emanuele II, Milan, Italy. (Photographer:
Michael Bednar)

FIGURE 1-8 Interior view, Cleveland Arcade,
Cleveland, Ohio. (Architects: John Eisenmann
and George Smith. Photographer: Martin
Linsey, Historic American Building Survey,
Library of Congress)

FIGURE 1-9 Plan of the Reform Club in
London, England: (1) Coffee Room, (2)
Library, (3) Dining Room, (4) Saloon.
(Architect: Sir Charles Barry. Source: R.
Middleton, D. Watkin, *Neoclassical and 19th
Century Architecture,* Abrams, New York,
1980, Pl. 451 — redrawn)

the nineteenth and even the twentieth century. In some cases, the
cortile was covered with a solid roof. However, it was not until the
beginning of the nineteenth century, when iron and glass technology
was perfected, that the atrium* became a permanent feature in the
world of architecture.

FIRST EPOCH OF THE ATRIUM

With the arrival of the nineteenth century in France, England, and
America, the use of metal and glass as significant components in
architecture began to develop. Cast iron and wrought iron had been
available before 1800, but they were not widely used, and if used, were
usually enclosed in masonry. The search for greater structural spans
led to a rapid development of structural technology. There was a concurrent development in glass manufacturing, resulting in larger panes
which could be held in place with milled-iron frames. In 1855, Sir
Henry Bessemer invented a new method of making steel which resulted in larger and stronger structural components, leading to ever
greater spans of space.

The fascination with this new technology resulted in the development of a wholly new architecture, buildings made entirely of iron and
glass. Many of these were built in England and France: conservatories
(Palm House at Kew by Richard Turner, 1845–1848), train stations
(Paddington Station in London by Brunel and Wyatt, 1853–1854),
exhibition halls (Galerie des Machines, Paris, by Dutert in 1889), and
markets (Les Halles, Paris, by Baltard, 1853–1858). The culmination
of this development in both sophistication and scale was the Crystal
Palace in Hyde Park, London, by Joseph Paxton in 1851.[11] Here then
was an architectural space of unprecedented scale (1848 feet long by
456 feet wide), completely transparent, and defined only by a matrix
of iron structural members. Moreover, it was made entirely of prefab-
ricated parts and could be disassembled and moved, as indeed it was to
Sydenham in 1852.

Concurrent with the development of the all-glass-and-iron building, there were many explorations in combining this new technology
with traditional masonry building forms. These explorations resulted
in the genesis of two new spatial types, the arcade and the atrium. In
both of these cases, traditional masonry forms were utilized for the
vertical enclosures and supports. The exposed iron and glass structure
was utilized primarily in the public spaces of these buildings.

The *arcade* is ''a glass covered passageway which connects two busy
streets and is lined on both sides with shops.''[12] It developed and
prospered during the course of the nineteenth century in England,
France, Italy, Germany, and America. Its invention was based on the
specific needs of society during that century for a public space, protected from traffic and the weather, which would aid in the marketing
of luxury goods being rapidly produced by industry. Perhaps the best-
known of these arcades is the Galleria Vittorio Emanuele II in Milan,
built in 1867 by Mengoni. Its scale is that of the Roman baths, with a
cruciform plan and a glazed dome at the crossing (Figure 1-7). The
best example in the United States is the Cleveland Arcade in Ohio,
built in 1890 by John Eisenmann and George Smith. Its scale is monumental, 390 feet long, 103 feet wide, and 104 feet high. The propor-

---

* The term *atrium* will be utilized hereafter to refer to the glass-roofed atrium as
distinguished from the open-air Roman atrium.

1-7

1-8

tions are such that the linearity is not overwhelming, resulting in an elegant Victorian gathering place full of life and light (Figure 1-8). The development of the arcade is certainly tangential to that of the atrium, and there are many similarities between these two spatial types. The arcade, however, is for exclusively commercial purposes, whereas the atrium (as we shall see) has much wider functional applications. In a recent book entitled *Arcades,* J. F. Geist has written an excellent account of this spatial type.[13]

Thus we arrive historically at the birth of a new spatial type, the atrium. There were many precursors to the glass-covered atrium. One of the earliest was the Consuls Office at the Bank of England where from 1792 to 1794 John Soane built a lantern of iron and glass to cover a 20-foot oculus.[14] Undoubtedly there were others, most likely in France and England.

The first known atrium was in the Reform Club by Sir Charles Barry in London (1837–1841). Barry used the Pallazzo Farnese as his model for the Club's building plan and form (Figure 1-9). However, in the design of the court, he took the next historical step and roofed it over with a vaulted structure of metal which was infilled with glass (Figure 1-10). Thus, for the first time the court became an interior room, fully protected from the weather but enjoying the light of an outdoor court. Starting at the second level, the atrium in this building was two stories high, surrounded by galleries, and it was used as a saloon for the club. Bridgewater House, designed in 1847 by the same

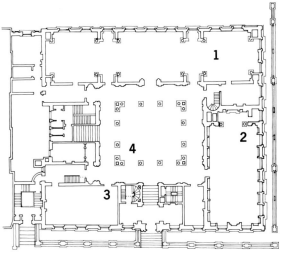

1-9

architect, has a longer rectangular atrium, which is covered by a
glazed roof and surrounded by galleries leading from a grand staircase.[15]

Another British example from this period is the London Coal Exchange on Lower Thames Street, designed in the years 1846 to 1899
by J. B. Bunning.[16] The building form is two masonry pallazzo blocks
linked by a round tower forming an atrium. The interior of this four-
story atrium was formed in iron, and the dome was covered in glass,
forming an airy and elegant space.

In France at this time there were many atria being built (termed
galleries) as glass-roofed courts in large department stores. This use of
the iron and glass roof was an outgrowth of the many commercial
arcades and passages being concurrently built. No less than thirty-
nine of these markets (*marché*) were known to be built in Paris between 1843 and 1879.[17] Most of them had glass-roofed courts. The
Bon Marché of 1876 by Boileau and Eiffel is one of the best-known
examples. It occupied an entire block with continuous subdividable
space and many light wells. The structure was an iron skeleton with a
glass roof, creating tremendous daylit spaces.

The French began to exploit the atrium spatial type and utilized it
for many different kinds of buildings, including hotels, offices, museums, apartments, libraries, and even garages (see Table 1-1).

1-10

1-11

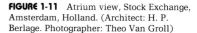

FIGURE 1-11 Atrium view, Stock Exchange, Amsterdam, Holland. (Architect: H. P. Berlage. Photographer: Theo Van Groll)

The most influential European atrium building from this era was the Amsterdam Stock Exchange, designed by H. P. Berlage between 1898 and 1903. Its influence upon the history of architecture was primarily for its Romanesque facades and its sincerity in expressing the materials of its construction, including the exposed iron structure of the three glass-roofed halls.[18] The atrium space for the Commodity Exchange is the largest of these halls and dominates this building (Figure 1-11). It is surrounded on three levels with galleries and offices. The structure is a triple, articulated, arched girder with exposed tie bars. The Corn Exchange Hall has offices on three levels along one side, as does the Stock Exchange Hall. Berlage used exposed iron and glass only for the roofs of these three halls, the remaining iron structure being totally encased in brick and stone. This same mode of expression was to be subsequently utilized in the United States.

The first half of the nineteenth century in England and France can be viewed as the *first epoch* of the atrium, during which it was invented and explored as a spatial type. The excitement in Europe began to wane toward the end of the century as architectural styles and forms began to change. The fire hazard was a very real reason for the waning, as people discovered that iron or steel and glass structures could not withstand the intense heat of urban fires. Many of the iron and glass buildings burned and collapsed.

TABLE 1-1
Early French Atria

Structure	City	Designer	Date
Museum of Natural History and Zoology	Paris	Jules Andre	1877–1889
Catholic Library	Paris	Eugene Dupuis	1878–1880
Verriere Convent	Paris		1896
Garage, rue de Ponthieu	Paris	A. and G. Perret	1907
Bibliothèque Nationale	Paris	H. Labrouste	1868
Cité Napoleon	Paris	Marie-Gabriel Veugny	1849–1853

FIGURE 1-12 Ground floor plan, Pension Building, Washington, D. C. (Architect: Montgomery Meigs. Source: National Building Museum — redrawn)

FIGURE 1-13 Atrium view, Pension Building, Washington, D. C. (Architect: Montgomery Meigs. Photographer: Michael Bednar)

1-12

SECOND EPOCH OF THE ATRIUM

The second epoch of the atrium took place in the United States at the turn of the nineteenth century. The buildings from this era were based upon the earlier European models, which many of the designers had read about and/or visited. As a group, they were all masonry buildings on the exterior, with iron, steel, and glass being used only in the atrium space itself. More than likely, this design strategy was a response to the fire problems encountered in Europe. All of these atria were either square or rectangular in plan and multistoried in section. In many of the buildings, the glazed roof was placed at an intermediate level in the light court rather than at the top of the building, so that the atrium and light court occupied the same plan position. These atria housed the same range of functions as their European models. They were geographically distributed throughout the country, although none were found in the South or Southwest, probably because of the more favorable climate in those regions.

The Pension Building in Washington, D.C., is at once the oldest known extant atrium building in the United States and the one with the most monumental atrium. It was designed by an army engineer, General Montgomery Meigs, in 1882 and completed in 1887 on a site north of Judiciary Square. The building's single tenant was the Pension Bureau, the equivalent of the present-day Veterans' Administration. It contained offices for 600 clerks located in galleries surrounding the grand atrium. As one of Meigs's primary concerns was the welfare of these workers, he wanted a thoroughly ventilated building, with no dark corridors, passages, or corners.[19] His scheme also served the pensioners who came there monthly. The ground floor had the scale of a civic square, complete with fountain, where the pensioners could gather and socialize. The building's planned future use will be as the National Museum of the Building Arts. The atrium, being one of the largest interior spaces in Washington, D.C., has been successfully used for eleven inaugural balls, seven of which were held between 1885 and 1909. Recent inaugural balls have been held there for Presidents Nixon, Carter, and Reagan (twice).

General Meigs cites the pallazzos of Rome (which he visited in 1867), the Pallazzo Farnese in particular, as the precedent for his Pension Building design. However, with the new iron and glass technology he was able to build a large-span, durable, and safe structure to cover the courtyard. Because of the elongation of the facade and the large clerestory roof, the resemblance to the Pallazzo Farnese is not evident, save for the height of the facade and the window designs. The loggias surrounding the atrium were based on those at the Pallazzo Cancellaria in Rome.[20]

At one time, the Pension Building was the largest brick building in the world. It occupies an entire city block and measures 200 feet by 400 feet in plan. The most dramatic feature is the atrium, 292 feet long, 92 feet wide (exclusive of loggias), and 159 feet high. The central portion of the huge clerestory roof is supported by two sets of four mammoth Corinthian columns which divide the atrium into three sections (Figure 1-12). The four levels of offices surrounding the atrium are accessed from arcaded galleries on the first and second levels, a parapeted walkway on the third level, and an iron balcony on the fourth level (Figure 1-13). Curiously, the building has no skylights; all natural light enters through gable-end clerestories over the atrium.

1-13

Among the most interesting aspects of General Meigs's design scheme are the energy-conserving features. The narrow band of offices receives daylight from the large exterior windows and the atrium, achieving good balanced visual conditions. The heavy brick masonry structure has both heat- and cold-retaining properties to offset diurnal and seasonal temperature variations. All windows are double-paned, and the roof has an unusual tile insulation system. A natural ventilation system has been built into each office, reputedly resulting in an air change every 2 minutes. Fresh air enters through ventilation slots under each window. It is heated by steam radiators, one under each window, and the heat naturally flows through archways into the atrium (no office doors were planned). The heated air rises to the top of the atrium, where it is exhausted through movable clerestory windows operated by pulleys, thus maintaining a continuous flow of fresh air.[21] These energy design lessons are certainly very relevant to us today.

The model for many present-day atrium plan office buildings is seen in the Bradbury Building in Los Angeles, designed by George Wyman in 1893.[22] The atrium serves as a magnificent interior lobby, with a pedestrian scale, to which each of the tenants is directly related. Each office entrance opens onto a gallery which surrounds the 47-foot by 119-foot atrium. The five levels of offices are contained within a restrained Italian Renaissance exterior built of brown brick and terra cotta. The building has been recently restored and renovated (Figure 1-14).

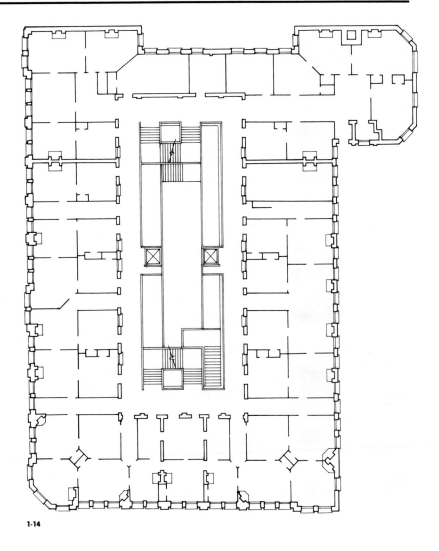

1-14

The Bradbury Building atrium is among the best-designed spaces of its kind to be found anywhere. It has the architectural character of a fine Victorian street lined by brick facades. The clear-glass skylight provides abundant daylight, replicating outdoor lighting levels. At opposite ends of the atrium are elegant stairways with Belgian marble treads and black wrought-iron guardrails. Opposite each other on the long sides are fascinating, open-cage, counterweighted traction elevators, which provide a mechanical animation in contrast to the human animation on the stairways. The "lacy" quality of the black iron elevators, stairs, and balustrades is in quiet contrast to the rich color and texture of the Mexican tile floors. The resulting ambience is alive with visual interest without harsh contrasts, since the materials and their colors absorb some of the brightness from the skylight (Figure 1-15).

Like the Pension Building, this building was a low-energy design scheme, calling for balanced daylighting and natural ventilation. Since Edison had not yet invented the light bulb, gas lamps were installed; provisions for electric lights came later. Fireplaces or stoves around the building perimeter yielded the minimal heating required in the Los Angeles climate. Fresh air entered through exterior windows and flowed through door transoms. Pivoted windows, at the top of the wall just below the skylight, served as outlets for venting. The Bradbury Building was the only building designed by George Wyman

1-15

and the only one built by Lewis Bradbury, but it stands as a shining example of high-quality atrium design.

The atrium in a single-tenant office building assumes a semipublic or private role. This is the case in Frank Lloyd Wright's 1904 Larkin Building in Buffalo (now demolished). The floor of the atrium was used as a work space overlooked by five levels of offices, bringing the entire work force into a sense of cohesiveness (Figure 1-16). The building plan, with its stair and duct shafts in each corner and entrance bay to the side, was extremely well organized (Fig. 1-17). It was the first air-conditioned office building. The skylights over the atrium brought daylight to those interior offices which surrounded it. Brick piers supported the floors around the atrium (referred to as a nave), giving it a gothic strength. The serenity of the space was such that the owners eventually installed an organ.[23]

In 1888, Henry C. Brown, a Denver realtor and builder, engaged Chicago architect Frank Edbrooke to design a truly unique and superb hotel. When it opened in 1892, the Brown Palace, as it came to be known, was the first hotel ever designed with an atrium at its center. This truly precedent-setting scheme was to serve as the inspiration and model for the many dramatic and exciting atrium hotels of the present era.

Frank Edbrooke's design was to rise ten stories on a triangular site.

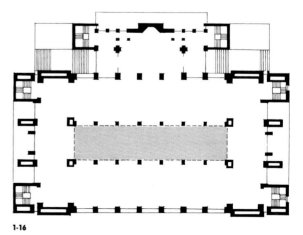

1-16

FIGURE 1-17 Atrium view, Larkin Building, Buffalo, New York. (Architect: Frank Lloyd Wright. Photograph courtesy of The Frank Lloyd Wright Memorial Foundation)

FIGURE 1-18 Atrium view, Brown Palace Hotel, Denver, Colorado. (Architect: Frank Edbrooke. Photograph courtesy of Brown Palace Hotel)

1-17

1-18

At its center is a trapezoidal atrium of matching height, covered by a square, double-domed skylight with patterned and colored glass (Figure 1-18). Galleries with wrought-iron balustrades surround the atrium on all sides, giving access to the guest rooms. The sumptuous atrium links directly with the main entry and serves as the hotel lobby, from which all guest services are accessed. The Brown Palace was the second fireproof building in America, with partitions and floors of terra cotta and an exterior of brown sandstone and red granite, all supported on a steel frame.

The atrium (here termed a "rotunda") is the living room for the Brown Palace Hotel. It is furnished with fine residential period pieces; its marble floors are covered with oriental rugs. The piers and fireplace are finished in exquisite onyx. Symbolically, the atrium was and is the living room for the state of Colorado. Here the rich and powerful, and all in between, come to stay and be seen. Debutantes make their appearance at the annual Christmas Ball. Hereford bulls are exhibited along with Titan missiles.[24] The atrium space serves admirably for all of these functions. The Brown Palace is much more than a hotel; it is a cultural institution for all of Colorado.

Daniel H. Burnham, known for his major contributions to city planning, civic design, and the *Chicago school* of architecture, also contributed significantly to the history of the atrium. Burnham himself is not generally considered to be the actual designer of these buildings, although he surely had a role in their conception. Until his death in 1891, John Wellborn Root was the major designer in the Burnham and Root firm. In the subsequent firm of D. H. Burnham and Company, Charles Atwood was the principal designer.

At least eleven major atrium buildings can be attributed to Burnham and Root or D. H. Burnham and Company, as shown in Table 1-2. Individually, none of these buildings is very outstanding as a work of architecture, with the exception of The Rookery. As a group, however, they represent significant advancement in the development of the

TABLE 1-2
Atrium Buildings Attributed to Burnham and Root or D. H. Burnham and Company

Building	Description	City	Date
Burlington & Quincy General Office Building	Six-story atrium with glazed roof at the top within a 199 foot by 122 foot corporate office block[25]	Chicago	1882–1883 (now demolished)
The Rookery	Ten-story speculative office building with a two-story atrium, 71 feet by 62 feet, formed by a glazed roof with a light court above[26]	Chicago	1885–1888
Society for Savings Building	Ten-story bank and office building with a ten-story atrium, 34 feet by 56 feet in plan; skylight at roof-level and an inner, leaded-glass ceiling at 26 feet[27]	Cleveland	1887–1890
Rand-McNally Building	Ten-story corporate office building with a two-story atrium, 67 feet by 67 feet 6 inches in plan; floor used as an accounting department[28]	Chicago	1888–1890 (now demolished)
Masonic Temple	A twenty-story, multiuse commercial building with a narrow, twenty-story atrium[29]	Chicago	1890–1892 (now demolished)
Mills Building	Ten-story office block with a two-story, 56-foot 8-inch by 50-foot 6-inch atrium surrounded by shops[30]	San Francisco	1890–1892
Equitable Building	Eight-story office block; both building and light court are trapezoidal in plan; one-story atrium[31]	Atlanta	1890–1892 (now demolished)
Ellicott Square	Ten-story office block with a large light court roofed at the second story with a heavy steel, clear-span structure to form an atrium (Figure 1-19)[32]	Buffalo	1895–1896
John Wanamaker's Department Store	Seven-story atrium within a twelve-story building with a five-story light well above[33]	Philadelphia	1902–1911
Marshall Field Store	Southwest section rebuilt around a small atrium[34]	Chicago	1907
Railway Exchange Building	Large, seventeen-story office block on Michigan Avenue with a sizeable light court glazed at the second floor to form an atrium[35]	Chicago	1903–1905

1-19

FIGURE 1-19 Atrium view, Ellicott Square, Buffalo, New York. (Architects: D. H. Burnham and Company. Photograph: © Stephen S. Mangione)

high-rise building through the use of the steel structural frame, passenger elevators, and the light court and/or atrium. For the most part, these atria served as public lobbies and circulation centers with adjacent elevator banks. They often featured a centrally located grand sculptural stair. The lower floors were usually surrounded by shops or offices serving the public.

Abundant light and air were the reasons for these building forms. Architects had convinced their clients that bringing natural light and fresh air to the office workers was worth the sacrifice in additional office space. When the glass and steel atrium roof was located at the ceiling of the second level, it was to maximize the amount of light and air to the offices above, which faced the light court. The light court walls were painted white to increase reflection of daylight down to the bottom. When the skylight was located at the top of the building, the atrium interior was designed in such a way that nothing would obstruct the daylight. This can be seen at the Society for Savings Building in Cleveland, where the walls are of white marble, the gallery guardrails are of metal filigree, and the gallery floors are covered with translucent glass lights (Figure 1-20).[36]

The Rookery in Chicago is significant both for its development in skeletal construction and its plan form, with a light court in the center of the building rising the full ten-story height. The lowest two floors of this light court are covered with a magnificent iron and glass roof, an outstanding example of this construction type. The offices facing the light court from above vicariously participate in the atrium by views through its glass roof. These offices were considered to be as desirable as those facing the street. A focal point in the atrium is the grand stair leading to the galleries around the second level. A daring cantilevered iron stair continues the procession from the second to the third floor, through the glass roof, and into an oriel stair rising the full height of the light court (Figure 1-21).

Burnham also incorporated the atrium in two department stores, following the earlier French tradition. In 1907, he rebuilt the southwest section of the Marshall Field Store in Chicago around a small atrium which was distinguished by its glass dome, designed by Louis

1-20

1-21

Comfort Tiffany.[37] Burnham's best atrium store design is at the John Wanamaker's Department Store in Philadelphia (1902–1911).[38] This atrium is a vertical shaft of space rising seven stories within the twelve-story height of the building. The original glazed roof unfortunately no longer brings in daylight. The atrium is surrounded with columns as in the porticoed Renaissance courtyard, which was the inspiration for this scheme.

The significance of the Wanamaker atrium is in the role it plays within this 2 million square foot department store. Surrounded on all sides by commercial floors, it provides a welcome point of orientation and spatial relief. The ground floor has commercial sales and displays but primarily serves as circulation space. The focal point is a large bronze eagle sculpture, which is a traditional meeting place for Philadelphians. During the Christmas season, the atrium is where children and adults alike gather to enjoy the Christmas tree and to witness the magic of the light show staged on the atrium's end wall. It also houses a large pipe organ from the 1904 Louisiana Purchase Exposition in St. Louis (Figure 1-22).

The use of the atrium was very appropriate to monumental civic buildings, such as post offices, courthouses, and city halls, which had to accommodate large throngs of people requiring a multitude of services. Many such buildings no longer serve their original purpose. In Buffalo, near Ellicott Square, the Old Post Office was renovated in 1981, appropriately for use as a community college (see Design Study 18). It was originally built in the years 1894 to 1901 by architects O'Rourke, Aiken and Taylor. The courtyard, based upon Richardson's Allegheny County Courthouse, is roofed over in iron and glass, form-

1-22

1-23

ing a grand four-story atrium with walls which reflect the exterior facades.[39] In St. Paul, the old Federal Courts Building was originally designed under the direction of W. J. Edbrooke and James Knox Taylor between 1892 and 1902.[40] The building, restored by Perry, Dean Rogers & Partners, is now Landmark Center, a public cultural center with a magnificent four-story central atrium (Figure 1-23). Another success story is the Old City Hall in Richmond, Virginia, designed by Elijah E. Myers between 1887 and 1894. This gothic revival building with its ornate atrium has been restored as an office building by Landmarks Design Associates (Figure 1-24). In Washington, D.C., the Old Post Office, originally designed in 1899 by supervising architect of the U.S. Treasury Department W. J. Edbrooke, has also undergone renovation for federal offices and multiuse commercial space.[41] The scheme by Arthur Cotton Moore/Associates was the result of a long campaign to save this prominent building on Pennsylvania Avenue (see Design Study 39). A new skylight installed at the roof level of the light court has heightened the original one-story atrium. The clock tower at the end of the new nine-story atrium is an attractive visual focus.

In 1902, nine years after McKim, Mead and White designed a Renaissance pallazzo — with a fine courtyard — for the Boston Public Library, Isabella Stewart Gardner built a palace in Boston (called the Gardner Museum or Fenway Court) that makes a direct association between the atrium and its Renaissance precursor.[42] Gardner, with her architect William T. Sears, created a faithful reproduction of a Venetian Renaissance pallazzo to house her great art collection of tapestries, paintings, prints, etchings, sculpture, furniture, books, and artifacts from every part of the world. The skylight over the courtyard, which was surrounded by balconies, provided a climate like that in southern Italy and allowed for year-round displays of flowers and exotic plants. To visit the Gardner Museum is to step into another culture and another century. It is incongruous in Boston but its "sense of place" is nevertheless compelling. (Figure 1-25).

The Gardner Museum served as a precedent for many subsequent museums to incorporate skylit courtyards for displays, as gardens, and/or as places of repose. Cram, Goodhue, and Ferguson designed a Japanese garden court in the Boston Museum of Fine Arts in 1910.

1-24

1-25

John Russell Pope also included skylit courtyards in his National Gallery of Art in Washington, D.C. (1941), as did I. M. Pei, much later, in the magnificent atrium of the East Building (1978) (Design Study 25). In 1959, F. L. Wright took the Gardner Museum spatial concept and twisted it, in his Guggenheim Museum, into a spiral form with a skylit central atrium. Thus, the Gardner Museum established a precedent by creating an inspirational place based upon a historic form.

This second epoch of the atrium came to an uncertain close in the years following World War I. The late nineteenth and early twentieth century had been an era of great exuberance and architectural spirit that saw the atrium plan adapted to many different building types and utilized in buildings of many styles, including Italian Renaissance, Romanesque, Victorian, Second Empire, and Chicago school. The reasons for the atrium's demise at the beginning of the twentieth century are uncertain. Certainly the atria in the United States, like the atria in Europe, were plagued by fire hazards. Probably the International Style, with its new plan types, was beginning to influence architects, as did the contracting postwar economy. The buildings which did incorporate the atrium during this era had a certain forthright presence and civic grandeur, a legacy which is being rediscovered in the present day.

THIRD EPOCH: THE NEW ATRIUM

After a dormancy of two-thirds of the twentieth century, the atrium is enjoying an unparalleled resurgence of interest and development. The reasons, as cited in the Introduction are many. To reiterate, they are marketing economics, energy consciousness, technological advancement, programmatic needs, and architectural invention. This trend is primarily evident in the United States, where the developments have been rapid and revolutionary, with the promise of an exciting future.

The third epoch of atrium design had several precursors in the period of relative dormancy in this century. Perhaps the earliest of these was Wright's Marin County (California) Civic Center of 1957. The form of this building was more akin to an arcade than an atrium. The spatial concept was adopted to a new functional purpose, that of a county services building. Minoru Yamasaki designed two small-scale atrium buildings in Detroit, both of which won American Institute of Architects (AIA) Honor Awards and therefore received wide publicity. The McGregor Conference Center (1959) at Wayne State University was a simple-parti, two-story building in which the atrium as a space simultaneously divided the building into two components and then united them into a cohesive whole. The Reynolds Metals Regional Office (1961) was the classic square atrium within a square plan surrounded by galleries on two levels.

One of the most well-conceived and well-executed atrium designs of this era is the University of Pennsylvania Women's Dormitory in Philadelphia, designed by Eero Saarinen in 1961. The building is related to a medieval castle in both plan and image. The atrium and two roof decks are formed by a solid perimeter of dormitory rooms (which face the street), a corridor, and an inner ring of service spaces and lounges which overlook the atrium. The atrium itself, a circulation and informal meeting space on the first floor, overlooks a dining hall on the lower level. The roof decks at either end give the atrium better proportions while allowing ample daylight to enter through the glazed end

FIGURE 1-26 Atrium view, University of
Pennsylvania Women's Dormitory,
Philadelphia, Pennsylvania. (Architects: Eero
Saarinen and Associates. Photographer:
Michael Bednar)

FIGURE 1-27 Atrium view, Hyatt Regency
Atlanta, Atlanta, Georgia. (Architects:
Edwards and Portman. Photograph: John
Portman Associates)

walls. Additional balancing daylight is brought in through clerestories (Figure 1-26). The entire ensemble of spaces and relationships is highly appropriate to this dormitory building. The atrium is full of light and life, a place for both spontaneous occasion and formal social event.

The two buildings which heralded the epoch of the "new atrium" were built in the consecutive years of 1967 and 1968. They were the Hyatt Regency Hotel in Atlanta by Edwards and Portman and the Ford Foundation Headquarters in New York City by Roche and Dinkeloo. Here were two buildings with atria of such vertical scale and sheer architectural bravura that they summoned the attention of the entire world of architecture. They were both daring and brilliant in conception and execution. Their creation expanded the horizons of atrium design and initiated a new era of possibilities and opportunities.

John Portman had set as his goal the design of a new type of hotel. He was dismayed by the dullness of the typical central-city hotel with dimly lit corridors, nondescript rooms, and a dreary lobby. He had seen the Brown Palace in Denver, but the extent of its influence upon him is uncertain. In 1965 Portman's firm completed the Antoine Graves Homes in Atlanta (Design Study 38), a housing project for the elderly with a six-story atrium subdivided by a bank of elevators and stairs at its center. He later said:

> I wanted to explode the hotel; to open it up; to create a grandeur of space, almost a resort, in the center of the city. The whole idea was to open everything up; take the hotel from its closed, tight position and explode it; take the elevators and literally pull them out of the walls and let them become an experience within themselves, let them become a giant kinetic sculpture.[43]

The resulting Hyatt Regency Hotel in Atlanta was an extravaganza, like no hotel the world had seen before. On the exterior, this twenty-three-story hotel appears to be a rather subdued modern concrete building with horizontal bands of balconies. However, the interior does "explode" as Portman had desired. At the center is a square atrium, 120 feet on each side, rising the full height of the building,

1-26

1-27

covered by an intriguing skylight, and surrounded by a clerestory (see
Design Study 27). This grand atrium is surrounded by galleries and
balconies (supporting planters) which serve as single-loaded corridors for the guest rooms, which also overlook the city. The elevators
have indeed been pulled "out of the walls" and placed in the atrium.
The cars are lighted Plexiglas capsules which truly form a "giant
kinetic sculpture" as they zoom up and down, adding mechanical
animation to this grand space. The elevators shoot through the skylight and arrive at a domed revolving restaurant with magnificent
views of Atlanta. One final feature is the cocktail lounge, which is
suspended in the atrium by a single steel cable, allowing it to gently
sway (Figure 1-27).

The Hyatt Regency Hotel in Atlanta took the hotel world in this
country by surprise. It was such a bold scheme that its very uniqueness assured it of a competitive advantage over other hotels. Its atrium
became the hallmark of the Hyatt hotel chain, with over thirty hotels
completed. Moreover, many other hotels have adopted atrium plan
designs in order to successfully compete in the lucrative hotel market.

The Ford Foundation Headquarters in New York had as provocative
an influence upon the future of office-building design as the Hyatt
Regency in Atlanta had upon hotel design. Large-scale atria had been
used in many turn-of-the-century office building schemes. The Ford
Foundation Headquarters was a rejuvenation of the atrium scheme,
which had been dormant for two-thirds of a century. The uniqueness
of this scheme was the placement of the atrium in the corner of the
almost square building plan, permitting the south and east facades,
ten stories of steel and glass, to be open to the city. The other two sides
of the atrium are surrounded by offices in an L-shaped configuration,
except on the tenth and eleventh floors, where the office plan becomes
a square doughnut. The offices directly overlook the atrium through
clear-glass sliding windows. There are no intervening circulation galleries (see Design Study 6).

The atrium in the Ford Foundation Headquarters is a highly urban
gesture. It serves as a transition space between the city outside (42nd
Street, the adjacent city play park, and neighboring Tudor City with its
parks) and the private inside (the office spaces of the Ford Foundation). It is designed as an indoor park to be used year-round by city
residents, the general public, and the occupants of the office building.[44] It is not a space necessary to the functioning of the office building, since there is an entrance lobby off of 43rd Street. There is a
secondary entrance from 42nd Street with stairs leading to the reception area. Admittedly, the atrium is an inside space by virtue of its
enclosure with glass. But therein lies its unique quality. Prior to this
time, most public spaces in the city were outdoor plazas open to the
sky. This is a new kind of public urban space; though enclosed, it
nevertheless represents a gift to the street (Figure 1-28).

The Ford Foundation atrium is also a highly institutional gesture,
because it gives this organization a communal focal space. Virtually
all spaces of the building have direct contact with the garden atrium.
The floor-to-ceiling glass walls cause all personnel, including the
president, to see each other across the atrium. This fosters a sense of
oneness, belonging, and common purpose among foundation employees. The atrium is also an amenity for the personnel, a gift from
the institution. It is a place of repose — to have lunch, to rest and chat,
to relieve the stresses of work.

The realization of the Ford Foundation Headquarters caused many office-building designers to reconsider the possibilities of the atrium form. Although, and perhaps because, this building was designed for a prestigious client by an inventive architect with a big budget, its impact upon office-building design was not immediate. Designers had to evaluate the atrium concept relative to the individual projects at hand. Neither was the impact as directly observable as in the case of hotels. But this building did rekindle the interest in atrium plan office buildings, as is evidenced by the many which have been and are being built.

In the period since 1967, the atrium concept has enjoyed a great revival among architects, clients, and the general public. About 200 buildings with atria have been built in the United States, and many more are in the planning and design stages. The analysis of this third epoch of atrium design, and the planning and design criteria that have emerged for use by architects and engineers, form the major topic of this book.

Not only have an unprecedented number of atrium buildings been built in this era but the concept has also been adapted to new roles and extended to new kinds of development. In recent years atria have been used in hospitals (Philadelphia Children's Hospital), schools (Erie County Community College in Buffalo, New York), merchandise exchanges (Atlanta Apparel Mart), libraries (Exeter Academy Library), city halls (Dallas City Hall), and specialized housing (Antoine Graves Homes in Atlanta, Georgia). New design concepts have evolved. Atria of unprecedented scale and complexity have been used as focal spaces in multiuse centers, such as Omni International in Atlanta, Galleria II in Houston, and the First Source Center in South Bend, Indiana. Some designers have used atria as the major element in an energy conservation strategy as at the Tennessee Valley Authority (TVA) Office Complex in Chattanooga or the Gregory Bateson State Office Building in Sacramento, California. The use of multiple-stacked atria in high-rise buildings as at 875 Third Avenue in New York City is another recent development.

This chapter has been an exploration of the evolution of the atrium throughout the course of architectural history. The origins of the concept were in the Greek and Roman houses of antiquity. In spirit, the concept was evidenced in the many cloisters and courtyards built before the end of the eighteenth century. The first epoch of the atrium took place in Europe during the first half of the nineteenth century, when the development of iron-and-glass technology permitted the covering of large courtyard spaces. This development was continued during the second epoch of the atrium during the last half of the nineteenth and the beginning of the twentieth century in the United States. After another period of relative dormancy, the atrium building type was rediscovered, partly in response to vital economic, aesthetic, and environmental concerns. This third epoch, of the new atrium, which began in the 1960s, continues through the present day. How long this third epoch will last or whether the atrium will become a permanent spatial type, thus making the notion of future epochs unnecessary, remains to be seen. What is known at this time is that the atrium is a vital and exciting aspect of the present architectural era, making it highly worthy of study and analysis, now and for the foreseeable future.

notes

[1] S. K. Leung et al., "Thermally Induced Ventilation in Atria: A State-of-the-Art Report," Eureka Laboratories, Sacramento, Calif., 1981, p. 7.

[2] Amos Rapoport, *House Form and Culture,* Prentice-Hall, Englewood Cliffs, N.J., 1969, p. 81.

[3] E. Camesasca, *History of the House,* Putnam, New York, 1971, p. 32.

[4] Ibid., p. 46.

[5] Ibid., p. 50.

[6] Vitruvius, *The Ten Books on Architecture,* H. M. Morgan (trans.), Dover, New York, 1960, pp. 176–180.

[7] Camesasca, op. cit., p. 53.

[8] R. Sturgis, *A Dictionary of Architecture and Building,* Volume I, Macmillan, New York, 1901, p. 50.

[9] J. Fleming, H. Honour, and N. Pevsner, *The Penguin Dictionary of Architecture,* Penguin, Middlesex, England, 1966, p. 64.

[10] H. Mansart, P. Bourget, and G. Cattavi, *Jules Hardouin Mansart,* Vincent Freal, Paris, 1956, Pl. LXXIX.

[11] John Hix, *The Glass House,* Phaidon, London, 1974, pp. 133–150.

[12] J. F. Geist, *Arcades,* MIT Press, Cambridge, Mass., 1983, p. 3.

[13] Ibid.

[14] H. R. Hitchcock, *Architecture: Nineteenth and Twentieth Centuries,* Penguin, Middlesex, England, 1958, p. 171.

[15] Alfred Barry, *The Life and Works of Sir Charles Barry,* Benjamin Blom, New York, 1972; London, 1867.

[16] Hitchcock, op. cit., p. 180.

[17] B. Marrey and P. Chemetov, *Architectures Paris 1848–1914,* Exhibition Catalog, Secretariat of Culture, Paris, 1972.

[18] Sigfried Giedion, *Space, Time and Architecture,* Harvard University Press, Cambridge, Mass., 1962, pp. 306–314.

[19] Chris Bene, "The Pension Building: Smithsonian Museum of Architecture," Thesis, University of Virginia School of Architecture, Charlottesville, Va., 1975.

[20] Ibid.

[21] Cynthia Field, "Energy Conscious Design: The Pension Building," in *Blueprints,* Committee for a National Museum of the Building Arts, Washington, D.C., July, 1980.

[22] Visitor Information, Bradbury Building Manager, Los Angeles, 1980.

[23] Giedion, op. cit., pp. 416–419.

[24] "The Brown Palace Hotel," Brown Palace Hotel, Denver, 1967.

[25] Donald Hoffman, *The Architecture of John Wellborn Root,* Johns Hopkins University Press, Baltimore, 1973, pp. 30–32.

[26] Ibid., pp. 65–83.

[27] Ibid., pp. 121–126.

[28] Ibid., pp. 132–137.

[29] Ibid., pp. 196–202.

[30] Ibid., pp. 206–211.

[31] Ibid., pp. 207–215.

[32] F. R. Kowsky et al., *Buffalo Architecture: A Guide,* MIT Press, Cambridge, Mass., 1961, p. 81.

[33] G. B. Tatum, *Penn's Great Town,* University of Pennsylvania Press, Philadelphia, 1961.

[34] O. W. Grube, P. L. Pran, and F. Schulze, *100 Years of Architecture in Chicago,* J. Philip O'Hara, 1973.

[35] T. S. Hines, *Burnham of Chicago,* Oxford University Press, New York, 1974, pp. 276–278.

[36] D. Hoffman, op. cit., p. 83.

[37] Grube et al., op. cit.

[38] Tatum, op. cit.

[39] Kowsky, op. cit., p. 82.

[40] "A New Landmark Center for St. Paul," *Architectural Record,* December 1978, pp. 100–105.

[41] Lois Craig, "Competitions: In Search of Quality," *Architectural Record,* December 1978, pp. 88–91.

[42] J. L. Eldredge, *Architecture Boston,* Boston Society of Architects, Boston, 1976, pp. 87–90.

[43] J. Barnett and J. Portman, *The Architect as Developer,* McGraw-Hill, New York, 1976.

[44] J. T. Burns and C. R. Smith, "Charity Begins at Home," *Progressive Architecture,* February 1968, pp. 92–105.

2 Urban Design

OVERLEAF: *Atrium rendering,*
Hercules Plaza, Wilmington,
Delaware. (Architects: Kohn Pedersen
Fox Associates)

The atrium is emerging as one of the most versatile and useful urban design elements available to contemporary architects and urban planners. Its utility for purposes of urban renewal with respect to the contextual influences of geometry, street pattern, and building mass is becoming readily apparent. Moreover, atria have the capacity to integrate old and new buildings, thus playing an active role in historic preservation strategy. Most important, atria add to the inventory of public spaces available to the pedestrian, joining inside and outside and enriching the urban experience.

Since its inception in Roman times, the atrium has served the needs for privacy, control, light, and air created by the urban condition. (Some atrium buildings are located in nonurban contexts, but they are the result of extenuating programmatic or site conditions.) Increasingly, its urban design potential is being acknowledged and realized, as evidenced by the examples in this chapter. The future promises even more atria in those cities and for those projects in which the integrity of the urban fabric and the richness of pedestrian life are important urban design criteria.

URBAN FORM

For at least three decades, the freestanding tower on an open plaza has been the prevailing urban building typology. In many cities, such as New York, this building form has been encouraged by incentive zoning that grants building height bonuses, or floor-area increases, based upon the creation of a public plaza amenity. In many cases, these plazas have become marginal amenities devoid of the design features necessary to make them useful public spaces. William H. Whyte has documented this well in his book *The Social Life of Small Urban Spaces.*[1] The corporate office buildings fronting on these plazas are aloof and detached from the street, often detracting from the historical continuity of urban commercial frontage and disrupting the pedestrian experience.

An atrium can be thought of as a public plaza which is enclosed, providing weather protection and its attendant benefits. In many instances it can be more beneficial to the public than an outdoor plaza. In the late 1960s, the New York City zoning law was amended to allow zoning incentives for covered pedestrian spaces, retail malls, and through-block arcades. In the case of atria, building floor-area increases could be granted on an equal basis with outdoor plazas.[2] The design of access and circulation is important to the success of atria as public amenities. At Citicorp Center (Design Study 46), this aspect has been well handled, assuring public availability. At the Park Avenue Atrium Building (466 Lexington), on the other hand, the circulation to and through the atrium is not encouraged by the design, making its public value suspect. Many atria have been built in New York under these zoning incentives, and more are surely to be built, since the "covered pedestrian space" provision has been retained in the most recent zoning revisions.

A concomitant feature of atrium building forms is usually lower, wider massing, which maintains urban street facades. This is very important in cities where the proliferation of plazas has destroyed the definition of the street as the most significant urban space. The continuity of street facades allows buildings from different eras to take their place within a prescribed relationship to each other and with common allegiance to the street. The viability of commercial districts often depends upon this continuity of street shop frontages to maintain vitality. Where atria, arcades, malls, or galleries are built, care must be taken to maintain this continuity of the shopping experience by providing good pedestrian connections. Shops facing atria can usually have frontage on the street as well.

In Washington, D.C., there has been a long tradition of building to the street plane. L'Enfant's plan of 1791 created a system of wide avenues intersecting civic squares. This wealth of open space, combined with a height limit of 160 feet established in 1910 in order to preserve views of the Capitol, has resulted in a proliferation of buildings with open-air courtyards.[3] Recently, atria have been taking the place of courtyards, as at 1201 Pennsylvania Avenue (Figure 2-1), 1300 New York Avenue (Design Study 7), and International Square. The usual floor-to-area ratio is 10, resulting in buildings of eleven, twelve, and thirteen stories with generous-sized atria. In each of these office buildings, the street frontages feature shops or services which also open onto the atrium. The overall result is a city with a high

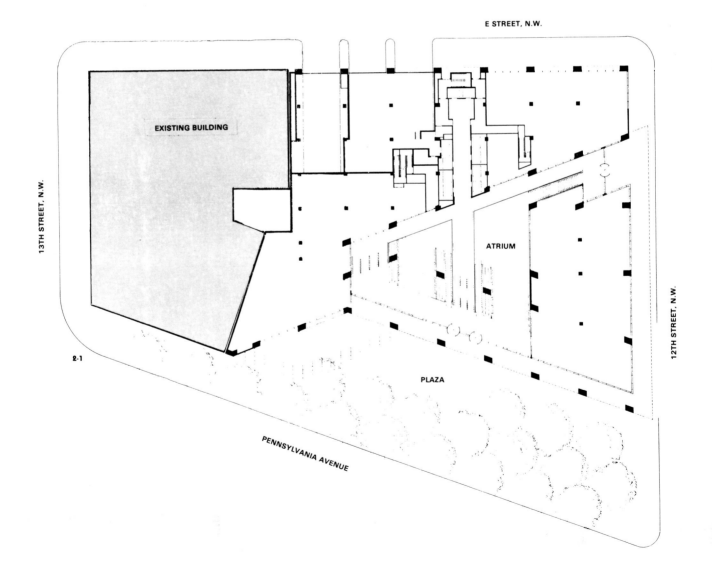

degree of urban design integrity, where the limits of building height and building density have yielded a clear spatial hierarchy.

Given equal area, atrium buildings hold many other advantages over towers. (The economic advantages are analyzed in Chapter 3.) But the urban design advantages are perhaps the most significant. For years to come, our culture's greatest architectural legacy will be the quality of life provided by our urban spaces.

THE ATRIUM AS PUBLIC PLACE

One of the most exciting urban design values of atria is their contribution toward the development of meaningful pedestrian sequences in the city. Until recently, urban designers have primarily had to utilize exterior spaces such as streets, arcades, plazas, and miniparks as passages for pedestrians. Atria add a new dimension to this inventory because they are enclosed and therefore offer a conditioned climate. This fact alone extends their usefulness to more hours and days per year, since weather is no longer a major determinant of use. Additional amenities and features can be offered, such as landscaping, artwork, fountains, and exhibitions. Transitions from outside to inside are available to extend the richness of the pedestrian experience.

Good examples of atria which have been successfully incorporated into the pedestrian network are readily available. In Wilmington, Delaware, the atrium of the new Hercules Plaza forms a link between the downtown and a park bordering Brandywine Creek (Figure 2-2). The lobby presents a choice of three paths: one up to the offices, a second around the retail arcades at the sides, and a third down through the indoor garden to the riverfront park (Design Study 8). In Sacramento, the atrium of the Gregory Bateson Building forms a spatial linkage between the park on the east and the plaza on the west, with walk-throughs encouraged by the positioning of the entrances (Design Study 3). At the Philadelphia Stock Exchange (Design Study 1), pedestrians are encouraged to walk through the block-long garden via entrances at both corners on Market Street.

An excellent example of coordination between an atrium building and an urban pedestrian sequence exists in San Antonio, Texas. Here the Paseo del Rio (river walk) is located one level below the street with a new connection to the historic Alamo (Figure 2-3). The Hyatt Regency San Antonio (Design Study 34) is located where the new "spur" joins the old river loop. The running water and pedestrian way pass right through the hotel atrium. The atrium embraces all aspects of the

FIGURE 2-2 Site plan, Hercules Plaza, Wilmington, Delaware. (Architects: Kohn Pedersen Fox Associates)

FIGURE 2-3 Site section, Hyatt Regency San Antonio, San Antonio, Texas. (Architects: Thompson, Ventulett, Stainback & Associates with Ford, Powell & Carson)

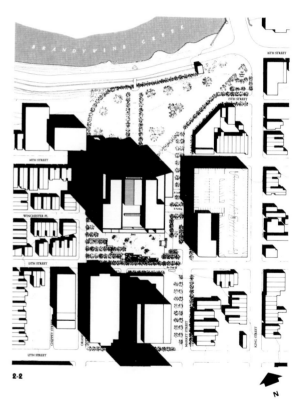

2-2

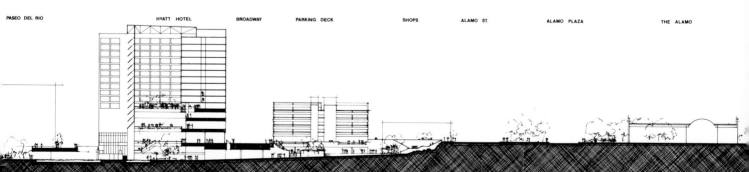

2-3

FIGURE 2-4 Master plan, Embarcadero Center, San Francisco, California. (Architects: John Portman & Associates)

FIGURE 2-5 Site plan, Hennepin County Government Center, Minneapolis, Minnesota. Architects: John Carl Warnecke Associates— redrawn)

FIGURE 2-6 Site plan, National Gallery of Art, East Building, Washington, D. C. (Architects: I. M. Pei & Partners)

hotel, both visually and spatially, relating the river walk to the hotel lobby, restaurants, and guest rooms.

At the Embarcadero Center in San Francisco, the Hyatt Hotel atrium forms the terminus to a pedestrian sequence and yields access to an urban plaza. John Portman entered the scene after several buildings had been constructed on top of a three-story parking garage. Portman developed a new master plan (Figure 2-4) which placed the parking underground to serve four office towers. A series of above-grade plazas was developed with places for shopping and eating continuing in a sequence toward the bay. Here the sequence reaches a major urban plaza with a direct connection, at the third level, to the atrium of the Hyatt Regency Hotel (Design Study 26). This pedestrian sequence is quite spectacular, with the drama of the enormous atrium making it an appropriate terminal space.

Relating an atrium to a civic space is another means of achieving pedestrian and spatial integration with the urban fabric. At the Hennepin County Government Center in Minneapolis (Design Study 11), the building straddles the street to create two plazas, integrating the open, two-block site. The southern entrance plaza leads pedestrians up through the linear atrium to a civic plaza in front of the historic courthouse (Figure 2-5). The Dallas City Hall scheme (Design Study 22) has a linear atrium connected to a grand civic plaza via a monumental entrance, with strong visual relationships between these two major spaces. In Washington, D.C., a civic plaza was created to relate

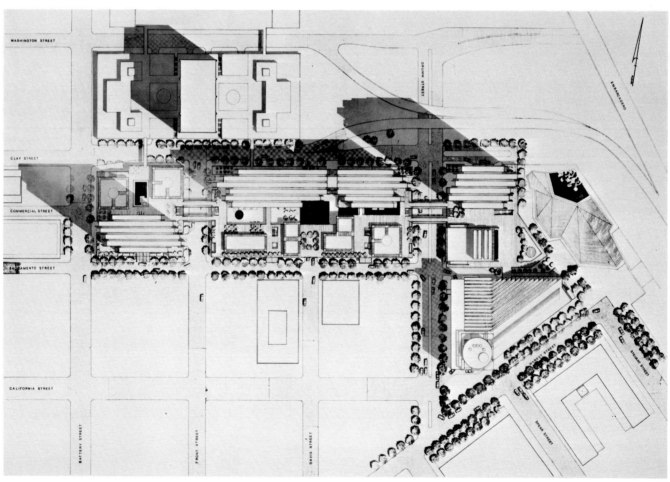

2-4

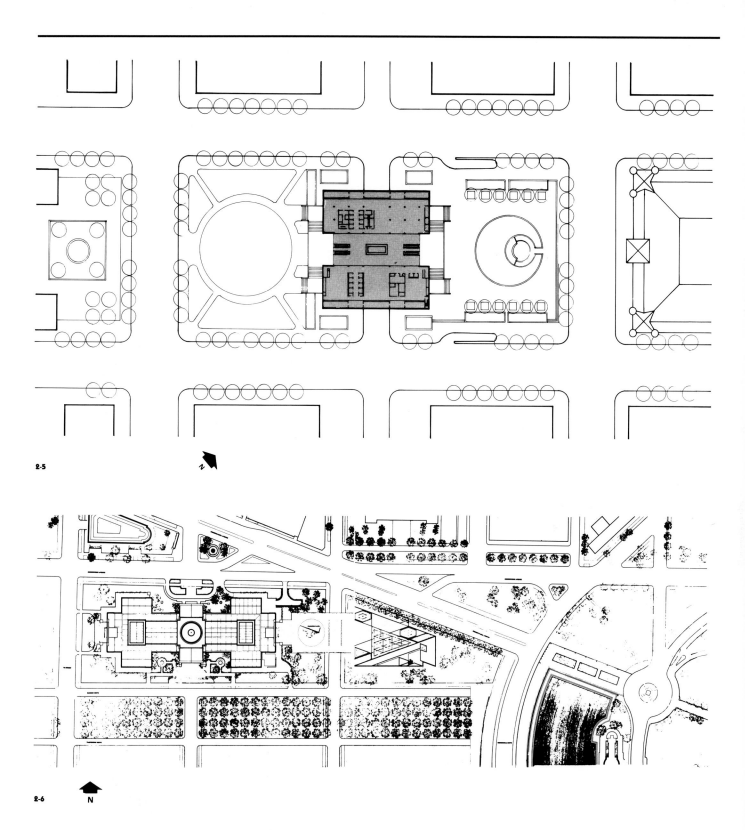

2-5

2-6

N

the new East Building of the National Gallery of Art to the main building (Figure 2-6), with the atrium linked to the plaza through an entry
and lobby (Design Study 25).

Another important type of urban connection is between the atrium
and the public transit system. In this case, the atrium serves as a
transition space between the underground subway station and the

exterior street system. At International Square in Washington, D.C., these transitions have been handled very well. The project occupies an entire block, with a new Metro station at one corner generating a diagonal concourse through the building, and the atrium is at its center (Figure 2-7). The atrium floor is one level below street grade, with a direct connection to the subway station, and there are retail activities at both Metro and street levels. This type of connection is handled similarly at Citicorp Center in New York City, except that there is a below-street-level plaza which relates the Lexington Avenue Subway to the commercial atrium (Figure 2-8).

In some cities, atria are being connected to each other through systems of pedestrian bridges and tunnels, open arcades, and covered plazas. A well-developed system exists in downtown Houston, where a series of pedestrian bridges and tunnels has evolved over a number of years to connect the partial atria and lobbies of many buildings. The below-grade tunnel system is the more extensive, connecting many older buildings to newer projects. At Pennzoil Place, a floor well, three cylindrical one-story elevators, and an escalator relate the street level to the tunnel level. More interesting to the pedestrian are the bridges which traverse streets and link atria together. A diagonal bridge connects the atrium of the Hyatt Regency Houston to the two-story wraparound atrium at 1100 Millam Street. The new Houston Center office complex has a multilevel concourse which is connected across McKinney Avenue with two pedestrian bridges to the linear atrium within the multiuse center called The Park (Figure 2-9; Design Study 44). Of course, the street-level system is also being developed with interconnecting plazas. However, due to the hot, humid climate, the pedestrian routes which connect air-conditioned spaces are preferable for much of the year.

In Atlanta, Georgia, architect and developer John Portman has made a valiant effort to relate three major atrium buildings — Hyatt Regency Hotel (Design Study 27), Peachtree Plaza Hotel, and the Apparel Mart (Design Study 41) — to office towers and parking garages within the

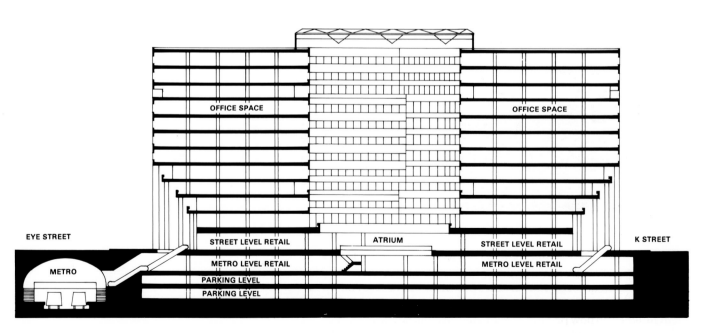

2-7

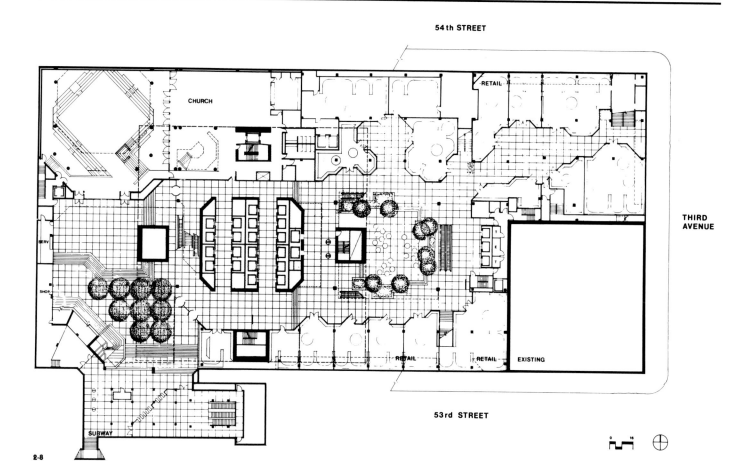

54 th STREET

CHURCH

RETAIL

THIRD
AVENUE

SERV.

SHOP.

RETAIL   RETAIL   EXISTING

53rd STREET

SUBWAY

2-8

2-9

nine-block Peachtree Center complex. However, the pedestrian bridge connections are long and in most cases are not well related to the atria. Being above street level in each case, the atrium floor does not relate well to the street pedestrian system.

An interesting new piece of urbanism has taken shape in Manhattan on two adjacent blocks between Madison and Fifth Avenues and 55th

FIGURE 2-10 Two-block urban space plan, New York, New York. (Architects: Swanke Hayden Connell)

FIGURE 2-11 Atrium view, Trump Tower, New York, New York. (Architects: Swanke Hayden Connell. Photographer: Michael Bednar)

FIGURE 2-12 Interior view, IBM garden plaza, New York, New York. (Architects: Edward Larrabee Barnes Associates. Photographer: Michael Bednar)

and 57th Streets (Figure 2-10). The pedestrian sequence begins on Fifth Avenue at the entrance to the Trump Tower (Design Study 47) and continues through a two-story interior passage to an opulent six-story commercial atrium (Figure 2-11). From there one can proceed to the triangular glazed court at the back of the IBM Tower (Figure 2-12). An enclosed arcade at the back of the Trump Tower is meant to connect across 56th Street to the half-vaulted, open-air retail arcade at the back of the AT&T Building, but they do not quite line up. The base of the AT&T Building is largely open, except for the cores and a small lobby, with a monumentally scaled arcade along Madison Avenue. There are many incongruities in scale, geometry, alignment, and architectural treatment which make this an uncoordinated, though interesting, assemblage of spaces.

As far as social availability is concerned, atria can be designed as private, semipublic, or public spaces or as variations of these. Classically, the primary courtyard or atrium in a building was a private space created for exclusive use and control, such as at the Reform Club in London. In some instances, the atrium has been a semipublic space for conditional public use, as are the lower two commercial floors at The Rookery in Chicago. Only the atria in public buildings, such as the Pension Building in Washington, have provided more than the semblance of public use and access. Such a tripartite scheme of social availability, however, has recently evolved into one of greater sophistication with more variation in the kind of access.

Of particular interest from an urban design point of view are those

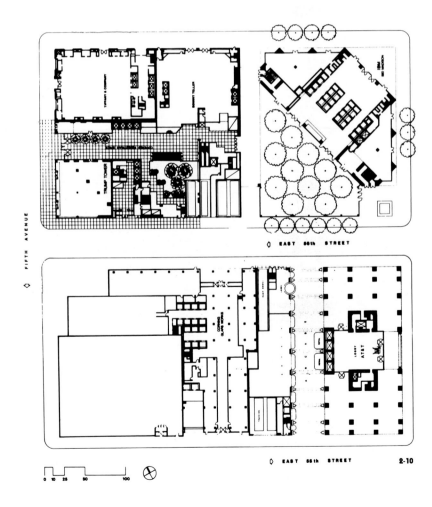

2-11

2-12

essentially private entities which have created atria that are jointly shared with the public. The most notable is at the Ford Foundation in New York (Design Study 6), where an indoor garden has been created in a twelve-story atrium for enjoyment by staff, visitors, and public alike. The Philadelphia Stock Exchange (Design Study 1), a speculative office building, and Hercules Plaza in Wilmington, Delaware (Design Study 8), have similar indoor gardens as public amenities. On

FIGURE 2-13 **FIGURE 2-13** Atrium view, ChemBank, New York, New York. (Architects: Haines Lundberg Waehler. Photographer: Michael Bednar)

2-13

Park Avenue in New York, ChemBank has covered the plaza at the base of the office tower it occupies with a block-long interior garden (Figure 2-13).

The proliferation of urban atria has created the need to direct or control access for public, semipublic, and private users. One way of achieving access control is through vertical separation. At Houston Center, for example, public access is limited to the street level, semipublic circulation is via bridges and tunnels, and private access is via high-rise elevators. Connections between public and semipublic floors are controlled by escalators, open stairs, or low-rise elevators, whereas access to the private floors is controlled at elevator lobbies, which are often not located at street level. At the Hyatt Regency San Antonio (Design Study 34), strictly public uses take place at the Paseo del Rio level and hotel uses at street level. Discontinuous vertical circulation aids in this circulation control; elevators and/or escalators from parking, commercial, or transit levels stop at the private lobby level, where new banks of elevators take over.

In all public and semipublic atria, regardless of functional use, access control and security have become a serious issue. The access control designed into a building is almost always supplemented by security personnel. For access to private levels, proof of identity and registration are becoming the rule rather than the exception. In other cases, security forces maintain control through direction-giving, user-questioning, general surveillance, and an authoritative presence. No doubt, security adds significant costs to the operation and maintenance of public access spaces of all kinds.

An interesting question regarding access control lies in the legal issue of private versus public space. In buildings or spaces owned by governmental entities, free access is usually available. But what about access and use of private and semipublic buildings? Who has the right to determine which individuals can use the space? And when does discrimination begin to occur? How can so-called undesirable elements be kept from loitering? The phenomenon of religious groups soliciting funds at airports and shopping malls has highlighted this issue in recent years. Solicitation, public protest, and political activity could easily become future issues in large-scale atria in hotels, museums, commercial buildings, and office towers.

HISTORIC PRESERVATION

Preservation of historic buildings has been an important urban design strategy in the United States during the last two decades. No longer is the clearance of old buildings accepted as a necessary means to urban renewal; it is too disruptive on many counts, often leading to sterile projects lacking continuity with historic urban patterns. This practice has been replaced by historic preservation, the effective integration of old structures and new development, resulting in urban projects which are more economically viable, interesting, and respectful of local traditions.

The atrium concept has had a significant role in the preservation movement. Its usefulness has been demonstrated in preservation, adaptive reuse, and integration of new with old structures. Its rediscovery and resurgence can be somewhat attributed to the increased historical knowledge and awareness of architects and urban designers. In fact, the growth of these two design phenomena are approximately parallel in time.

The restoration and/or preservation of certain significant atrium buildings have either taken place or been proposed. The Bradbury Building in Los Angeles and the Arcade in Cleveland have been accurately restored, with no change in use. The Pension Building in Washington, D.C., is awaiting preservation and adaptive reuse as the National Building Museum. The Old Post Office in Buffalo, New York, has already been converted to the Erie County Community College (Design Study 18). (All of these examples were presented in Chapter 1.) Other examples remain to be restored as warranted by their condition.

One of the great advantages of the atrium concept is that the designer is able to accurately restore the exterior of a building, thus maintaining the urban fabric, while giving the building a new interior. This allows a change of use, new vertical circulation, and a revised energy strategy, as well as the installation of new building services. Two approaches have been utilized in this process: covering courtyards and carving out atria.

Many nineteenth-century buildings had courtyards to admit light and air and to provide views. In their renewed life, these courtyards have been enclosed with glazing and converted into atria. Louis Sullivan's well-known Wainwright Building in St. Louis had a U-shaped courtyard which has now been enclosed as part of an overall scheme for changing the circulation system and providing energy efficiency (Figure 2-14). At the 1913 Biltmore Hotel in New York City, architects converted a similar courtyard to the Bank of America building with a twenty-seven-story atrium by relocating the elevator core (Figure 2-15).[4] However, the resulting 66-foot by 68-foot atrium is poorly proportioned for its height, and the interior facades are banal and uniform on all four sides.

Providing a glazed cover is a relatively easy means of converting a courtyard, which is already enclosed on four sides, into an atrium. The Philadelphia Bourse originally had a skylight over the trading floor with an open-air courtyard above (Design Study 42). A nine-story atrium was created by relocating the skylight at the roof level. Similar strategies have been utilized at the Old Post Office in Washington,

FIGURE 2-14 Exterior view, Wainwright State Office Complex, St. Louis, Missouri. (Architects: Mitchell/Giurgola. Photograph: © Copyright 1981 Sadin/Karant)

FIGURE 2-15 Bank of America plan, New York, New York. (Architects: Environetics — redrawn)

2-14

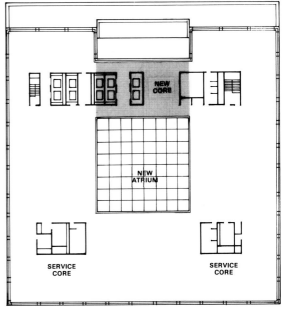

2-15

FIGURE 2-16 Atrium view, Tobacco Company
Restaurant, Richmond, Virginia.
(Photographer: Michael Bednar)

2-16

D.C. (Design Study 39), Landmark Center in St. Paul, Minnesota, and
the Erie County Community College in Buffalo, New York.

A very popular strategy, as judged by its frequent use, is actually
carving out an atrium within an old building by removing portions of
each floor from top to bottom. This can be readily accomplished in a
wood- or steel-frame building by taking out some of the beams and
columns. Atria were formed in this way in heavy timber-frame buildings such as Butler Square in Minneapolis (Design Study 45), the
Tobacco Company Restaurant in Richmond, Virginia (Figure 2-16),
and Boston's Mercantile Wharf (Design Study 35). This method
allows the possibility of various geometries in plan and section.
Usually the structural frame is left exposed to express the original
framing method and the subsequent atrium formation.

Some of the most ambitious preservation projects have utilized atria
to unite old and new structures, forming cohesive complexes of buildings. The atrium can be used to create a transitional space which

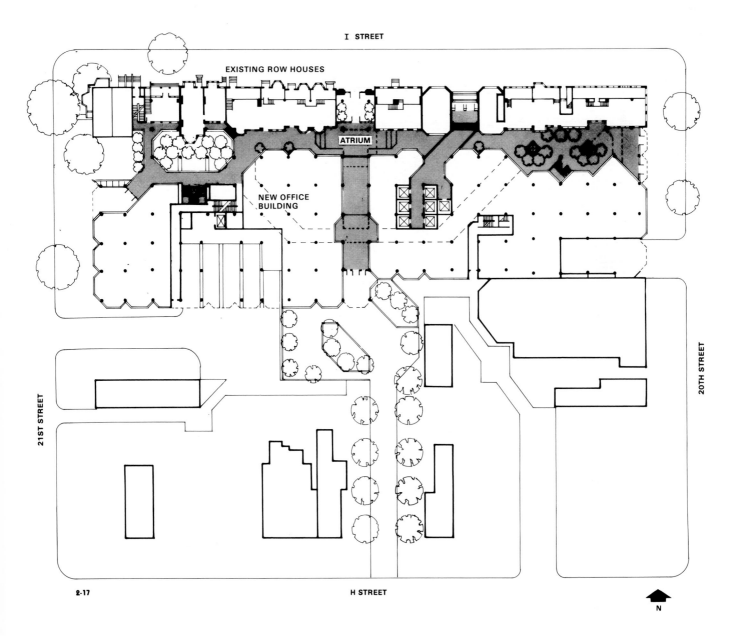

2-17

FIGURE 2-17 Street-level floor plan, 2000 Pennsylvania Avenue, Washington, D. C. (Architects: Hellmuth, Obata & Kassabaum — redrawn)

FIGURE 2-18 Atrium view, 2000 Pennsylvania Avenue, Washington, D. C. (Architects: Hellmuth, Obata & Kassabaum. Photographer: Michael Bednar)

2-18

unifies the project. At 2000 Pennsylvania Avenue in Washington, D.C., a new eleven-story office building has been placed behind a block of late nineteenth-century townhouses in order to preserve them. The skylighted space between is an interesting linear atrium formed by the juxtaposition of the new concrete and glass office building and the irregular brick facades of the old townhouses (Figures 2-17, 2-18). Another unique scheme can be found at the Board of Trade in Chicago (Design Study 15). A twelve-story atrium, starting at the twelfth floor, connects the original 1930 building to the new building addition.

All of these methods of utilizing atria in the interest of urban historic preservation will continue to be used in the future. Atria offer architects versatile and adaptable tools for the solution of difficult design problems. Moreover, atria can be used to give historic preservation projects new spatial identity, complementing the visual identity of the building's original facades.

FIGURE 2-19   Site plan, IDS Center, Minneapolis, Minnesota. (Architects: Johnson/Burgee — redrawn)

FIGURE 2-20   Exterior view, IDS Center, Minneapolis, Minnesota. (Architects: Johnson/Burgee. Photograph: Johnson/ Burgee)

FIGURE 2-21   Crystal Court view, IDS Center, Minneapolis, Minnesota. (Architects: Johnson/Burgee. Photograph: Johnson/ Burgee)

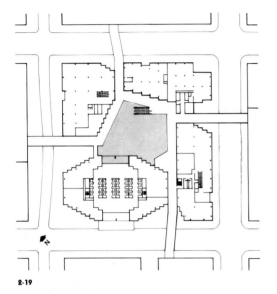

2-19

2-20

THE PLAZA ATRIUM

Out of the rapid evolution of the atrium during the last two decades a new spatial type has emerged: the plaza atrium. This atrium is no longer contained within a given building but rather serves to interrelate several buildings by forming an enclosed space which is shared. Analogous to a covered plaza, the space is large in scale and varied in function, and is intertwined with multileveled circulation systems. Usually it is well connected to the surrounding pedestrian spaces and streets, making the plaza atrium a unique twentieth-century urban spatial type.

The Crystal Court at IDS Center in Minneapolis, designed by Philip Johnson and John Burgee in 1973, marks the invention of this new spatial type. The IDS Center is truly a city center, at the nexus of commercial activity on the Nicollet Mall. The scheme draws together the circulation ''desire lines'' from surrounding blocks, already connected by a system of second-level bridges, or skyways. Four of these bridges come directly into the Crystal Court, two of them from the main department stores of Donaldson's and Dayton's. Under each bridge there is also a street-level entry. The Crystal Court is in the center of the block, surrounded by four new buildings: the fifty-one-story IDS office tower, a nineteen-story hotel (286 rooms), an eight-story office building containing the underground garage entrance, and a two-story Woolworth's. These four elements feed directly into the plaza atrium, which is surrounded by additional shops on two levels (Figures 2-19 and 2-20). The Crystal Court brings all of these elements together and allows them to become mutually supportive — it is the center of life for downtown Minneapolis, the main spatial event, the place to be.

The design and construction of the Crystal Court is as unique as the spatial concept. An irregular pentagon in plan, the atrium encloses a total of 20,000 square feet. In section, it rises in steps from two stories to seven stories at the IDS tower, the lower office floors of which command views onto the atrium. The roof structure is a unique steel crystalline space frame, painted white, with vertical clear glass and pyramidal, translucent acrylic skylights. Balcony walkways of blue-painted steel are suspended from this space frame. The spatial effect is breathtaking and the daylight quality excellent on both sunny and rainy days. The ground floor is quite open and unstructured, as in a plaza. Furnishings and plantings are sparse but will probably increase as the place matures (Figure 2-21).

The design of the Crystal Court is very pragmatic for this harsh northern environment of subzero temperatures, high winds, and frequent snows. The enclosed, climate-controlled atmosphere puts people at ease, allowing them to enjoy the activities there without worrying about the elements. The atrium's use extends into the night and to days when the weather curtails other activities. Merchants do not have to depend upon reasonable weather to spur sales. Although it takes a considerable amount of capital to construct such a place, and although operating and maintenance costs are high, in the long run increased commercial activity may justify these outlays.

Duality of function and image are inherent in the design of the Crystal Court. It is both a focal space for the pedestrian in the city and an entry to the four buildings on the block. The crystalline roof structure is ambiguous, being both opaque and transparent, closed and open. The solid surrounding masses give it spatial definition. The

tension, the duality between these opposites, imbues the Crystal Court with a sense of intrigue.

Construction of the Omni International in Atlanta in 1976 followed creation of the IDS Center in Minneapolis. The Omni, a mixed-use development, is also organized around a very large plaza atrium which serves to unify the complex of buildings. However, the Atlanta complex is more autonomous, being located away from the commercial core and built on air rights over railroad tracks. The intention of developers Tom Cousins and Maurice Alpert was to create a business and convention center in downtown Atlanta which could compete with the many outlying regional shopping centers and office parks. This was achieved in a rundown western part of downtown (Figure 2-22).

The plaza atrium at the Omni International in Atlanta is a colossus, exceeding the scale of the atrium of the historic Pension Building in Washington, D.C. It is clearly the largest atrium space known, enclosing some 11 million cubic feet. Although approximately trapezoidal in plan, the geometry develops complexities at both ends. The two office buildings flanking the long sides of the atrium, with their regular planar facades, add needed stability and definition to the space. It is truly a *mega*-atrium for a *mega*structure.

The atrium, referred to as "The Great Space," is intended to unify the several elements which constitute this mixed-use center: two eleven-story office buildings, a 500-room hotel, an indoor amusement park, 230,000 square feet of retail shops, ten restaurants, and six cinemas (Figure 2-23).

The plaza atrium is intended as a great public space, with an olympic-size ice-skating rink as its focus. It is ringed by four levels of galleries which serve the various facilities and has a bridge which crosses

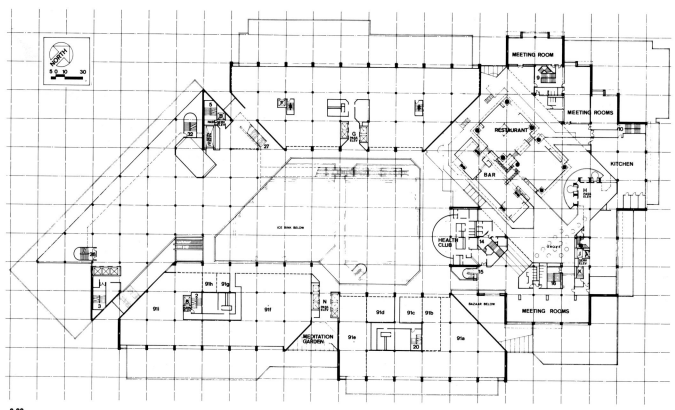

2-22

the ice rink. The hotel has its own terrace at the fourth level, giving it a separate spatial identity. It also has balconies which overlook the atrium. The varied geometry of the galleries tends to fragment the space at the lower four public levels. The ice-skating rink, used by only a small number, creates a peripheral circulation scheme that puts emphasis upon the galleries. Designing the ground floor as a public plaza would have enabled more people to occupy and experience the entire atrium.

The circulation system is ordered in such a way that it serves the separate elements. The lower four levels of commercial functions are served by escalators at the two ends of the atrium. Each office tower is served by a private elevator bank and lobby. The elevator bank for the hotel is removed from the main atrium, with four glass observation cars indicating its presence. The grand circulation event is an eight-story escalator offering a two-minute ride to the amusement world, which unfortunately is no longer in operation. The escalator is poised as a linear element along one side of the atrium and offers an exciting, dynamic way to experience "The Great Space" (Figure 2-24).

The success of Omni International is equally attributable to the attraction of the components (parking structure, sports coliseum, multiuse center, and convention center) and the quality of the architecture. Thompson, Ventulett, Stainback & Associates, the architects from Atlanta, designed buildings with a significant degree of boldness and clarity without sacrificing accommodation of user needs. This design attitude is epitomized in the atrium, a "great space" which is awesome in scale, yet memorable at a personal level.

In San Francisco, Welton Becket and Associates have designed a one-block complex of offices and retail called One Market Plaza. Bliss and Faville's 1916 Southern Pacific Building faces Market Street and serves as a main entry to the complex. The U-shaped courtyard of this

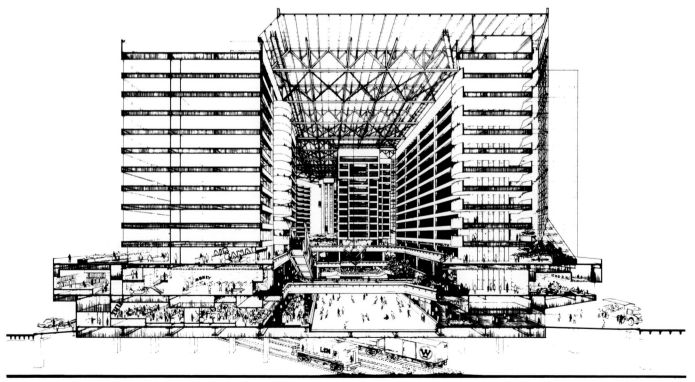

2-23

2-24

building was made into a partial atrium, from which a pedestrian galleria now extends through the block to Mission Street (Figures 2-25 and 2-26). A twenty-eight-story and a forty-two-story office tower straddle this galleria, rising out of a six-story base of offices and retail, with open-air terraces on the roof. The pedestrian arcade on all four street sides allows shops to have double frontage. The skylighted pedestrian spaces on the interior of the block tie the elements of the complex together, while providing a gracious public amenity.

In South Bend, Indiana, Murphy/Jahn Architects have created First Source Center, a 27,000 square foot piazza atrium relating a 150,000 square foot bank and office building to a 300-room hotel, with a 520-car parking garage underneath. The atrium has a formal, semicircular entrance from a parking plaza, with through-the-block visual and pedestrian connections to a nearby park. The piazza gradually gives way

FIGURE 2-24   Atrium view, Omni International, Atlanta, Georgia. (Architects: Thompson, Ventulett & Stainback. Photographer: Alexandre Georges)

FIGURE 2-25   Galleria view, One Market Plaza, San Francisco, California. (Architects: Welton Becket & Associates. Photographer: Michael Bednar)

FIGURE 2-26   Site section, One Market Plaza, San Francisco, California. (Architects: Welton Becket & Associates — redrawn)

2-25

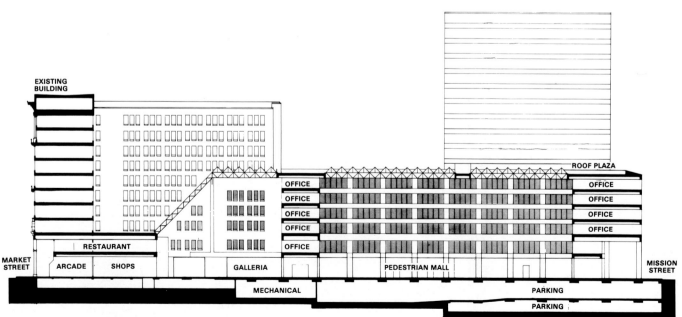

2-26

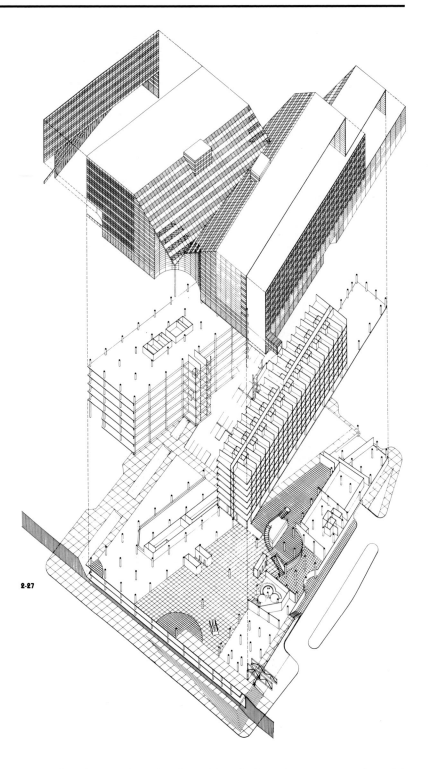

2-27

to the first floors of the bank and hotel, fostering a sense of spatial interrelatedness. The atrium form is unique, being trapezoidal in plan, with an inverted gable roof which reduces the enclosed volume considerably (Figure 2-27). The atrium is sheathed with alternating bands of clear glass and silver reflective glass stretched over an exposed steel structure. The complex geometry of the crystalline forms shimmers in the sunlight, with fascinating visual patterns being formed on the inside. A grand interior civic space has been created as a gift to the people of this small city (Figure 2-28).

2-28

The creation of the Crystal Court marked the invention of a new atrium type. What the nineteenth-century arcade did for the shopping street, the plaza atrium has done for the plaza. It has been enclosed and internalized to create an interior public space full of pedestrian amenities. Several large mixed-use projects have utilized the plaza atrium as a unifying spatial element, especially in climates that are either too hot or too cold. It has been demonstrated that this design concept, which has greatly improved the quality of urban life in cities in which it has been utilized, is viable both functionally and financially. More such projects are sure to be designed and built in the near future.

COMMERCIAL ATRIA

No analysis of the role of atria in urban design would be complete without a discussion of the urban shopping center. Fundamentally, this is not a new spatial form, for it grows out of America's two-decade love affair with the suburban shopping mall, which had its antecedents in the nineteenth-century commercial arcades. However, the introduction of the enclosed shopping mall into the core of many cities

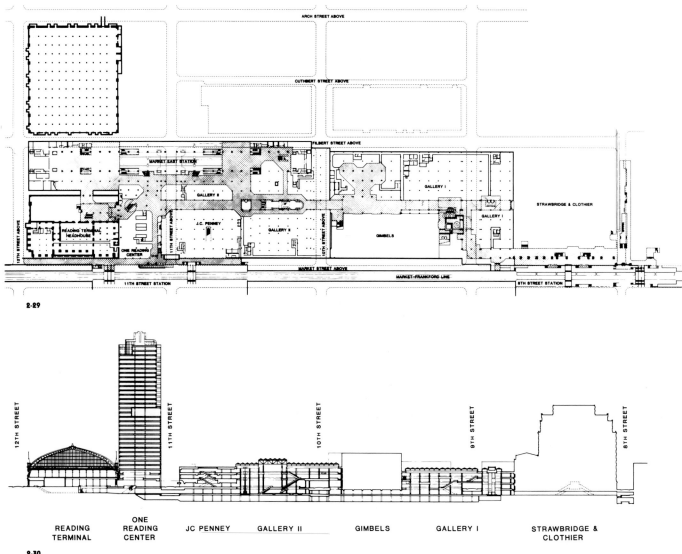

2-29

2-30

has caused it to change, to become more vertical and more spatially complex, while simultaneously accommodating to a variety of contextual forces.

After World War II, the suburban shopping center movement grew very rapidly in the United States, resulting in many large complexes of stores surrounding open-air, landscaped malls. In 1956, Victor Gruen designed and built the Southdale Mall in Minneapolis, the first enclosed shopping mall.[5] The mall was more compact than previous open-air malls and comprised two stories; the high cost of enclosing and conditioning a large common space was one factor that influenced the design. The advantages to the shopper were obvious: less walking, in a pleasant, weather-free environment. The advantages to the retailer were a captive commercial audience and the ability to control merchandising, while keeping undesirable influences outside. Now, some three decades later, there are enclosed shopping malls in every corner of the United States.

Victor Gruen also created the prototype for the urban shopping center when in the years 1956 to 1962 he designed the Midtown Plaza in Rochester, New York.[6] The mall was created at the back of two existing department stores and a hotel, connecting them to a new eighteen-story office-hotel, a bus terminal, a 2000-car underground garage, and fifty shops. However, this prototype was not adopted as readily as its suburban counterpart. Although many urban shopping centers were planned and designed, few, if any, were built.

Among the first of the new generation of urban shopping centers to be built with an enclosed linear atrium was Gallery I in Philadelphia, completed in 1977. The second phase, Gallery II, was completed in 1983. Located along East Market Street between Eighth and Twelfth streets, this project extends from the existing Strawbridge and Clothier Department Store on the east to the 1893 Reading Terminal on the west, with two new department stores, 400,000 square feet of shops, a thirty-one-story office building, and two parking garages (Figures 2-29 and 2-30). The whole is spatially connected by a four-story linear atrium which begins one level below the street. This allows pedestrian traffic to flow beneath existing vehicular cross streets. It also brings the above-ground pedestrian in at midlevel, a design decision based on the supposition that it is always easier to go down than up, even on an escalator. A glazed entrance atrium at Ninth Street creates a vertical circulation node and a spatial focus for special events (Figure 2-31). A similar spatial focus occurs in Gallery II (Figure 2-32). Both of these atrium nodes feature fountains, extensive landscaping, and mobiles hung from the skylight structure.

The Gallery at Market East took the shopping street and moved it to the middle of the block, enclosed it with skylights, and intensified the availability vertically to four levels. It is unfortunate that the new buildings had to turn their backs to the street, detracting from a wider range of pedestrian activities. However, the advantages of the new enclosed shopping street to the pedestrian are considerable, including safety from traffic, freedom from noise, lack of precipitation, and climate conditioning. The linear atrium has been designed as a pedestrian street with full-width skylights, brick pavers, street lighting, full-size trees, water features, and landscaping. The architecture is subdued so as to highlight the stores and the activities of the shoppers.

By every measure, this project is a great success. New economic vitality has come to what was once a blighted section of the city. After

FIGURE 2-31 Gallery I view, Market Street East, Philadelphia, Pennsylvania. (Architects: Bower & Fradley. Photograph: Bower & Fradley)

FIGURE 2-32 Gallery II view, Market Street East, Philadelphia, Pennsylvania. (Architects: Bower Lewis Thrower. Photograph: Bower Lewis Thrower)

2-31

one year of operation, sales were reported to be over twice the average for a suburban shopping mall.[7] This level of sales in the three department stores is crucial to the long-term stability of this center, for it represents sales to middle-class residents, not tourists. The direct, unembellished architecture supports this marketing strategy. Shoppers enjoy the convenience of access from subways, trains, and on-site parking garages. A vital new piece of the city has been created after a long period (since 1958) of gestation and planning.

The typology of a commercial base with offices above, both surrounding an atrium, has been utilized since Burnham and Root developed it at the end of the last century. Several atrium buildings from that era utilized this arrangement. Two excellent rehabilitated examples are the Philadelphia Bourse (Design Study 42) and the Old Post Office in Washington, D.C. (Design Study 39).

Two recent projects in Houston, Texas, have been able to success-

2-32

fully integrate linear shopping malls with office towers above, both uses sharing a common atrium. Galleria II (Design Study 43) is a mixed-use center in a suburban location which uses an atrium to integrate five different functions: parking, shops, offices, department store, and hotel. The central vertical atrium is directly shared by parking, shops, and offices, with consistent design treatment yielding well-defined and ordered spaces.

The Park in Houston Center (Design Study 44) is a two-block-long, mixed-use development joined by pedestrian bridges to office towers across McKinney Avenue. The two-level shopping mall sits above a parking garage with a twelve-story office slab rising above. A large-scale, half-vaulted skylight encloses the retail mall and four floors of offices which overlook it. The development of new retail uses within this corporate office sector will make it a more enjoyable place to work. Its success as a commercial venture has been greatly enhanced by the multiplicity of pedestrian connections: tunnels, street-level walkways, and bridges.

Another version of this mixed-use concept can be seen at Citicorp Center (Design Study 46) and Trump Tower (Design Study 47), both in New York City. In these two schemes the commercial atrium is separate from the rest of the building except for common entrances and ground-floor circulation.

Since the agora of ancient Greece, western culture has placed great value on making the marketplace also a meeting place, through architecture which incorporates a public open space. In the nineteenth century, these commercial centers became enclosed; steel and glass technology made possible great market halls, arcades, gallerias, and *grands magasins*. Contemporary urban commercial centers featuring linear atria maintain the historic continuity of this typological tradition.

After three decades of retail migration to the suburbs, the return of retail to urban centers is certainly a hopeful sign of revitalization. The success of enclosed suburban shopping malls is due in part to their amenities and environment. Designers of recent urban shopping centers are borrowing upon this experience with the intention of making shopping fun again. The atrium space has a vital role to play in this regard. The design danger is introversion; these new urban centers must not become exclusive and inward-oriented. They must be good pieces of urban design tied into existing pedestrian, transport, and service systems, while acknowledging historic contextual forces. Only in this way can they contribute to a healthy urban fabric.

NOTES

[1] William H. Whyte, *The Social Life of Small Urban Spaces,* The Conservation Foundation, Washington, D.C., 1980.

[2] Ibid., Chapter 8.

[3] "The Pennsylvania Avenue Plan 1974," Pennsylvania Avenue Development Corporation, Washington, D.C., 1974, p. 85.

[4] J. B. Gardner, "Structural Design Ingenuity Aids Historic Hotel Transformation," *Architectural Record,* January 1983, pp. 128–133.

[5] V. Gruen and L. Smith, *Shopping Towns, USA,* Reinhold, New York, 1960.

[6] "Center for Rochester," *Architectural Forum,* June 1962, pp. 108–113.

[7] David Morton, "Suburban Shopping Downtown?" *Progressive Architecture,* December 1978, p. 64.

3 Design Analysis

OVERLEAF: *Rendering of atrium,*
State of Illinois Center, Chicago,
Illinois. (Architects: Murphy/Jahn.
Renderer: Kevin Woest)

As revealed in Chapter 1, "Historical Development," the concept of an atrium has evolved and changed considerably throughout the course of history. It originated as the primary space of a Roman house, the communal space to which all other rooms were related. It was also a place of arrival and circulation which brought light and air to the center of the house through the roof. In the evolution of this concept, many of these characteristics have been retained and others added, most notably that of an atrium as an enclosed interior space.

SPATIAL TYPOLOGY

In an effort to define the contemporary concept of the atrium, its recent development has been analyzed with a view toward the historical evolution of the form. The salient characteristic is spatial and leads to a new definition of the term:

ATRIUM: *a centroidal, interior, daylit space which organizes a building.*

Centroidal is a key word in this definition, because if a space is in the center of a plan and extends vertically through the building in section, then it has the potential to spatially organize that building. The atrium need not be in the geometric center to achieve this purpose; it can be centroidal in its spatial role as long as the majority of spaces relate to it. The atrium at the John F. Kennedy Library (Design Study 20), although not in the center of the plan, is still considered to be centroidal since the research floors and lobby overlook it. An atrium must also be an interior space, that is, a space enclosed and protected from the weather. Otherwise, it should be called a courtyard. It must also be daylit, with some measure of direct natural lighting. The central space at the new Long Wharf Marriott Hotel in Boston, for example, cannot be termed an atrium — although it is centroidal and interior — because it has no natural light. Finally, an atrium must be within a single building. Atria which meet these conditions but spatially relate several different buildings to each other should be termed *plaza atria.*

An atrium can organize a building in several ways. It should be established as a place of orientation. Horizontal and vertical circulation elements which either define or relate to it can reinforce this role. The atrium can organize a building functionally by accommodating a purpose shared by all occupants, serving as a lounge, reception, or exhibition area. In some buildings it serves as a social, institutional, or symbolic organizer. In others, atria serve to channel, modify, and distribute the natural flow of energy. However, in all cases the atrium should serve an organizational role for the entire building. If it relates to only a part of the building, it is a partial atrium.

The recent confusion regarding the atrium has been in part a problem of terminology, since an accurate definition does not currently exist. Those writing about or discussing architecture have thus used the term *atrium* to refer to the Roman type, and other terms (*court, galleria, covered plaza, square, cortile, rotunda, pavilion, literium*) to refer to the new type. Hopefully, adopting the definition developed here for the term *atrium*, while using the term *Roman atrium* to refer to the ancient form, will end this confusion.

Theories of architectural typology have begun to reemerge in recent years as part of an effort to systematically analyze architecture. The

FIGURE 3-1 Closed atrium diagram.
(Delineator: Michael Bednar)

FIGURE 3-2 Open atrium diagram.
(Delineator: Michael Bednar)

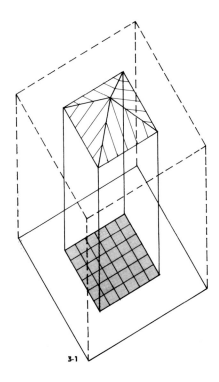

3-1

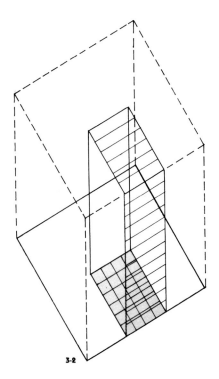

3-2

atrium building is a spatial type (also referred to as a formal type) which constitutes a given set of spatial relationships. The definition of the type is inherent in the definition of the term *atrium*. An atrium is inextricable from the building which contains it, for it is by this organizational relationship that the formal type is defined. The atrium type is distinguished from the courtyard type by being enclosed; it is distinguished from the arcade type, a form of covered street which relates buildings across a civic space, by being within a single building. The distinctions between atrium buildings, arcades, and plaza atria can, however, become ambiguous (see Chapter 2, ''Urban Design'').

What follows is a taxonomy of the atrium building type. (A similar taxonomy is used by Richard Saxon in his book *Atrium Buildings*.)[1] It is organized according to four plan subtypes of full atria, followed by the partial atrium subtype. The design studies in Part II of this book are organized according to this taxonomy, with relevant examples of each subtype.

Closed Atrium The classic or standard subtype defined on all sides by occupied zones; it is the most prevalent subtype; it can be any shape in plan, including square, rectangular, circular, or triangular. The only source of daylight and view is the skylight or roof clerestory. (Figure 3-1)

Open-Sided Atrium An atrium subtype with one, two, or three sides partially or completely glazed; the roof may or may not be glazed; the open sides are very sensitive to manipulation for view, daylight, and solar radiation. (Figure 3-2)

Linear Atrium Subtype with occupied zones on opposite sides of the atrium and circulation connections across; usually an elongated rectangle in plan; ends may be glazed or defined by building elements. Skylight or roof clerestory is the major source of view and daylight. (Figure 3-3)

Multiple Lateral Atria More than one atrium within a building, each laterally disposed and spatially organizing a section of the building. Each one is usually a complete atrium subtype in its form. Two atria with circulation elements between them is the most common variant. (Figure 3-4)

Partial Atrium Any atrium which spatially organizes only a part of a building; can be a tower base form with the atrium in the base; can be a vertically stacked form with multiple atria in a high-rise building, each one relating only a set number of floors; can be an adapted form spatially relating an old and new building. (Figure 3-5)

Classifying atria according to subtype is not always easy, since variants of these defined subtypes frequently occur, forming hybrids. For example, if the atrium embraces all of the retail space, but only part of the office space in a mixed-use building (see The Park in Houston Center, Design Study 44; Galleria II, Design Study 43), should it be classified as a partial or a linear atrium? When does a closed atrium become a linear atrium and vice versa? The classification of subtypes is not absolute, but is only for the purpose of analysis. It is based upon judgment born of a comparison of charcteristics.

Variations in building section further enrich the design possibilities

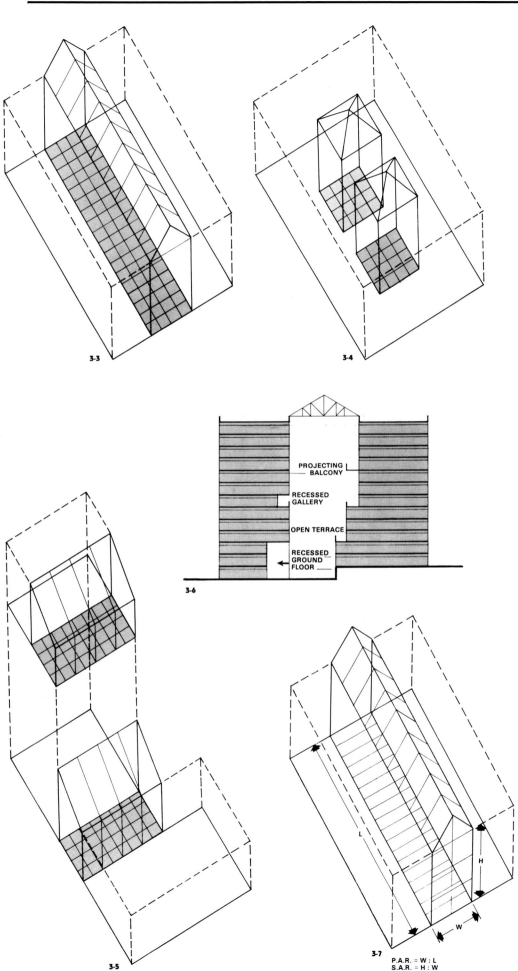

FIGURE 3-3 Linear atrium diagram.
(Delineator: Michael Bednar)

FIGURE 3-4 Multiple lateral atria diagram.
(Delineator: Michael Bednar)

FIGURE 3-5 Partial atrium diagram.
(Delineator: Michael Bednar)

FIGURE 3-6 Atrium section variations.
(Delineator: Michael Bednar)

FIGURE 3-7 Aspect ratio diagram.
(Delineator: Michael Bednar)

3-3

3-4

PROJECTING
BALCONY

RECESSED
GALLERY

OPEN TERRACE

RECESSED
GROUND
FLOOR

3-6

3-5

3-7

P.A.R. = W : L
S.A.R. = H : W

(Figure 3-6). Most atrium sections are uniform from top to bottom, with visual relief created on the interior facade by projections and setbacks. Arguments have been made for making the atrium space progressively narrower from top to bottom so that a part of each floor would have direct contact with the skylight. The opposite sectional scheme (progressively wider from top to bottom) would allow each floor to shade the one below it, where solar gain is an issue. Many variations of these three basic sectional types are in evidence. The most common variation opposes the sides, stepping one side and keeping the others vertical. In open-sided and partial atria, stepped and sloped glazed facades add a great deal of spatial interest.

The definition of every atrium space is subject to given proportions in plan and section. The plan proportion is termed *plan aspect ratio* (P.A.R. = width to length). The section proportion is termed *section aspect ratio* (S.A.R. = height to width) (Figure 3-7). An analysis of these proportions was undertaken for the atria presented in Part II. Measurements have always been taken to the actual facade of the atrium, not including galleries. Only atria with quadrilateral plans and sections were included, always using the shortest and longest dimensions. A cursory examination of these data reveals that for linear atria the P.A.R. is below 0.40, for rectangular atria between 0.40 and 0.90, and for square-plan atria 1.00 or close to 1.00. An atrium with an S.A.R. of less than 1.00 can be considered shallow, whereas an S.A.R. above 2.00 yields a tall and/or narrow proportion. The large majority of S.A.R. figures are between 1.00 and 2.00, a reasonable proportion for effective daylight penetration.

It is not possible to make absolute recommendations regarding atrium plan and section proportions. There are too many other variables which influence proportions, such as site restrictions, building program, and energy strategy. (Those related to energy are discussed in Chapter 4.) Proportions can only be evaluated relative to the circumstances of each project; this is done in Part II, "Design Studies," though only when the proportions are somehow problematic. An atrium's proportions are usually perceived from its ground floor as tall and narrow (the vertical surfaces dominate) or low and wide (the roof or floor dominates). When none of these surfaces dominates, our perception of the proportions may be closer to ideal. It is always interesting to compare perceptions to numerical ratios as a means for honing judgment.

PROGRAMMATIC ROLE

As the dominant space in a building, the atrium plays a specific functional, spatial, and social role, depending on the building type and the intentions of the designer. Defining this role is important in programming and designing a successful atrium building.

The role of an atrium in collective housing would seem to be a derivation from its Roman origins. However, one of the primary concerns in collective housing is the maintenance of privacy, which is antithetical to the social cohesiveness that an atrium engenders. Thus, atria are usually utilized only for specialized housing, such as dormitories, hotels, or housing for the elderly. In these cases, the need for privacy is subordinated to the values an atrium can offer. The Atrium on the Bayshore in Tampa, Florida (Design Study 29), a highrise condominium building, is a notable exception to this general rule.

The luxury hotel has been one of the most prevalent atrium building types to emerge in recent years, to the extent that it has become the standard for the hotel industry. The atrium in a hotel usually has a dual role: as a communal social space and a place of orientation; as a common living room and a pallazzo courtyard. John Portman, who developed the modern atrium hotel, usually designs the space as a courtyard but furnishes it as a living room. Since the rooms of a hotel often form the walls of the atrium, vicarious participation in this communal space is a constant feature. Moreover, orientation within the hotel is excellent, lending a degree of security to the transient guest. Circulation within the hotel, which is explicitly related to the atrium, makes movement an enjoyable procession.

For purposes of housing, atrium schemes have been utilized when the occupants share common values and/or characteristics. The Women's Dormitory at the University of Pennsylvania is a good example (p. 25–26). Recently, a nursing home and several housing projects for the elderly have made very appropriate use of the atrium as a common living room for social events and meetings. This communal aspect is crucial for those who are facing a time of alienation and loneliness. At the C.A.B.S. Nursing Home in Brooklyn, New York, the atrium is shared with the surrounding community for socializing, playing games, or just passing the time of day (Figure 3-8). In addition, the door of each room or apartment facing the galleries surround-

3-8

ing the atrium can be observed from a single location on each floor. This makes surveillance by staff, a guard, or residents very easy and lends a sense of security to the elderly residents.

The role of atria in office buildings varies depending upon the tenants of the building. Atria in public office buildings usually serve the public first and the government workers second. Atria in multiple-tenant buildings are shared by the general public and the collective tenants, usually with some access and use controls. Atria in single-tenant buildings, such as corporate headquarters, often become combined reception areas, employee lounges, and/or public amenities. Although the atrium floor of Wright's 1904 Larkin Building was utilized as work space, this example has not been followed except in some vertical stacked atria. Of course, variations upon these roles and combinations of roles occur in some buildings.

The precedent for atria in public buildings was established in the Pension Building in Washington, D.C. (1882–1887), where in scale and treatment the ground floor was designed as a civic square. This precedent was followed in the Hennepin County Government Center in Minneapolis (Design Study 11), where the atrium floor, designed as an extension of the exterior civic plaza, relates the old and new municipal buildings. At the Gregory Bateson State Office Building in Sacramento, California (Design Study 3), the atrium is both a public plaza and an employee lounge. In each of these cases, the offices surround the civic space, indirectly sharing it with the public.

The precedent for atria in multiple-tenant buildings was established by the Bradbury Building in Los Angeles (1893), where the atrium is a magnificent lobby used jointly for circulation and access. The historical continuity of this role is evidenced by several contemporary buildings, notably 1300 New York Avenue in Washington, D.C. (Design Study 7), Enerplex in Plainsboro, New Jersey (Design Study 5), and One West Loop Plaza in Houston, Texas (Design Study 9). At the Philadelphia Stock Exchange (Design Study 1), the atrium is designed as an indoor garden for joint use by tenants and the public at large.

In single-tenant and corporate office buildings, the atrium roles are generally more specialized. At the Boise Cascade Home Office (Design Study 2), the atrium is a symbol of corporate unity, with its elevator bank standing in the center of the space. At the Lockheed Missiles and Space Company (Design Study 10), the atrium is primarily an employee lounge. This is also the case at Deere West, with its luxurious interior garden. In two well-known instances, the Ford Foundation in New York (Design Study 6) and Hercules Plaza in Wilmington, Delaware (Design Study 8), the atrium space is used both to foster corporate cohesion and to create a public amenity. The ground floor of each of these buildings is designed as a public garden, as a philanthropic corporate gesture.

The role of the atrium in a commercial complex takes its precedent from the Galleria in Milan, Italy (1867), a well-known nineteenth-century arcade. The form is essentially that of a shopping street, covered with a metal and glass structure so as to create an environment protected from the climate. The design approach is one of building facades facing an interior street and defining this linear space. The space is usually designed as a street with hard paving, street lamps, benches, fountains, sculpture, street trees, and planting. This model has been adopted in countless suburban shopping malls and is now being utilized in new urban shopping centers.

FIGURE 3-9 Atrium view, Gould Hall, University of Washington, Seattle, Washington. (Architects: Streissguth & Zema. Photographer: Ari Cowan, Information Services, University of Washington)

Many of the early arcades, including the Galleria, were mixed-use centers with shops at the lower levels and housing or offices above, a model utilized today in developments such as the Philadelphia Bourse (Design Study 42), Galleria II in Houston (Design Study 43), and The Park in Houston Center (Design Study 44). These centers retain linear street forms, with the vertical dimension of the atrium acting as the unifier of uses. As mixed-use projects grow in scale and complexity, large-scale plaza atria will prove useful as spaces which bring identity, order, and cohesion. This has been demonstrated at Omni International in Atlanta, the IDS Center in Minneapolis, and the Plaza of the Americas in Dallas. Moreover, the atria in these developments can serve independent uses — as public plazas or skating rinks.

Atria also serve as focal spaces in many institutional and civic buildings. Their roles in each of these instances are uniquely suited to the given program and purpose. In educational institutions, the atrium can be used as a communal meeting space and for group functions. At the University of Washington's College of Architecture and Urban Planning, the atrium's ground floor accommodates a coffee shop on the east end and a variety of uses on the west end, including exhibitions, social events, and theatrical presentations. By encouraging communication and interaction between students and faculty, the atrium fosters a sense of unity and identity (Figure 3-9). In a hospital, an atrium can serve as a common space for snacks and relaxation, as at the New Thomas Jefferson University Hospital (Design Study 24). At the National Gallery of Art East Building (Design Study 25), large-scale artworks are exhibited in the unique triangular atrium. In other

3-9

museums and libraries, the atrium is mainly a spatial symbol for the institution. In the Dallas City Hall (Design Study 22), the atrium floor provides easy access to public services, while the space provides orientation within this large bureaucracy. The civic or institutional building type is perhaps the most interesting with regard to the atrium role because of its high variability and the need for specific adaptation.

In this analysis of the programmatic role of atria in different building types the emphasis has been upon the variation in functional, spatial, and social roles. It is indeed interesting to see the many ways in which this common spatial type can be adapted. Moreover, many new adaptations have occurred in the last two decades, as architects have become familiar with atrium design and have explored its potential.

There are commonalities as well as differences to be discerned from this analysis. An atrium by its very nature as a focal space provides orientation for building occupants and the public. To the extent that circulation is related to the atrium, this sense of orientation is reinforced. An atrium also imparts an image identity to the building, a memorable gestalt of its spatial organization. It gives a building a center of gravity, a *locus nexus,* a place of repose.

DESIGN ECONOMICS

Most developers' and building owners' first reaction to the atrium concept is that it is very exciting but obviously too expensive. How can any building which sets aside such a large space, often without functional purpose, be economically reasonable? The complexity of the skylight system alone is enough to make an atrium design appear unfeasible. A more compact building form using less land area must, it is assumed, be lower in cost.

Closer evaluation often reveals these initial reactions to be unfounded. Although an atrium may not have any functional purpose, the intangible image it contributes to a project usually improves profitability. The skylight may indeed be expensive, but it admits abundant daylight, thereby reducing energy costs. Tower forms occupying less land are usually more costly to build because of higher structural, facade, and elevator costs.

The economics of any project are crucial to its implementation and long-term viability. For purposes of analysis, this issue can be subdivided into four components: profitability, construction cost, operating cost, and financing. Only the first three will be discussed since it is assumed that there are few, if any, special considerations involved in financing an atrium building, except that it may have a somewhat shorter construction period. Because these components are interactive in nature, they cannot be evaluated separately. They constitute an economic equation which must be solved as a totality.

The profitability of an atrium building, in comparison to other building forms, is a function of its ability to attract higher rental rates, more sales, and/or higher occupancy rates. This is generally due to the strong identity of the building and the memorable image of the space. An atrium building is unique and it attracts attention. These factors set it apart from and ahead of the competition. The amenities offered further contribute to this distinction. With its sunlight, greenery, sculpture, fountains, and other features, an atrium is an asset which attracts people of all kinds. Advertisements feature it in words and pictures depicting a glamorous setting full of happy people.

The primary marketing advantage of a speculative atrium office building is the availability of additional windows with a view. For certain kinds of tenants that require a high proportion of private offices, such as law firms, this feature is extremely important. At 1201 Pennsylvania Avenue, offices for a law firm were arranged with junior partners overlooking the atrium and senior partners overlooking the street. The shallow-bayed office space could thus be used very efficiently, since there was no need for a large secretarial area. Having to rent less total area than in a conventional, deep-bayed building, the tenant was willing to pay a higher rental rate, thus justifying any increased construction cost attributable to the tower atrium scheme (Figure 3-10).

A similar situation occurs at other speculative atrium office buildings. At the Philadelphia Stock Exchange (Design Study 1), the developer chose to build only one-third of the permissible floor area, which surrounded a parklike atrium, in order to complete the building quickly and enter the rental market earlier than planned. Although this building did cost $15 per square foot more than a standard office building ($65 versus $50 per square foot in 1981), because of the atrium amenity, it rents for $4 per square foot more annually ($25 versus $21, for example).[2] Thus a high-quality office building often makes good business sense.

FIGURE 3-10 Atrium view looking up, 1201 Pennsylvania Avenue, Washington, D. C. (Architects: Skidmore, Owings & Merrill. Photographer: Michael Fisher)

3-10

The need for a sense of identity is important to many office tenants. At 1300 New York Avenue in Washington, D.C. (Design Study 7), the developer wanted a grand atrium scheme in order to attract tenants to this peripheral office site. Stacked atria in high-rise buildings also meet this need by allowing one tenant to rent the space surrounding the partial atrium. This occurs at 875 Third Avenue in New York (Design Study 16), where each of the four-story partial atria is rented by a prestigious tenant for use as a reception or library space. Rental rates are based on complete floors, as though the atria were not there. The building owner thus loses no rental profits as a result of the atria, while increasing the marketability of his project.

The energy-saving potential of this building type is another benefit. The owner who pays utility costs can offer lower rental rates. Conversely, the tenant who pays utilities may be willing to pay a higher rental rate, offsetting the cost of energy-saving features. Energy-saving buildings provide an advantage in a competitive rental market. One of the original design intentions of Enerplex in Plainsboro, New Jersey (Design Study 5), was to offer energy-saving inducements to attract tenants.

The atrium concept can lose its unique marketing advantage when there are too many of these buildings in any given area. This has occurred in Houston, where the speculative developers have turned the atrium office building into a cliché. The latest developer's fad, it is often ill-conceived and badly designed, relying upon a glossy image to gain an advantage in a cutthroat market. This is indeed unfortunate and may ruin the value of the concept in Houston.

The notion of an atrium, and the term itself in some instances, has become a matter of vogue. There are legitimate atrium buildings which have included the term in their names, such as 45 Broadway Atrium, Fashion Atrium, and Park Avenue Atrium, all in New York. However, others misuse the term, trading upon the name when the building only has a lean-to, partial atrium or a large-scale lobby. There is even a wooden-door manufacturer (Moulding Products, Incorporated, of Irving, Texas) that is marketing "The Atrium Door" as a registered trademark. This trend lessens the marketing value of the concept itself and will hopefully be short-lived.

In commercial retail centers, the atrium has a distinct marketing advantage, which is the ability to create a kind of captive audience. With all the shops related to the atrium, whether it be linear or vertical, they can be easily accessed. The climate is controlled and the ambience is pleasant, making shopping a pleasure and thereby increasing sales. The viability of the concept has certainly been well demonstrated. In its first year of operation (1978), The Gallery in Philadelphia grossed over $250 per square foot in sales, as compared to $100 per square foot in sales for an average shopping mall.[3] Other centers, such as Georgetown Park in Washington and Citicorp in New York, are also successful. The atrium itself is used as an inducement to attract shoppers. The Old Post Office in Washington, D.C., provides live entertainment for the enjoyment of retail and restaurant clientele.

In mixed-use projects, the components selected must have the potential to achieve a synergistic quality. They should support each other, relying upon a year-round captive audience of users. The plaza atrium holds the project together spatially, serving as a focal space accommodating a shared amenity. These principles are well demon-

strated at the Plaza of the Americas in Dallas, Texas (Figure 3-11).
This $200 million project, completed in 1980, contains two office
towers of twenty-five stories at each end, a 442-room, fifteen-story
hotel along one side, and an 1100-car high-rise parking garage along
the other side.[4] A fifteen-story-high plaza atrium with a landscaped
ice-skating rink, surrounded by two levels of retail, unifies the complex, with amenities for office workers, hotel guests, and visitors. The
project objective was to create a high-quality, self-contained mixed-
use corporate environment. A pedestrian skyway was constructed to
link this complex to other buildings in the financial district. The developers decided to build all elements simultaneously in order to
achieve the intended synergy from the outset. This strategy, which
delayed the project for two years while financing was being arranged,
was significant to the success of the project, which outperformed the
expected leasing schedule by two years.

3-11

The atrium hotel has secured a firm place in the luxury hotel market. It was pioneered by architect John Portman and the Hyatt hotel chain. In fact the atrium has become the hallmark of the Hyatt Regency hotel, with over thirty constructed since 1967. The success of the atrium hotel is attributable to its ability to make every hotel guest an active participant in a place of great drama and excitement. Staying or being in these hotels is a very memorable experience, causing people to return and to encourage their friends to visit.

The competitive advantage of the atrium hotel for the Hyatt Corporation is so strong that other hotel chains (Sheraton, Holiday Inn, Stouffer), as well as individual luxury hotels, have adopted this design concept. Hyatt claims that its Regency hotels (luxury hotel with at least 400 rooms, seven stories and an atrium) achieve an 8 to 10 percent higher occupancy rate than conventional hotels, in spite of the fact that rates are 10 to 20 percent higher.[5] These factors more than offset the 20 percent higher construction cost. Now that the competition has increased, Hyatt is adjusting its design concept from large atria surrounded by rooms with single-loaded galleries to smaller atria with double-loaded corridors (see Hyatt Regency West Houston, Design Study 30, and Hyatt Regency Cambridge, Design Study 33). While reducing construction costs, these schemes do not seem to reduce the excitement and aura of the great space.

Architects are greatly concerned with construction cost since it is directly related to their building design. A comparison of design alternatives and their attendant construction estimates should be undertaken during the initial stage of every project. Richard Saxon, in his book *Atrium Buildings,* has completed such a comparison between a four-story atrium design and a twelve-story tower design for an office building of equal program area on a 3 : 1 floor-to-area ratio site.[6] The results are very revealing, for they indicate that the tower scheme could cost 11.4 percent more while delivering only 90 percent as much usable area. The plan efficiency of the atrium scheme results from its capacity to serve larger floor areas from a single core. The cost differences can be compared by building system (equal quality construction and finishes were evaluated):

Structure Although the atrium building foundations cost more due to the greater area, the tower structural-frame cost outweighs this difference.

Roof The atrium roof is greater in area and unit cost because of the skylight system.

Stairs The atrium building has four stairshafts versus two for the tower, but overall fewer runs.

Facades The atrium building has a much better surface-to-floor-area ratio, resulting in a considerable saving.

Partitions Overall costs for the tower option are higher; there are no atrium walls in this scheme.

Mechanical Components Costs for the atrium scheme are somewhat higher because of the need for full conditioning and a sprinkler and smoke exhaust system.

Elevators The tower scheme has four elevators, versus two in the atrium building.

Contractor A tower takes longer to build, with more expensive equipment.

A higher density study (12 : 1 floor-to-area ratio) resulted in an atrium building seventeen stories high compared to a tower of twenty-seven stories. The tower cost an estimated 15 percent more to construct, while achieving less net usable area than the lower atrium scheme.[7]

The capital cost of an atrium building need not be higher than that of an equal-area conventional solution. Atrium buildings are generally more expensive due to higher-quality construction, finishes, and furnishings. But the advantages, such as profitability and energy savings, favor the atrium scheme. The point is that an architect should not initially dismiss the atrium design as unworthy of study simply because it appears to be too costly.

Operating costs, also known as life-cycle costs, are the third component of design economics. Over the life of a building, these costs total far more than the initial construction cost. Thus, reductions in operating cost through conscientious design are often economically prudent.

The greatest potential operating cost advantage of atrium buildings is lowered energy usage. An atrium building can be operated more efficiently than an equivalent conventional building because of its inherent passive energy potential. Capital expenditures on passive energy features, such as sunshades, fans, and thermal mass, will more than pay for themselves in the long run.

Figure 3-12 presents a chart comparing the projected annual energy performance of six atrium buildings discussed in Part II of this book. Their climatic situations vary, making direct comparisons impossible. However, as the chart reveals, each was able to achieve or far surpass the Department of Energy's ''Building Energy-Performance Standards'' for its given climate. Energy-saving potential was limited at Butler Square in Minneapolis and at the Wainwright Building in St. Louis, since these were renovations. The design of the State of Illinois Center did not seek to maximize energy savings. However, at the others this was an important design goal and the projected results are indeed remarkable.

FIGURE 3-12 Annual Projected Energy Performance of Selected Atrium Buildings[8] (Btu/sq ft/year)

FIGURE 3-12
Annual Projected Energy Performance of Selected Atrium Buildings[8]
(Btu/sq ft/year)

	Lighting	Heating	Cooling	Other	Total
Butler Square — Phase II Minneapolis, Minnesota	35,177 70.0%	2,780 6.0%	6,028 12.0%	6,407 12.0%	50,392 100.0%
Gregory Bateson Building Sacramento, California	13,134 66.0%	300 1.5%	100 0.5%	6,366 32.0%	19,900 100.0%
Wainwright Office Complex St. Louis, Missouri	19,700 (elec)	27,200	13,000	?	59,900
State of Illinois Center Chicago, Illinois	20,800 (elec)	6,700	12,900	?	40,500
Intelsat Washington, D.C.	4,150 14.2%	1,222 4.2%	11,300 38.6%	12,568 43.0%	29,240 100.0%
Tennessee Valley Authority Chattanooga, Tennessee	13,800 38.4%	1,800 5.0%	10,100 28.3%	10,100 28.3%	35,800 100.0%

Atrium buildings also have some possible increased operating costs. Maintenance is probably the most significant. Interior window walls and skylights must be cleaned often, requiring specialized equipment and personnel. If there is interior landscaping, it must be watered, fertilized, cleaned, and sometimes replaced. This again requires special equipment and personnel or a private contractor. Increased security may also be necessary because of additional entrances and public use spaces.

In solving the economics equation, the highest value must be sought from the design solution. The economic goals of the developer or owner must be explicitly stated to the architect and contractor. Only then can the trade-offs between profitability, construction cost, and operating costs be considered in the design process. The atrium form does have significant advantages over other building forms when it is appropriate to the economic goals of the owner, the site circumstances, and the building program.

DESIGN GUIDELINES

Finally, here are some design guidelines, or recommendations, drawn from the analyses in this book, discussions with architects, and many site visits to atrium buildings. Although they appear in other chapters, it seems useful to summarize them here.

1. **Make the design address the context** Evaluate the atrium building form in terms of its site massing and contextual role; connect the atrium to streets, plazas, courtyards, arcades, pedestrian bridges, tunnels, and subways; maximize public access and use; make it visible by giving it exterior expression; provide public amenities in the form of seating, services, exhibitions, landscaping, and artwork.

2. **Organize the sequence** Structure the spatial experience from outside to inside; treat the entry as a transition; use vertical transportation to exploit the space; create a sense of orientation by relating the circulation to the atrium; provide viewpoints from several vertical locations; make emergency routes safe and simple to use.

3. **Give it a program role** Give people reasons to be there; provide a formal program, such as shopping, dining, entertainment, a library, or reception; or provide an informal public purpose, such as an exhibition, information, lounging, or waiting; avoid completely unprogrammed space.

4. **Use furnishings to enhance the space** The atrium is the feature; furnishings should enhance it; use planters and trees to define subspaces; use plants to soften gallery guardrails; make planting a part of the architecture; make the water feature a visual focus; don't let the artwork and architecture compete for attention; limit artwork to a few large-scale pieces placed to define a subspace; avoid residential-scale and -style furnishings; make artificial lighting unobtrusive.

5. **Use it to save energy** Consider the value of the buffer effect; maximize passive energy flows; maximize daylight availability and distribution; consider leaving the atrium unconditioned; utilize the stack effect to advantage; make it a part of the mechanical system as an air plenum; evaluate solar orientation for gain and shading.

6. Use economic advantages creatively Maximize profitability by creating identity, image, and environmental quality; take advantage of zoning bonuses; take advantage of operating energy savings; design for building service and circulation efficiency; maximize atrium perimeter for office views and commercial frontage; reduce costs of skylight systems, atrium finishes, and fire prevention systems.

7. Make it memorable Define and articulate the spatial subtype; make the space "read" clearly; give it a strong organizational role; create a building section responsive to spatial perception; use daylight to bring the space to life; emphasize the power of the space by avoiding visual clutter; give it human scale by articulating floors, terraces, balconies, or special windows.

Choosing the atrium form as a building concept is a profound design decision; developing it into a successful scheme is equally important. This book is intended to aid in both phases by offering the background necessary to understand the atrium building and the technical information needed to develop one. Choosing the atrium as a parti does not mean the project is halfway completed. There are as many poorly designed atrium buildings as there are good ones. The evaluations presented with the design studies in Part II will help develop a sense of design discernment. The foregoing design guidelines can serve double duty as evaluation measures.

NOTES

[1] Richard Saxon, *Atrium Buildings,* The Architectural Press, London, 1983, pp. 74–75.

[2] Carleton Knight, "Soaring Space Behind Sleek Facade," *AIA Journal,* May 1983, p. 195.

[3] David Morton, "Suburban Shopping Downtown?" *Progressive Architecture,* December 1978, p. 64.

[4] S. L. Rogel, "Plaza of the Americas," *Urban Land,* April 1983, pp. 16–19.

[5] A. O. Dean, "A Hotel Chain Built upon an Architectural Concept," *AIA Journal,* July 1978, pp. 64–71.

[6] Saxon, op. cit., pp. 160–162.

[7] Ibid., pp. 163–164.

[8] Based upon a variety of published sources.

4 Energy Performance

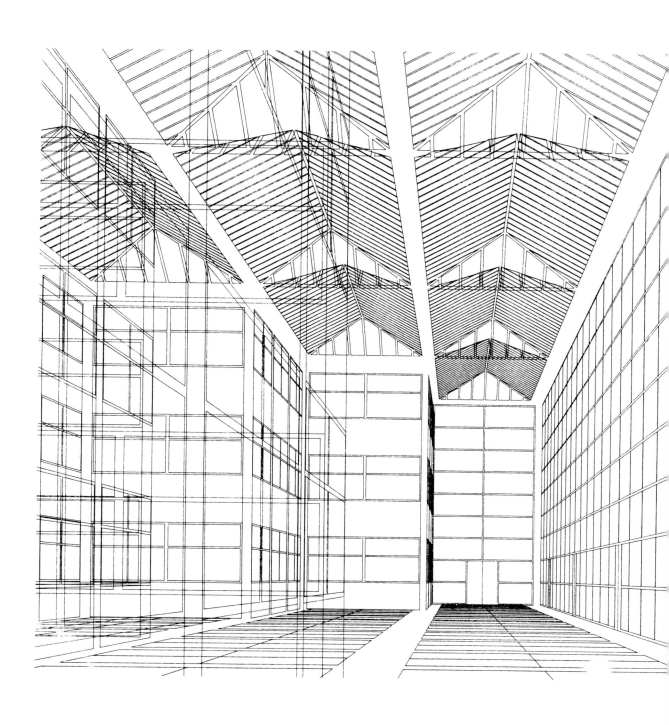

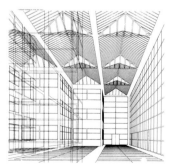

OVERLEAF: *Computer drawing,*
Enerplex-South, Plainsboro, New
Jersey. (Architects: Skidmore, Owings
& Merrill — New York)

Although there are many reasons for the current resurgence of atrium buildings, none is more significant than the inherent energy potential of this spatial type. An atrium contributes to passive heating, is useful in an overall ventilation and cooling strategy, and always makes daylight more available to the spaces which surround it. Thus it is no mere coincidence that the resurgence of this spatial type should take place concurrently with the resurgence of energy-conscious building design. The atrium is one of the generic strategies available to architects and engineers in their quest to provide more energy-efficient and environmentally suitable buildings.

During the last two decades, the energy potential of the atrium has not always been utilized to advantage. Various other factors, such as spatial image, construction economics, program requirements, and site characteristics, have caused building designers to downplay the value of energy conservation. However, there are many examples in which energy has been a primary form determinant, always resulting in a better overall building design. Ever-increasing fuel costs and the impending scarcity of energy will continue to elevate energy conservation as a design requirement. To design an atrium building without taking advantage of its inherent energy value is truly to miss an opportunity to create a more complete architecture.

ENERGY POTENTIAL OF ATRIA

One of the primary reasons behind the inception of the ancient atrium house form was its ability to enhance the climate. In a Mediterranean house, the atrium walls shade the space in summer. The night air cools the masonry atrium surfaces, allowing them to absorb heat from adjacent spaces during the daytime. Cross circulation from the perimeter of the house up through the atrium top is induced by thermal and wind-driven convection flows. Rainwater, which is stored in a cistern, provides additional evaporative and radiative cooling. In winter, the opening to the sky brings in solar heat to be stored in the masonry walls and floor. Daylight is available in all seasons to support the activities of living. All characteristics of this design work as a coordinated energy system which compensates diurnal and seasonal climatic variations by utilizing natural energy flows (Figure 4-1).

An atrium designed for energy efficiency should make maximum use of passive energy flows alone or in concert with mechanical energy systems. Not all of those features present in the open-air Mediterranean atrium house are realistically possible in the enclosed atria under consideration in this book. Nevertheless, the following means are readily available:

1. *Daylighting.* Effective transmission of natural light and balanced distribution
2. *Passive Cooling.* Shading of the atrium from direct sun and self-shading of interior surfaces
3. *Ventilation.* Cross ventilation and vertical ventilation, both natural and mechanically aided
4. *Microclimates.* Effective use of plants and water features to provide cool, refreshing zones
5. *Passive Heating.* Direct gain in the sunspace in addition to heat storage in thermal mass

An atrium has certain built-in features which heighten its potential

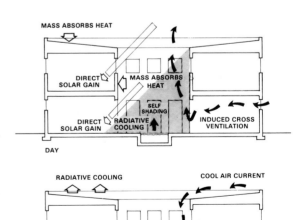

FIGURE 4-2 West atrium wall, Hyatt Regency San Antonio, San Antonio, Texas. (Architects: Thompson, Ventulett, Stainback & Associates with Ford, Powell & Carson. Photographer: Michael Bednar)

for achieving energy efficiency. These are *buffering, orientation control, aspect ratio, generated perimeter,* and *stratification.* They must be used to advantage in a coordinated system for the true energy potential of the atrium to be realized.

The concept of buffering is generic to energy control in buildings for it refers to any space which shields occupied spaces from the full impact of the climate. A buffer space is a transition space, an intermediary zone between inside and outside. An atrium can be thought of as a buffer space, for the occupied spaces which face onto it can make contact with the exterior climate only through this atrium. Thus the atrium acts as a shield and filter. The concept is similar to that of an envelope house, in which the faces of the outer wall have been separated, creating a buffer zone in between. In an atrium building this buffer space has assumed large proportions so as to become the focal space of the building.

An atrium absorbs the impact of solar radiation, temperature differ-

4-2

ential, and wind by providing a huge, contained air mass that serves as a buffer. The negative effects of solar radiation on occupied spaces can thus be ameliorated by being absorbed in the atrium; likewise, the cooling effects of winter winds and wind infiltration. Heat flows through walls are a function of the temperature differential between the two sides of the wall. When the temperature of an atrium air mass is between that of occupied spaces and the exterior environment, the rate of energy flow is slowed. This is best achieved when the atrium is not fully conditioned to the same temperature as the occupied spaces (this would defeat its purpose as a temperature buffer), and when the ratio of exposed surface to interior surface is at its lowest. In a cubic atrium with a skylit roof one exposed surface shields five interior surfaces of equal area (exposed-to-interior-surface ratio is 0.2), assuming the ground floor is not in contact with the earth. In taller skylit atria, this ratio can be even lower. The buffering effect yields benefits whether the occupied spaces are being heated or cooled, for the atrium efficiently reduces either heat loss or heat gain.

Orientation of exterior atrium surfaces is always a significant design factor. A skylight occupies the most neutral position, lending itself to all orientations or selective ones, depending upon the specific configuration. A skylight with a preferential orientation is essential if one is to maximize daylighting on sunny versus cloudy days and control solar radiation strategies for cooling or heating. Glazed atrium side walls afford more interesting possibilities for view and solar control. East- or west-oriented glazed walls should basically be avoided because of the difficulties of controlling the low-angled sun, unless the primary view is in that direction. At the Hyatt Regency San Antonio (Design Study 34), where the western wall overlooks the Paseo del Rio, a system of translucent sunshades was installed to control the sun without ruining the view. (Figure 4-2).

North- or south-oriented atrium walls are preferable, depending upon the energy strategy. In an office building (or other heavy thermal occupancy structure) in a warm climate, a glazed north wall is useful to avoid solar gain while preserving a glare-free view. At One West Loop Plaza in Houston, Texas (Design Study 9) a tinted glass, space-framed skylight and north wall preserve views while minimizing solar gain. In cool climates, a south-oriented atrium wall is the most useful, particularly if it is designed with sunshades to keep out the high-angled summer sun while admitting the low-angled winter sun for passive solar heating. The Children's Hospital of Philadelphia (Design Study 19) adopts this strategy utilizing open play decks as summer shading devices (Figure 4-3).

An inherent characteristic of all atria is their proportions, here referred to as *aspect ratios* (see page 66). These proportional characteristics determine the amount and location of solar radiation to impinge upon atrium surfaces, thus affecting the mechanisms of passive energy flow. The self-shading nature of atria is the issue, with the section aspect ratio (S.A.R.) being a more important proportion than the plan aspect ratio (P.A.R.). Correct solar orientation of the long axis is the crucial concern for all buildings.

The section aspect ratio greatly influences the daylighting, passive heating, and cooling of atrium buildings. High-S.A.R. buildings do not permit solar radiation to reach the floor of the building or lower portions of the interior facades. Conversely, the concentrated solar radiation at the top generates thermal convective flows useful in passive

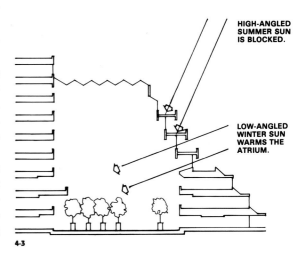

HIGH-ANGLED SUMMER SUN IS BLOCKED.

LOW-ANGLED WINTER SUN WARMS THE ATRIUM.

4-3

cooling. The taller the atrium (high S.A.R.), the greater the stratification and therefore the higher the convection flow. Low-S.A.R. buildings are best for daylighting, passive heating, and radiative cooling. For every climate and building use, there is probably an ideal combination of S.A.R., P.A.R., and orientation which will support intended passive strategies. The Thermally Induced Ventilation in Atria Project (TIVIA) had analyzed vernacular atria relative to their climate zone as a preliminary basis for developing aspect ratio guidelines.[1] However, research funding was terminated before empirical data gathering and analysis could take place.

An atrium's primary value in terms of daylighting optimization is in the generated perimeter of occupied spaces which face it. A courtyard scheme, finger plan, or tower slab achieve the same purpose but at the cost of expensive exterior walls which must be built to withstand the elements and directly address the climate. In an atrium scheme, this daylight-absorbing generated perimeter is achieved with considerable economy of means. The atrium walls can be made of interior materials, with maximal use of clear glazing for daylight. Moreover, the atrium scheme creates a controlled viewing environment, which is often a necessity on restricted urban sites (see Design Study 32, Vista International Hotel). An elongated, rectangular-plan atrium generates the greatest perimeter for the least enclosed volume, followed by triangles, squares, and circles, in that order.

Another characteristic of tall atrium spaces is the tendency for air stratification to occur, with the cool air at the bottom and hot air at the top. This phenomenon is exaggerated in skylit atria, where the air at the top is overheated by the sun. The most useful benefit of stratification is in the so-called stack effect or chimney effect. The hot air at the top will escape if louvers are provided. This action will in turn create vertical air circulation, venting and thus cooling the atrium. Fresh air or cool air must be introduced at the bottom of the space for this ventilation cycle to continue. The spaces surrounding the atrium can in this way also be ventilated. This method has been used to great advantage to provide a form of natural air conditioning at the Pension Building in Washington, D.C. (see page 13), and the Bradbury Building in Los Angeles (see page 14).

In the following sections of this chapter, the energy characteristics of atria will be analyzed relative to the needs for daylighting, cooling, and heating in buildings. Limitations of space do not allow a presentation of general principles related to these needs. The reader is referred to the many excellent books written in the last decade which treat these topics in detail. The analysis here will concentrate on the atrium's role in supplying building energy needs; the design studies presented in Part II of this book will serve as examples. (References to solar orientations are for the northern hemisphere.)

DAYLIGHTING

The value of daylighting is universal to good architecture. All architecture until the advent of electric lighting addressed this issue as a primary form determinant, leading to many creative solutions. The atrium concept allows the innovative exploitation of daylighting by bringing natural light into the centers of buildings, thus eliminating deep, dark spaces. The generated interior facades, in tandem with the exterior facades, serve to balance the distribution of daylight within the occupied zones.

The use of daylighting, a free energy source, can offset the cost of electricity, the most expensive energy source. This is particularly appropriate in commercial and institutional buildings where high light levels are required during the daytime. Each unit of artificial lighting energy utilized requires the expenditure of an additional one-half unit of energy for air conditioning to offset the heat generated by the lights, thus compounding the energy usage. Daylighting has a short payback period in all climates, for many building types, when designed in a coordinated system with artificial lighting.

The analysis of daylighting in atria can be organized around three considerations:

1. *Daylight Source.* How is the daylight brought into the atrium?
2. *Light Box.* How is the daylight distributed within the atrium?
3. *Illumination.* How is the daylight utilized within occupied spaces?

The prevailing sky conditions in the area along with local contextual circumstances are the most important factors to consider when choosing a daylight source. Some form of overhead source is the optimal choice, both for quantity of available daylight and the control opportunities. Although there have been many atria designed with glazed side walls, this scheme is usually utilized to capture long-distance views or to relate the atrium to an exterior space. At the Hyatt Regency Cambridge (Design Study 33), views across the Charles River to Boston were the primary reason for the great southeast window. Views to the sea were a primary design determinant at the John F. Kennedy Library in Boston (Design Study 20), and views to the Paseo del Rio determined the glazed west facade of the Hyatt Regency San Antonio atrium (Design Study 34). At the Ford Foundation (Design Study 6) in New York, the two glazed side walls establish a visual relationship between the indoor garden, the street, and neighboring Tudor City. Similarly, a glazed wall was necessary in each atrium at Enerplex in Plainsboro, New Jersey (Design Study 5), in order to effectuate relationships between them across an open court. Although these glazed side walls act as daylight sources, the quantity available is not optimal under cloudy sky conditions, and neighboring obstructions usually reduce the daylight under sunny sky conditions. The quality of daylight is directional and can be harsh if not controlled by the fenestration design. Reflective or tinted glass is often used to control glare, although it also restricts availability of light. Exterior shading devices (vertical on the east and west, horizontal on the south) are the most effective in controlling daylight under sunny conditions.

Under prevailing cloudy sky conditions, clear-glazed, nondirectional skylights will bring in the most daylight, since the sky-dome is brightest at the zenith. This can be seen in the gable-roofed, steel-truss-supported skylights at the Philadelphia Stock Exchange (Design Study 1) or the Old Post Office in Washington, D.C. (Design Study 39). However, if and when the clouds disappear, problems begin to occur and the interior atrium facades must become the location of daylight control. Although the sun might be welcome in the winter to provide direct-gain heating, there is no way to keep it out in the summer. This skylight form, although initially inexpensive to install, lacks the design sophistication to accommodate dynamic sky conditions. In some cases, methods other than clear-glazing can be employed to ameliorate this situation, as at the National Gallery of Art East Building (Design Study 25) where the trihedron skylights are fitted with delicate aluminum sunscreens to filter the natural light (Figure 4-4). Another possi-

FIGURE 4-4 Skylight, National Gallery of Art, East Building, Washington, D.C. (Architects: I. M. Pei & Partners. Photographer: Michael Bednar)

4-4

FIGURE 4-5 Skylight detail, Yale Center for British Art, New Haven, Connecticut. (Architects: Louis I. Kahn; completed by Pellecchia and Meyers — redrawn)

FIGURE 4-6 Skylight systems, Enerplex — North and South, Plainsboro, New Jersey. (Architects: Skidmore, Owings & Merrill — New York)

bility can be seen at the Yale Center for British Art (Design Study 23), where a system of metal baffles is mounted above the skylights to modify the incoming daylight (Figure 4-5).

A saw-toothed skylight with vertical glazing facing north or south is the most effective under clear sky conditions. Although there is less daylight available from the sky-dome, this skylight form can best control the direct sun. A roof overhang or horizontal sunshades are necessary to keep the high southern summer sun from penetrating. A north-facing monitor requires no such controls. A case can be made for

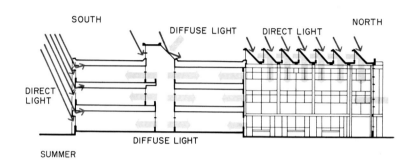

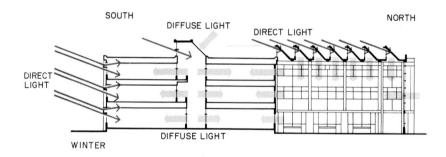

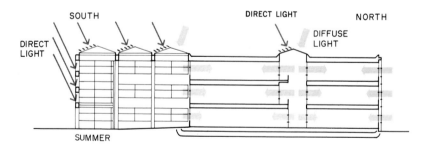

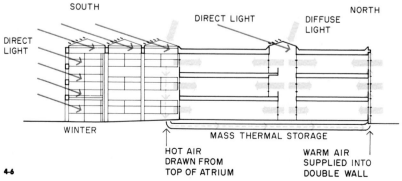

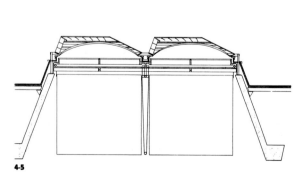

4-5

4-6

admitting both southern and northern daylight components: the southern for its intensity and golden color and the northern for its constancy and even color. Enerplex in Plainsboro, New Jersey, has exceptionally well-designed skylight systems. The South Building has individual roof monitors with vertical glazing and horizontal sunshades facing south and clear sloped glazing facing north. On the North Building, pyramidal skylights have metal louvers over the south-facing portions, angled to admit winter sun but to exclude summer rays (Figure 4-6).

The next level of sophistication is a dynamic system which is capable of responding to changing sky conditions. The south-facing monitors at the Gregory Bateson Building in Sacramento, California (Design Study 3), have motorized vertical louvers which change angles to keep out the summer sun but admit the winter sun. The most advanced system was designed for the Tennessee Valley Authority (TVA) Office Complex in Chattanooga (Design Study 13), where large motorized louvers over the atrium skylight were to be automatically controlled. On sunny winter days, the mirrored side of the louvers would be used to beam sunlight to mirrored reflectors at each balcony. On sunny summer days, the louvers would constantly adjust to keep out direct sun but admit diffused light reflected from their surfaces. On cloudy days, the louvers would be opened to admit maximum daylight. At night, they would be closed to serve as an insulating barrier. However, the system proved uneconomical and was never installed (Figure 4-7).

In hot climates, the need to restrict solar gain is the paramount concern in daylight design. Clerestories surrounding the atrium on all sides are very effective, especially with exterior sunshades. This scheme has been utilized with success at the Hyatt Regency in West Houston (Design Study 30), where the reduced daylight levels establish an atmosphere of refreshing coolness. The opaque insulated roof in this building shields the atrium from the high-angled summer sun. Another strategy can be seen at the Dallas City Hall (Design Study 22), where only north light is admitted to the atrium from three half-vaulted monitors which extend for its entire length.

After the daylight sources, the next concern is the light box itself, the atrium design as a means of light distribution. There are three factors: the section aspect ratio, the sectional scheme, and the atrium surfaces (Figure 4-8).

The section aspect ratio (S.A.R.), or proportion of the atrium section, establishes the conditions for the amount of daylight which will reach the atrium floor and the spaces which surround it. This is a significant parameter in evaluating the daylighting design, since important activities usually take place in these locations. It is difficult to specify optimal S.A.R. values; there are too many other design factors involved which can either improve or negate any given S.A.R. Undoubtedly, the lower the S.A.R., the easier it will be to provide adequate daylight at the atrium floor. Conversely, there are some atria which are basically too tall and narrow (high S.A.R.) for effective daylight to penetrate to the bottom. Examples are usually found in high-rise urban hotels and office buildings such as the Houston Hyatt Hotel or the Bank of America in New York City (S.A.R. 5.4). For daylight to reach the bottom of a tall atrium it must be reflected many times from the vertical surfaces which define the space. With each reflection some component of light either enters surrounding spaces or is absorbed. Even in an atrium with highly reflective surfaces, such

FIGURE 4-7 Skylight louver system, Tennessee Valley Authority Building, Chattanooga, Tennessee. (Architects: The Architects Collaborative. Source: *AIA Journal*, September, 1979, p. 89 — redrawn)

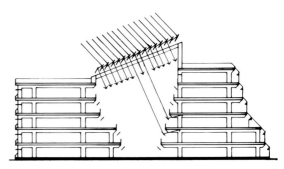

DIRECT SUMMER SUN IS BLOCKED BY REFLECTIVE LOUVERS PRODUCING DIFFUSE BEAM DAYLIGHTING AND SOLAR HEAT REJECTION

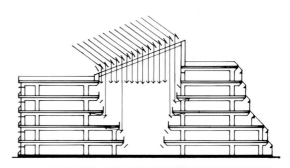

TRACKING MIRRORED LOUVERS CAPTURE WINTER SUN FOR DIRECT BEAM DAYLIGHTING AND PASSIVE SOLAR GAIN.

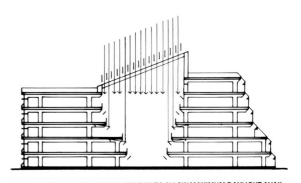

LOUVERS REMAIN OPEN ON CLOUDY DAY TO ALLOW MAXIMUM DAYLIGHT AVAILABILITY FROM SKY-DOME.

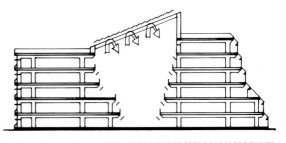

LOUVERS CLOSED DURING WINTER NIGHTS WITH REFLECTIVE SURFACE DOWN TO CREATE INFRARED BARRIER TO HEAT LOSS.

4-7

FIGURE 4-8 Atrium daylight distribution diagram. (Delineator: Michael Bednar)

FIGURE 4-9 Atrium view, Bank of America, New York, New York. (Architects: Environetics. Photographer: Michael Bednar)

as the Bank of America (Figure 4-9), the high S.A.R. reduces daylighting penetration.

The sectional scheme can contribute greatly to daylight distribution. A stepped building section with each floor projecting into the atrium further than the floor above it gives a portion of that floor its own view of the skylight source. This scheme can be seen at the historic Bradbury Building as well as at the contemporary TVA Office Complex. A stepped building section can be an effective design device, but it does reduce the atrium floor area while making each office floor progressively deeper and therefore more difficult to daylight. The new office building at 1300 New York Avenue in Washington, D.C. (Design Study 7), has an intriguing reverse-stepped section which brings daylight from the south into a centrally located atrium, while shading the office floors which face the skylight source. The Philadelphia Stock Exchange Building (Design Study 1) makes effective use of a wide array of projecting terraces, recessed balconies, bay windows, and stepped plan corners, all to creatively utilize the daylight available from the skylight.

The designer must also deal with the surfaces which describe the atrium relative to their daylight significance. Opaque surfaces which are light-colored, smooth, and reflective are the most advantageous for distributing daylight. A ground floor with the same characteristics is useful for projecting daylight into spaces which surround it. Off-white paving tiles and pools of water in the atrium hotels designed by John Portman are effective in this regard. Dense planting, heavily foliated trees, and brick pavers make the floor space a light-absorbing area.

Another significant design issue is the treatment of the gallery guardrails. Once again, smooth, light-colored, solid surfaces are best for distributing daylight within the atrium. Many designers like to hang vines over these guardrails, visually softening the space but rendering the guardrails much less effective as reflecting surfaces. The other notable trend is to use glass or open metal guardrails, thus enabling the floor of the gallery to reflect light onto the ceilings of surrounding spaces. If light-colored reflective gallery floors are utilized, this can be an effective means for projecting daylight deep into occupied zones.

The last major daylighting design consideration concerns illumination of the occupied zones around the atrium. The fenestration design of the atrium facades should acknowledge the differences in daylight levels between the top and bottom of the space by utilizing different amounts of glass or different kinds of glazing.[2] Likewise, treatment of the various sides of an atrium should acknowledge their respective solar orientations, as is the case with good exterior facade designs. However, this does not usually occur. The most prevalent design mode is to install floor-to-ceiling clear glass on all facades on all levels. Shades, drapes, or blinds are then necessary to give the occupant control over brightness, glare, and daylight levels.

The amount of daylight reaching the occupied zone is significantly influenced by its distance from the atrium facade. Flush glazing is used in many office buildings, as at Irving Trust in New York (Design Study 12). At the Lockheed Missiles and Space Company in Sunnyvale, California (Design Study 10), there is no atrium glazing, although this is not usually wise because of the need for acoustic and climatic separation. Galleries remove the occupant from direct contact with the atrium. They also shade each other, cutting down on the amount of usable daylight. On the south side in direct sun, this characteristic may be useful, but it is detrimental on the north side. All of

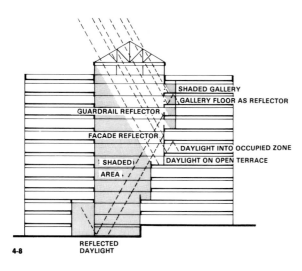

SHADED GALLERY
GALLERY FLOOR AS REFLECTOR
GUARDRAIL REFLECTOR
FACADE REFLECTOR
DAYLIGHT INTO OCCUPIED ZONE
SHADED
AREA
DAYLIGHT ON OPEN TERRACE

REFLECTED
DAYLIGHT

4-8

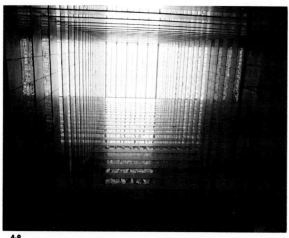

4-9

these concerns relate only to the occupied zone nearest the atrium.

The most difficult problem in daylighting design is how to project sufficient ambient light deep into the occupied zone. A light-colored, reflective ceiling is appropriate for this task. The shallower the bay, the easier the task. However, the higher the ceiling, the better the results. Thus the ceiling of the Lockheed Missiles and Space Company slopes from 15 feet at the glazing to 10 feet at the center of a 90-foot-wide office bay. Figure 4-10 gives the daylighting profile for a typical south bay of this building (field measurement on January 31, 1983, 9:00 a.m., 30 inches above the finished floor with no furniture and no electric lighting).[3] The significantly higher light levels in the exterior half of the bay are due to the higher daylight levels outside the building and the use of a light shelf.

A light shelf has been effectively used in several daylighting designs to reflect light onto the ceiling and thus deep into the occupied zone. At Shell Woodcreek in Houston, the light shelf was devised to carry the HVAC ducts, thus freeing the ceiling for use as a reflective surface (Figure 4-11). Louvers and an exterior beam were added to shade the

FIGURE 4-10 South bay daylighting profile on January 31, 1983, 9:00 a.m., Lockheed Missiles and Space Building, Sunnyvale, California. (Architect: Leo A. Daly. Source: *Architectural Record,* January, 1984, p. 142 — redrawn)

FIGURE 4-11 Typical office cross section. (Source: B. J. Evans, *Daylighting,* McGraw-Hill, New York, 1982, Figure 6-31 — redrawn)

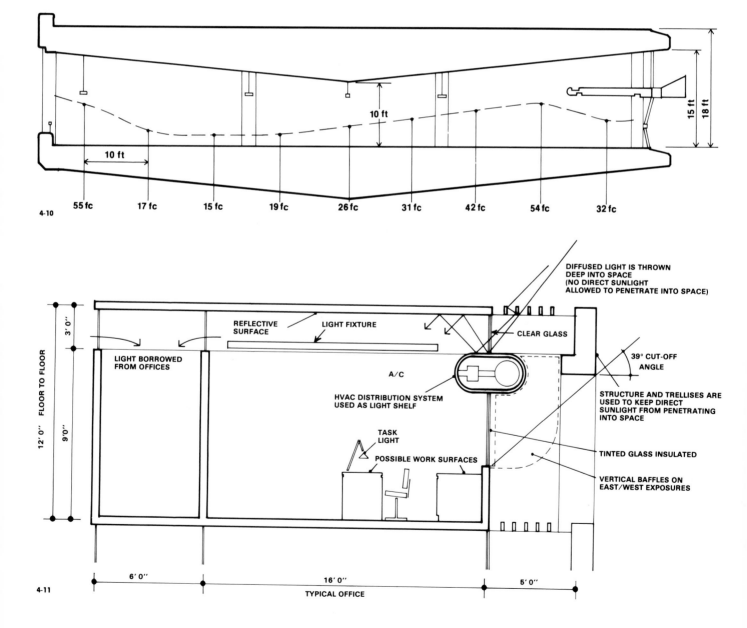

4-10

4-11

sun. This same wall section was utilized on the exterior and facing the atrium. Model studies were confirmed by measurements in the full-scale mock-up and demonstrated in the completed building. Supplementary electric illumination may be needed only in the offices at the bottom of the atrium.[4] Light shelves in atrium interiors are most effective when the atrium section is stepped, being wider at the top than at the bottom.

A daylighting scheme cannot stand alone but must be complemented by an efficient artificial-lighting system. A task-ambient concept is the most reasonable. Ambient artificial lighting can add to the existing levels of natural illumination by using the same surfaces as distributors of light. Artificial lights directed toward the ceiling can be set on automatic dimmer controls to keep the ambient light at a constant level. This scheme can adjust for changes in sky conditions and time of day, while using available daylight to save electrical energy. Individual, user-controlled task lights at each desk provide increased illumination when critical visual tasks are involved.

COOLING

Most atrium buildings are thermally heavy (high internal heat gains) and used during the hottest part of the day, making cooling a very important concern. It is a bigger concern in hot-arid and hot-humid climates, although thermally heavy buildings in cold climates may also require cooling for the majority of annual operating hours. Cooling requires a higher level of energy expenditure per degree of temperature reduction than does heating per degree of temperature increase. Daylighting has compound energy benefits because it not only saves electricity for lighting but also reduces cooling loads resulting from heat generated by electric lights.

There are potentially four passive cooling techniques available for use in atrium buildings. They are control of solar heat gain (shading), use of thermal mass, radiative cooling, and convective cooling. None of these techniques, alone or together, can be relied upon in its natural form to completely or effectively cool large-scale, enclosed atrium buildings. However, they can be very helpful in reducing cooling needs and thereby aiding the mechanical air-conditioning system. In this way, the use of these concepts can contribute to energy efficiency.

Shading is a defensive cooling strategy which relies upon keeping solar heat out of the space to be cooled. Solar orientation is important in this regard because walls of the atrium can be in shade and/or shade other walls and the floor. Atria with high section aspect ratios are the most effective, if they are enclosed on all sides except the skylit top. In hot climates, north orientation of vertical glazing and skylight monitors admits daylight without solar heat gain. The fully glazed atrium facade of One West Loop Plaza in Houston, Texas (Design Study 9), faces north for this reason. Where this is not possible, reflective insulated glass in other than north orientations will aid in the same purpose.

In climates which have both heating and cooling seasons, horizontal sunshades on southern orientations can keep out high-angled summer sun while admitting low-angled winter rays. At the Children's Hospital of Philadelphia (Design Study 19), the entire south facade is stepped, utilizing play decks as summer shading devices. At Enerplex (Design Study 5), fixed metal sunshades on the outside of the skylights and roof monitors serve the same purpose. At the Gregory Bateson Building (Design Study 3), motorized louvers on the outside of south-facing monitors can be adjusted for shading or heating as needed. These sunshades must be proportioned correctly to produce effective shading of the glazing. Moreover, they should be on the outside of the glass.

The thermal mass of a building can aid in the cooling strategy by reducing building temperature at night so that internally generated heat can be absorbed during the day. This concept works well in climates where the night temperature goes below 68 degrees Fahrenheit and the diurnal temperature swing is 15 to 20 degrees Fahrenheit. The cool night air must be flushed through the building in abundance to reduce the temperature of its mass components. The Gregory Bateson Building was designed to actively utilize this strategy. A high-thermal-mass concrete structure was chosen and left exposed to optimize thermal transfer. Cool night air (25 to 30 degrees Fahrenheit lower than daytime temperatures) is mechanically forced through the building, flushing out hot air and cooling the structure. Two 660-ton rock beds beneath the atrium are cooled in the same way. During the day, these cooled rock beds absorb heat from the warm return air circulated from office spaces (Figure 4-12). This night ventilation scheme accounts for a projected 70 percent of the summer cooling load while the rock bed meets a projected 23 percent of the annual cooling load. Virtually no refrigerant air conditioning is thus required.

FIGURE 4-12 Passive energy system, Gregory Bateson Building, Sacramento, California. (Architect: Office of the California State Architect, Sim Van Der Ryn—redrawn)

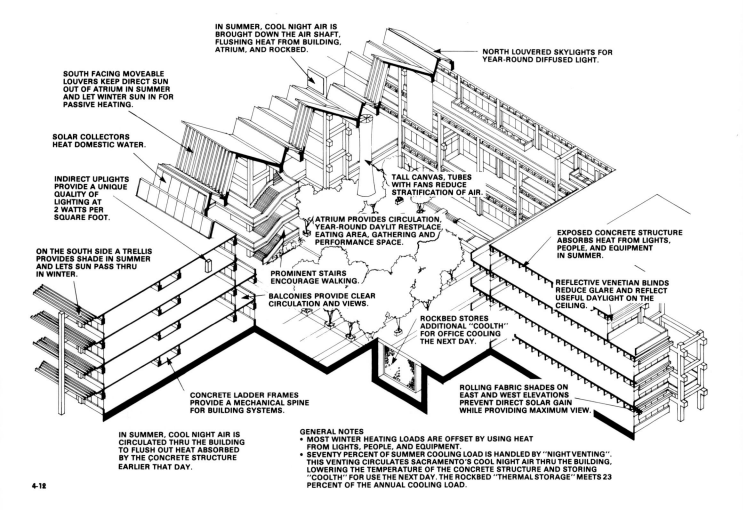

IN SUMMER, COOL NIGHT AIR IS BROUGHT DOWN THE AIR SHAFT, FLUSHING HEAT FROM BUILDING, ATRIUM, AND ROCKBED.

NORTH LOUVERED SKYLIGHTS FOR YEAR-ROUND DIFFUSED LIGHT.

SOUTH FACING MOVEABLE LOUVERS KEEP DIRECT SUN OUT OF ATRIUM IN SUMMER AND LET WINTER SUN IN FOR PASSIVE HEATING.

SOLAR COLLECTORS HEAT DOMESTIC WATER.

INDIRECT UPLIGHTS PROVIDE A UNIQUE QUALITY OF LIGHTING AT 2 WATTS PER SQUARE FOOT.

TALL CANVAS, TUBES WITH FANS REDUCE STRATIFICATION OF AIR.

ATRIUM PROVIDES CIRCULATION, YEAR-ROUND DAYLIT RESTPLACE, EATING AREA, GATHERING AND PERFORMANCE SPACE.

EXPOSED CONCRETE STRUCTURE ABSORBS HEAT FROM LIGHTS, PEOPLE, AND EQUIPMENT IN SUMMER.

ON THE SOUTH SIDE A TRELLIS PROVIDES SHADE IN SUMMER AND LETS SUN PASS THRU IN WINTER.

PROMINENT STAIRS ENCOURAGE WALKING.

BALCONIES PROVIDE CLEAR CIRCULATION AND VIEWS.

REFLECTIVE VENETIAN BLINDS REDUCE GLARE AND REFLECT USEFUL DAYLIGHT ON THE CEILING.

ROCKBED STORES ADDITIONAL "COOLTH" FOR OFFICE COOLING THE NEXT DAY.

CONCRETE LADDER FRAMES PROVIDE A MECHANICAL SPINE FOR BUILDING SYSTEMS.

ROLLING FABRIC SHADES ON EAST AND WEST ELEVATIONS PREVENT DIRECT SOLAR GAIN WHILE PROVIDING MAXIMUM VIEW.

IN SUMMER, COOL NIGHT AIR IS CIRCULATED THRU THE BUILDING TO FLUSH OUT HEAT ABSORBED BY THE CONCRETE STRUCTURE EARLIER THAT DAY.

GENERAL NOTES
• MOST WINTER HEATING LOADS ARE OFFSET BY USING HEAT FROM LIGHTS, PEOPLE, AND EQUIPMENT.
• SEVENTY PERCENT OF SUMMER COOLING LOAD IS HANDLED BY "NIGHT VENTING". THIS VENTING CIRCULATES SACRAMENTO'S COOL NIGHT AIR THRU THE BUILDING, LOWERING THE TEMPERATURE OF THE CONCRETE STRUCTURE AND STORING "COOLTH" FOR USE THE NEXT DAY. THE ROCKBED "THERMAL STORAGE" MEETS 23 PERCENT OF THE ANNUAL COOLING LOAD.

4-12

FIGURE 4-13 Thermally driven and wind-induced atrium convection. (Delineator: Michael Bednar)

FIGURE 4-14 Natural ventilation scheme, Atrium on the Bayshore, Tampa, Florida. (Architects: Rowe Holmes Barnett)

The cold night sky and the polar sky during the day can serve as a heat sink for the radiative cooling of a building. Heat will flow from a warm atrium to cooler areas of the sky. The horizontal surfaces that face the sky without obstruction achieve the greatest radiative heat loss; vertical surfaces achieve the least. In the case of enclosed atria, the roofs have this unobstructed potential whereas the floors can only achieve indirect radiative cooling. As the humidity and cloud cover increase, the radiative cooling potential of the sky decreases. In atria with low section aspect ratios (large roof and floor surfaces), radiative cooling can be of some limited use in hot-arid climates.

Convective cooling is the most useful direct technique for passively cooling atrium buildings. Thermally driven convection is based upon the stack effect in atria with high section aspect ratios. These tall atria naturally stratify air of different temperatures, and therefore densities, creating a vertical pressure differential. The hot air wants to escape through the top of an atrium, drawing air from surrounding spaces to fill the vacuum and thereby setting up convective flows (Figure 4-13). This scheme can best be used at night, when cool air is drawn in at the bottom and used to cool the building interior. During the day, convective air movement can aid in user comfort through evaporative cooling to reduce skin temperature.

Thermally driven convection provides some degree of cooling in almost all atria. It is often mechanically aided by exhaust fans at the top of the space. This method is used to draw warm air from occupied

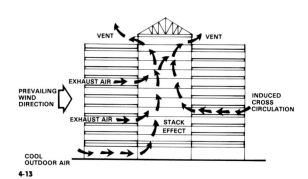

4-13

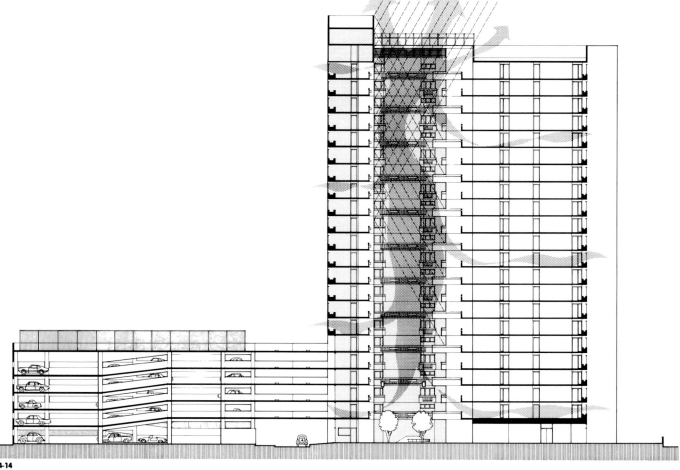

4-14

zones when the atrium is used as a heat sink, a place to dump used air before it is exhausted.

Wind-induced convective cooling can also be functionally effective. Air entering the windward side of a building is redirected to exit through the atrium top. Wind flowing over the top of a building creates a pressure differential, naturally drawing the air out of the exhaust vents. A negative pressure is created on the leeward side of the building, drawing air into and out of the atrium. Wind-induced convective cooling has been used to great effect at The Atrium on the Bayshore in Tampa, Florida (Design Study 29). This high-rise condominium tower has a high degree of wind exposure which is utilized to create a system of mechanically aided cross ventilation in the apartment units (Figure 4-14).

The location and sizing of vents is the same for thermally driven and wind-induced convection. Exhaust vents should always be at the highest point in the atrium, on the leeward side if wind-induced. Raising the roof of the atrium above the surrounding roofs gives a location for these vents and creates a hot air reservoir which is above the occupied zones. The cool-air intake should be as low as possible and approximately one-third to one-half the area of the exhaust vent, with the larger size being used in warm-humid climates. For wind-induced convection, the intake vents should be on the windward side facing directly into the prevailing breeze. Additional rules of thumb and formulas for calculating ventilation flows and rates are given in the TIVIA Report.[5]

Filling the atrium with conditioned air and drawing this air into surrounding occupied zones, as needed, allows the atrium to serve as a supply-air plenum. The constant air circulation results in the reduction of temperature differences between bottom and top, which is useful when there are galleries, balconies, or terraces. Under this system, the entire atrium, including the ground floor, is totally conditioned to full comfort levels. Therefore, spaces surrounding the atrium on all levels can open directly onto it without intervening glazing. Large air supply ducts are not needed, saving space and construction cost. This scheme works well in warm climates where cooling is required year-round. Shading of the skylight reduces the detrimental heat gain. Smoke control measures must be compatible, reversing the direction of air flow to exhaust smoke from the top of the atrium.

Historical notions about the atrium as garden or courtyard have influenced many contemporary design schemes. Controlling the microclimates at the occupied levels can produce cooling effects. Plants and trees absorb heat and light. Tree canopies produce shade and hold cool air near the ground. Water features such as pools and fountains produce evaporative and radiative cooling in their proximity. These effects can be measured as temperature changes and air movements although in actuality they are minute. More significant are the psychological effects, the associations between greenery and water and cool gardens or courtyards. The Hyatt Regency West Houston with its large pools of water and lush greenery is like an oasis set within that hot-humid climate.

HEATING

The atrium can contribute to the heating function of the building it serves through passive solar heating, more efficient mechanical system operation, and/or conservation of building heat. In most commercial, institutional, and office buildings, heating is not as significant a concern as lighting and cooling because these buildings have a heavy thermal load with large amounts of heat generated by occupants, artificial lights, and office machines. The heating problem increases in importance in cold climates and in other building types such as hotels, housing, and museums. Thus in general, heating considerations play only a tertiary role in the design of atria.

An atrium must have south-facing glazing in order to effectively contribute to passive solar heating. Skylights are not optimal for they favor the high-angled summer sun. In the northern hemisphere, glazing on the south facade is ideal, for it allows low-angled winter rays to penetrate. Sloped glazing is also possible as long as the tilt angle is not lower than the latitude in degrees of the location. Orienting and proportioning the atrium to achieve maximum southern exposure increases the solar potential. The atrium at 1300 New York Avenue in Washington, D.C. (Design Study 7), is ideal in this respect. There is a large southern exposure, and the surface-to-volume ratio is high, allowing surfaces to be warmed and heat to be stored.

In terms of passive solar heating, the most effective mode of operation for an atrium is as a sunspace within an isolated gain system. In this passive heating scheme, the solar energy is collected and stored in a space separate from the living space, with provisions for its transfer to the living space as needed. The sunspace must have a direct, glazed southern exposure, with the solar mass storage either located in the sunspace or thermally linked to it. Walls and floors of the sunspace as well as remotely located rock beds or pools of water can be used to store heat. The means, whether natural or mechanically aided, for distributing the stored heat to the living spaces is the crucial control consideration. To the extent that a sunspace or atrium is also considered as a living space, it functions as a direct-gain system. In this case, the sun warms the atrium first, with excess heat being stored for later use in mass storage elements. Dark-colored, low-reflectance, dense-mass surfaces are the most efficient for storing heat when placed in the direct sun. This factor negates their use for distributing daylight; other surfaces must assume this role.

Few large-scale atria have been designed as isolated-gain passive heating systems, due to the inefficiency of using a large volume of air as a solar collector. The designers of the atrium at the North Building of Enerplex made it an effective solar collector by stretching it across the entire southern facade and reducing its plan depth. In winter, the superheated air is drawn from the top of this atrium and ducted through insulated underground concrete pipes which serve as mass storage elements. The warm air is then used to temper the envelope air space between the double walls on the north, east, and west facades before it is returned to the atrium to be reheated (Figure 4-15; see also Figure 4-6).

A more economical strategy is to use the advantages of an atrium to augment the mechanical system which is necessary in large-scale buildings. Using the space as a return-air plenum has proven to be a very useful scheme. Air supplied to heat the occupied zones can be reused to heat the atrium. This return air can be partially reheated by the solar radiation coming through the atrium glazing. Fresh make-up air can be introduced into the atrium for preheating. It will naturally stratify in such a way that it can be drawn from the top of the space and

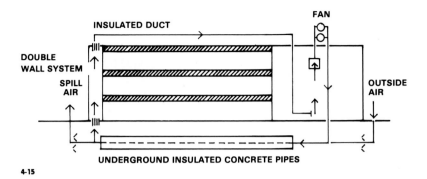

recycled through the heating system, exhausting stale air and adding fresh air as necessary. Using the atrium in this manner considerably reduces the cost of the return duct system. This scheme was utilized at the Children's Hospital of Philadelphia, saving over $100,000 in construction costs.[6] The ground floor of this atrium is air conditioned, with temperature and humidity suitable for plants and people. From the second through eighth floors, return air is discharged from spandrel slots surrounding the atrium. Since the south wall is glazed, the return air is solar heated. Although the roof has a clear glazed ridge-and-furrow skylight, it does not contribute much to the solar heating of return air because of the low sun angles in winter.

An energy analysis of Phase I of Butler Square (1975) (Design Study 45) led to a 50 percent improvement in energy performance for Phase II (1980). A key factor in the Phase II energy system was the use of the atrium as a return-air plenum. In Phase I, both supply and return air flowed through air-handling units along the building's perimeter. This caused a downward flow of cold air in the atrium that was further induced by kitchen exhaust fans in restaurants on the lower two levels. In summer, the skylight overheated the atrium, adding heat gain to the surrounding offices. Using the atrium as a return-air plenum in Phase II reversed the downward flow of cold air in winter. In summer, exhausting the return air prevented heat buildup under the skylight (Figure 4-16).[7]

Most atria will function as direct-gain spaces, retaining heat due to the greenhouse effect, whereby shortwave solar radiation can penetrate glazing but longwave heat radiation cannot as easily escape. If atria can be used as unconditioned circulation spaces, they will require no net energy expenditure. Additional tempering can be gained from surrounding occupied spaces, depending upon the thermal separation between them and the atrium. Warm air from the atrium top can be recirculated to the floor, providing virtually free heating.

Conserving the heat within is the final consideration in heating atrium buildings. The exterior enclosure is the primary concern, since it usually has a high percentage of glazing. Insulating glass is certainly to be recommended as being cost-effective in terms of energy savings. This is especially true for skylights where the radiative heat loss to the zenith of the winter night sky is greatest. New glazing materials with low emissivity (passage of radiant heat energy) but high transmittance (passage of visible light) promise even better energy efficiency. A high degree of insulation in opaque roof and facade elements as well as thermal-break sash and skylight framing should also be carefully evaluated.

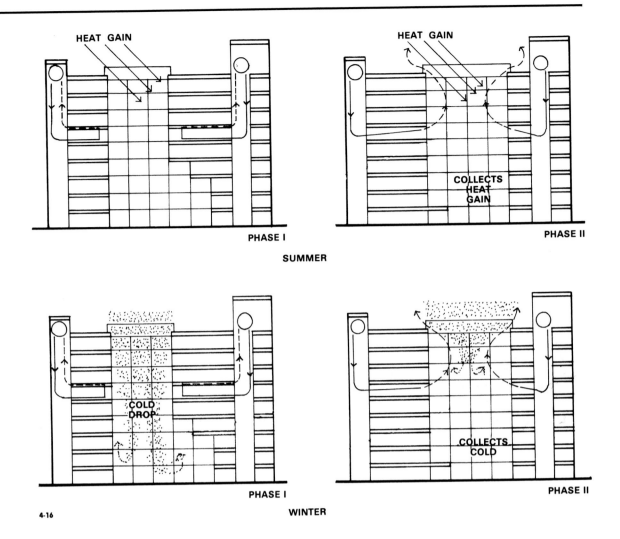

HEAT GAIN

COLLECTS
HEAT
GAIN

PHASE I   **PHASE II**

SUMMER

COLD
DROP

COLLECTS
COLD

PHASE I   **PHASE II**

4-16   **WINTER**

The nature of the wall separating occupied zones from the atrium depends upon the degree of thermal uncoupling dictated by the overall energy strategy. If the atrium is unconditioned, this wall may be treated as an exterior wall in terms of insulating value and infiltration. If the atrium is fully conditioned, the separating wall may be completely removed. However, air movements may still need to be controlled by mechanical systems rather than by natural convection. This interior facade also controls the transmission of light from the atrium to surrounding zones. Thus, in almost all cases, it should be made of clear glass, since maximizing daylighting is a primary benefit of atria. During the course of this study, the use of reflective or highly tinted glass has been observed on interior facades of several atrium buildings. This is certainly a highly questionable design practice.

ENERGY STRATEGY

In the last analysis, the architect and mechanical engineer must solve the energy equation for a building while utilizing the potentials of the atrium concept.

The factors in this equation are several:

Climate Local climatic conditions including heating degree days, cooling degree days, temperature extremes, and diurnal swings

Site Solar orientation, prevailing wind directions, existing trees, water bodies, surrounding buildings

Building Use Heavy thermal versus light thermal, daily and seasonal use patterns, user needs

Atrium Use Programmed versus intermittent, ground floor or entire height

Economics Capital cost versus operating cost, fuel costs and availability

Climate has the most profound influence for it establishes the conditions which a building design must address. Donald Watson has developed a chart which relates atrium energy design principles to climate categories as an aid in developing an energy strategy (Figure 4-17).[8] Local site conditions establish limitations upon available design options. The building use determines the user needs and internal energy use patterns, which ultimately must be reconciled with the external climate conditions. Atrium use will determine comfort ranges required and the degree of conditioning necessary. Economic factors are the bottom line in establishing goals for energy conservation and overall energy design.

Taken together, an analysis of these factors can lead to an effective energy strategy for the project in question. To be sure, difficult trade-offs must be made in an effort to optimize the result. That is the essence of the design act, to weigh the factors and create a scheme leading to a balanced solution. Establishing programmatic goals regarding energy conservation before design begins will aid in the process of evaluating alternative design schemes and developing the finished building.

Computer models with which to analyze the interactive factors of energy performance for any given building design are now available. Vladimir Bazjanac of the College of Environmental Design, University

FIGURE 4-16 Atrium air flows, Butler Square, Minneapolis, Minnesota. (Delineator: Bradley J. Kramer, University of Minnesota — redrawn)

FIGURE 4-17 Relative importance of design principles in various climates. (Source: Donald Watson, "The Energy Within the Space Within," *Progressive Architecture*, July, 1982, p. 100)

FIGURE 4.17
Relative Importance of Design in Various Climates

ATRIUM ENERGY DESIGN PRINCIPLE	COLD/CLOUDY	COOL/SUNNY	WARM/DRY	HOT/WET
Heating				
To maximize winter solar heat gain, orient the atrium aperture to south.	O	□	△	
For radiant heat storage and distribution, place interior masonry directly in the path of winter sun.	△	□	O	
To prevent excessive nighttime heat loss, consider an insulating system for the glazing.	O	□		
To recover heat, place a return air duct high in the space, directly in the sun.	□	O	△	
Cooling				
To minimize solar gain, provide shade from the summer sun.		□	□	O
Use the atrium as an air plenum in the mechanical system of the building.	□	□	□	□
To facilitate natural ventilation, create a vertical "chimney" effect with high outlets and low inlets.	□	□	□	O
Lighting				
To maximize daylight, use a stepped section (in predominantly cloudy areas).	□	△		
To maximize daylight, select skylight glazing for predominant sky condition (clear and horizontal in predominantly cloudy areas).	□	□	□	□
Provide sun and glare control.	□	□	O	□

Key: O Very important   □ Positive benefit   △ Discretionary use

FIGURE 4-18 Energy analysis, Wainwright Building. (Delineator: Vladimir Bazjanac, Ph.D., University of California at Berkeley — redrawn)

DESIGN ALTERNATIVES
1 As Designed
2 Double Glazing
3 100% Artificial Lighting
4 With Window Management (Blinds)
5 Heating Thermostats at 68°F.
6 Heating Thermostats at 60°F.
7 With Air Conditioning

A As Renovated
B Without Air Conditioning
C Clear Glazing (Limited Daylighting)
D With Window Management (Blinds)
E Incandescent Lights
F Atrium Triple-Glazed
G Atrium Thermostat Settings 60–85°F.
H Atrium Unconditioned (Single-Glazed Inside)

of California at Berkeley, has been performing energy analyses using the DOE-2.1 computer simulation model. These studies analyze heating and cooling loads and the energy demands of light fixtures and user-generated equipment. They do not include the energy use of mechanical systems. Separate daylighting simulation models are utilized. Bazjanac's comparative analysis of the old and new high-rise Wainwright Building (see Figure 2-14) arrives at some interesting conclusions.[9] Daylighting of offices in the renovated building is not as good, since offices do not face the atrium directly and the daylight transmission has been reduced by double glazing (tinted outside, clear inside) on the facades. The heat loss of the original building, with its high exterior surface-to-floor-area ratio, has been improved with the enclosure of the light court. But the removal of glazing in the light court now requires full conditioning of the atrium. Curiously, reducing the thermostat settings in the atrium or putting back the single glazing and not conditioning it both somewhat increase the annual energy consumption. This is due to the heat losses and heat gains between offices and the atrium resulting from temperature differen-

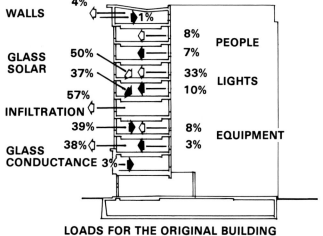

LOADS FOR THE ORIGINAL BUILDING

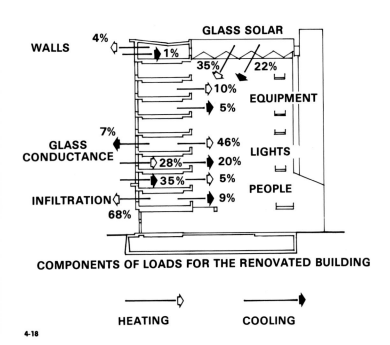

COMPONENTS OF LOADS FOR THE RENOVATED BUILDING

HEATING   COOLING

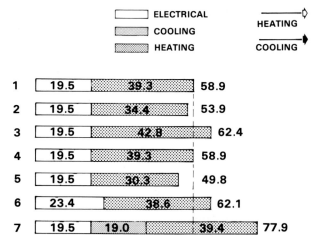

COMPARISON OF ANNUAL ENERGY PERFORMANCE (1000 BTU PER SQUARE FOOT PER YEAR)

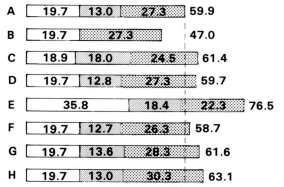

COMPARISON OF ANNUAL ENERGY PERFORMANCE (1000 BTU PER SQUARE FOOT PER YEAR)

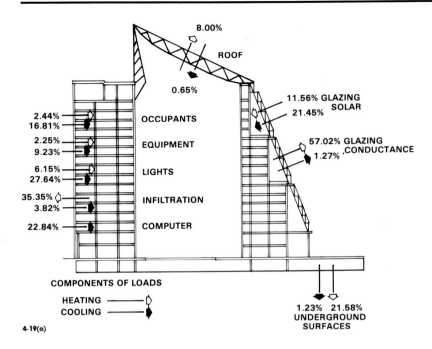

8.00%

ROOF

0.65%

2.44%
16.81% OCCUPANTS

2.25%
9.23% EQUIPMENT

6.15%
27.64% LIGHTS

35.35% INFILTRATION
3.82%

22.84% COMPUTER

11.56% GLAZING
21.45% SOLAR

57.02% GLAZING
.CONDUCTANCE
1.27%

COMPONENTS OF LOADS

HEATING
COOLING

4-19(a)

1.23% 21.58%
UNDERGROUND
SURFACES

FIGURE 4-19 Energy analysis, State of Illinois Center (Delineator: Vladimir Bazjanac, Ph.D., University of California at Berkeley — redrawn)

A As Designed (Atrium 68–78°F.)
B As Designed Except Atrium 60–85°F.
C As Designed Except Atrium Unconditioned
D As Designed Except Glazing All Clear, Double
E As Designed Except Glazing All Reflective, Double
F As Designed Except Glazing North Reflective, East, South and West Clear
G As Designed Except All Single Glazing
H As Designed Except All Triple Glazing
I As Designed Except Atrium Unconditioned and Double Skin
J Unconditioned Atrium and Double Skin, Atrium Glazing Reflective, Natural Atrium Ventilation

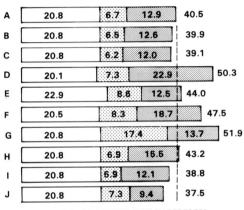

	Electrical	Heating	Cooling	Total
A	20.8	6.7	12.9	40.5
B	20.8	6.5	12.6	39.9
C	20.8	6.2	12.0	39.1
D	20.1	7.3	22.9	50.3
E	22.9	8.6	12.5	44.0
F	20.5	8.3	18.7	47.5
G	20.8	17.4	13.7	51.9
H	20.8	6.9	15.5	43.2
I	20.8	6.9	12.1	38.8
J	20.8	7.3	9.4	37.5

COMPARISON OF ANNUAL ENERGY PERFORMANCE (1000 BTU PER SQUARE FOOT PER YEAR)

4-19(b)

ELECTRICAL

HEATING

COOLING

tials and the high amount of surface area. The building as designed is the best option, except that triple glazing the atrium would have helped. Actually, the new building with air conditioning consumes only slightly more energy than the old building without air conditioning (Figure 4-18).

Bazjanac's energy analysis of the State of Illinois Center in Chicago (Design Study 4) does not compare the performance with and without an atrium but only considers modifications to the atrium design.[10] In actuality, the internal loads of this building are so large that changes in the operation of the atrium have only minor effects. The highly glazed grand space has such a low thermal mass that if left unconditioned it would be subject to overheating and undercooling. However, as a shaded and vented unconditioned atrium it could act as an effective heat sink, absorbing heat from the surrounding office spaces. As designed, the atrium is conditioned to vary between 68 and 78 degrees Fahrenheit. Treating it as an unconditioned but vented space with insulating reflective glass instead of clear glass would result in the greatest reduction in thermal loads (7.7 percent). In an unconditioned atrium, the probability of achieving a 68 to 78 degrees Fahrenheit temperature range during working hours would be 26 percent. This probability would increase to 56 percent if the temperature range was widened to 60 to 85 degrees Fahrenheit. Creation of a "double skin" exterior, where the office spaces step back in section from the sloped facade (Figure 4-19), would result in an additional 2 percent reduction in thermal load.

As these examples show, the trade-offs are complex and require careful study. Although the building use may be relatively constant throughout the year, the dynamic changes of the climate make it difficult to produce a static architectural solution which will be optimal under all conditions. The needs for heating versus cooling can change during the day and vary between areas of the same building. Daylighting performance changes with sky conditions and sun positions. Means to alter the building to respond to these processes are available in the form of mechanical controls, shading devices, and adjustable artificial lighting systems. Optimized energy performance is the goal; conscientious design analysis is the means to achieve it.

Conservation of building operating energy is increasingly a design goal of building owners. The atrium building has emerged as a generic spatial type which can be used to address many different energy conservation problems. However, not all of the thermodynamic processes are completely understood. Nor are the computer models sophisticated enough to evaluate all of the interactive trade-offs. Several research projects are under way at major universities to study the thermal performance, daylighting characteristics, ventilation rates, and their computer simulations in atrium buildings. In the meantime, the experience of many buildings has demonstrated the potential for energy conservation. The considerations outlined in this chapter should produce an awareness of the possibilities inherent in the atrium concept.

NOTES

[1] S. K. Leung et al, "Thermally Induced Ventilation Applications in Atria: A State-of-the-Art Report," Eureka Laboratories, Sacramento, California, 1981.

[2] Richard Saxon, *Atrium Buildings,* The Architectural Press, London, 1983, pp. 80–81.

[3] J. B. Gardner, "Daylighting Cuts Energy Use to 19,600 Btu per sq. ft. per year," *Architectural Record,* January 1984, p. 142.

[4] "Engineered Daylighting for an Energy Company in Houston," *Architectural Record,* Mid-August 1979, p. 105.

[5] S. K. Leung et al, pp. 74–76.

[6] David Morton, "Chopping Energy Costs," *Progressive Architecture,* May 1975, p. 49.

[7] Steve Steinberg, "Warehouse Conjures Savings Out of Air," *Building Design & Construction,* October 1981.

[8] Watson, Donald, "The Energy Within the Space Within," *Progressive Architecture,* July 1982, p. 100.

[9] Vladimir Bazjanac, "Energy Analysis," *Progressive Architecture,* November 1981, p. 107.

[10] Vladimir Bazjanac, "Energy Analysis," *Progressive Architecture,* February, 1981, p. 99.

5 Design Development

The atrium concept harbors a unique set of design challenges and opportunities. When considered during design development, they require a creative response if the resulting building is to fulfill its promise of design excellence. This chapter discusses those design development issues which are unique to the atrium building, along with relevant examples from the design studies in Part II. The issues include fire safety, vertical transportation, glazing systems, details, finishes, art, water, and plants. Although presented as individual concerns, in fact they must always be considered as part of the whole scheme. In the successful atrium building design, these components have both a balanced and a synergistic relationship.

FIRE SAFETY

The issue of fire safety is very significant to the design and development of every atrium building. Because of the restrictive nature of the U.S. building code system, no atrium building can be built unless the building official is satisfied that code provisions have been met. From a positive viewpoint, the architect and engineer should maintain the protection of life and property from fire as an important design objective. These issues have important implications for the design of the atrium and its parent building.

Until the mid-1960s the atrium building was considered unconventional. Thus building codes restricted its design and construction. Building officials faced with an atrium design were reluctant to grant approval since there were few precedents, little experience, and no fire research. There are many instances of bold architects being the first in their city to work with building officials in developing firesafe schemes. Architects such as John Portman led the way in developing the fire safety provisions which have now been incorporated into the building codes.

To be sure, the atrium building form presents certain unusual fire hazards:

- Smoke buildup in the atrium and smoke spread between floors via the atrium
- Rapid fire spread between floors via the unrestricted atrium; horizontal and vertical fire spread within the atrium
- Unprotected egress when the atrium is part of the escape route via galleries and/or stairs
- Fire-fighting problems due to the unrestricted nature of the fire and smoke source

The means to combat these hazards is the issue to be addressed.

Thorough analysis and responsive design are required to build a firesafe atrium building. Now there is the experience with hundreds of these buildings, including some actual limited fire experience. As of 1981, both the National Fire Protection Association (NFPA) Life Safety Code and the Building Officials and Code Administrators International (BOCA) Basic Building Code have incorporated fire safety provisions. The architect and the engineer should be motivated to go beyond the code in exercising their professional responsibilities. There is no substitute for thinking through the life safety problem using sound design judgment based on known safety principles. In fact, the 1981 BOCA Basic Building Code recognizes this avenue to code satisfaction (Section 620.2.1.5, Other Approved Methods) by

FIGURE 5.1
A Guide to Fire Protection Requirements for the Atrium Portions of Buildings

REQUIREMENT	1984 BOCA BASIC BUILDING CODE SECTION 620.0		1982 UNIFORM BUILDING CODE (SECTION 1715)		1981 LIFE SAFETY CODE (SECTION 6-2.2.3.1, EXC. 2)	1982 STANDARD BUILDING CODE (SECTION 510)	
FIRE SUPPRESSION	Supervised automatic sprinkers in all areas not separated from the atrium by rated construction per line 3 Table 401 [620.1.1]		Automatic sprinkler protection throughout [1715(a)]		Automatic sprinkler protection throughout Sprinklers may not be required at atrium ceiling greater than 55′ in height [6-2.2.3.1, Exc. 2(e)]	Automatic sprinklers in all areas not separated from the atrium by 2-hour construction Sprinklers not required at atrium ceiling greater than 55′ in height [510.3]	
FIRE DETECTION	Automatic sprinkler water flow alarms [620.1.1] Smoke detectors at atrium ceiling and underside of floors projecting into the atrium space [620.2.1.3]		Automatic sprinkler water flow alarms [1715(b)] Smoke detectors at atrium ceiling, perimeter, and unenclosed floors, within 15′ of atrium space [1715(b)]		Automatic sprinkler water flow alarms [6-2.2.3.1, Exc. 2(g)2] Smoke detectors at atrium ceiling and return air inlets from the atrium [6-2.2.3.1, Exc. 2(g)1]	——— Smoke detectors at atrium ceiling and underside of floors projecting into the atrium space [510.6]	
FIRE ALARM	In all buildings with an atrium, a fire alarm system shall be required for floors communicating with the atrium. Use groups A, E, or M must provide voice alarms [620.2.3]		———		———	Alarm at a constantly manned location activated by atrium smoke detectors [510.6]	
SMOKE CONTROL	[Section 620.2.1]		[Section 1715(b)]		Design must be acceptable to the authority having jurisdiction [6-2.2.3.1, Exc. 2(f)]	[Section 510.4]	
ATRIUM	<600,000 ft³	>600,000 ft³	<600,000 ft³	>600,000 ft³	———	<600,000 ft³	>600,000 ft³
Exhaust Air Location Capacity	ceiling 6 changes/ hr. and 40,000 CFM whichever is greater	ceiling 4 changes/ hr.	ceiling 6 changes/ hr. or 40,000 CFM, whichever is greater	ceiling 4 changes/ hr.	——— ———	ceiling 6 changes/ hr. or 40,000 CFM, whichever is greater	ceiling 4 changes/ hr.
Supply Air	Required [620.2.1.2]		Req. if atrium is greater than 55′ in height		———	Req. if atrium is greater than 55′ in height	
Location	<55′ in height, may be by gravity >55′ in height, must be mechanically at floor of atrium. >6 stories supplemental air at upper levels		Atrium floor		———	Atrium floor	
Capacity	50% of exhaust capacity volume located at the lowest level of the atrium [620.2.1]		50% of exhaust capacity		———	75% of exhaust capacity	
FLOOR	———		100% supply and exhaust, 6 air changes/hr.		———	100% exhaust, 6 air changes/hr. [510.8]	
ACTIVATION	By waterflow alarm, atrium smoke detector or manual controls. When activated, other air handling systems which may interfere with its function shall shut off automatically		By waterflow alarm, 2 atrium smoke detectors		By waterflow alarm, atrium smoke detectors, manual fire alarms	Atrium smoke detectors [510.6]	
ACCEPTANCE	By testing [620.1.5]		By testing [1715(i)]		———	By testing [510.9]	
MAINTENANCE	Test of operating parts every 3 months Functional test every 6 months [620.1.6]		Inspection of operating parts-3 months [1715(j)]		———	Testing every 6 months [510.10]	

stating, "Any other approved design which will achieve the same level of smoke control as described in this section may be used in lieu of these requirements."[1]

Building code developments concerning atria have been extensive in recent years. The Board for Coordination of Model Codes has worked to coordinate these provisions and to minimize discrepancies. Rolf Jensen & Associates, fire protection engineers, have analyzed these provisions and produced a comparison chart which is reproduced here as Figure 5-1. The chart shows many areas of agreement, without any significant disparities. Hopefully, this cooperation will continue as knowledge about and experience with this building form develops, and future revisions and additions are incorporated.

To begin with, atria themselves are not usually a great source of fire hazard, since only low-hazard uses are permitted, and any fire can be quickly detected because of the high visibility throughout. If the

REQUIREMENT	1984 BOCA BASIC BUILDING CODE SECTION 620.0	1982 UNIFORM BUILDING CODE (SECTION 1715)	1981 LIFE SAFETY CODE (SECTION 6-2.2.3.1, EXC. 2)	1982 STANDARD BUILDING CODE (SECTION 510)
EMERGENCY POWER	Stand by power source required for smoke control systems and activating devices [620.1.4]	Required for smoke control systems and activating devices [1715(g) & 1807(i)]	———	Required for smoke control system and activating devices [510.7]
ATRIUM ENCLOSURE	1-hour enclosure [620.2.2] Residential occupancy may be unprotected when each dwelling unit does not exceed 1,000 sq. ft. and each room or unit has an approved means of egress not entering the atrium	1-hour enclosure [1715(c)]	1-hour enclosure [6-2.2.3, Exc. 2(h)]	1-hour enclosure [510.5]
	A glass wall provided with sprinklers designed to wet the entire surface of glass when activated. (6'o.c. located on both sides within 1' of the glass). No obstructions between sprinklers and glass	Open exit balconies permitted Wired, tempered or laminated glass with gasketed frames and sprinkler both sides	A glass wall w/sprinklers spaced 6' o.c. located on both sides within 1' of the glass	A glass wall w/sprinklers spaced 6' o.c. located on both sides within 1' of the glass [510.5]
	3 floors may be unenclosed [620.2.2 Exc]	3 floors may be unenclosed [1715(c)]	3 floors may be unenclosed	3 floors may be unenclosed [510.5, Exc.]
ATRIUM EXITING Stair Enclosure	Unenclosed exit stair permitted for 3 levels [620.1.3]	Required	Required [6-2.2.3.1, Exc. 2(b)]	———
Travel Distance	150' when through atrium space [620.2.4]	100' when means of egress enters the atrium space [1715(d)]	———	———
ATRIUM USE	Low hazard	Occupancy separation not required B2, or A3, and R1 occupancies [1715(f)]	Low or ordinary hazard contents [6-2.2.3.1, Exc. 2(c)]	Low hazard [510.2]
	Any use when floor area is sprinklered [620.1.2, Exc]	Limited combustible furnishings [1715(k)]	Atrium area open and unobstructed [6-2.2.3.1, Exc. 2(d)]	Any use when floor area is sprinklered [510.2, Exc.]
ATRIUM SIZE	———	#Stories / Min. Dim. / Min. Area: 3–4 20 ft 400 sq ft; 5–7 30 ft 900 sq ft; 8+ 40 ft 1600 sq ft	Min. Dim. = 20' Min. Area = 1,000 sq ft	———
INTERIOR FINISH	———	Class I [1715(h)]	———	Class B [510.11]

FIGURE 5-2 Smoke control diagram.
(Delineator: Michael Bednar)

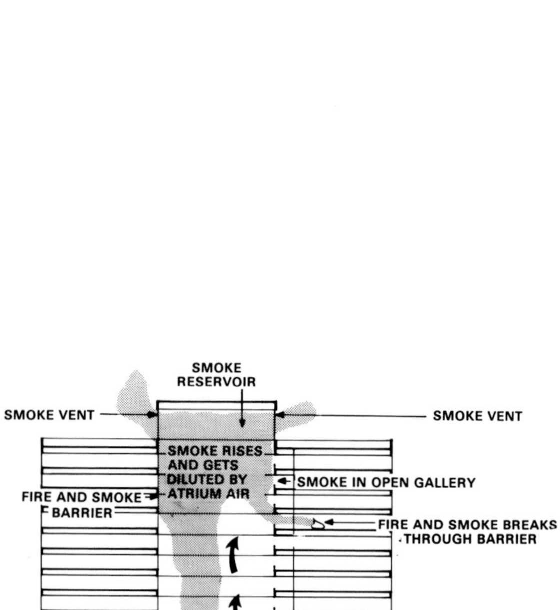

SMOKE
RESERVOIR

SMOKE VENT ——— — SMOKE VENT

SMOKE RISES
AND GETS
DILUTED BY ◄— SMOKE IN OPEN GALLERY
ATRIUM AIR
FIRE AND SMOKE ►
BARRIER
FIRE AND SMOKE BREAKS
THROUGH BARRIER

OUTDOOR AIR TO
REPLACE
EXHAUSTED GASES

5-2

atrium is used for other purposes, it must be sprinklered. The atrium as defined in the BOCA code includes all spaces not fire-separated from it. Only atria in buildings over two stories require these special fire safety measures. The BOCA code uses the general term "open well," with separate provisions for atria and floor openings.

Smoke control is the area of intensive concern in atrium buildings since this large connecting space provides a ready route for the spread of smoke throughout all occupied zones. Smoke from a fire in one of those zones will gather air and expand in volume moving along the ceiling. If the atrium is fully enclosed, the smoke should be mechanically exhausted from occupied zones via a smoke shaft or directly to the exterior. If the zone is open to the atrium, the smoke will escape into it, collecting at the atrium top, expanding to adjacent floors, and/or filling up the atrium. Although not yet required by model building codes, a smoke reservoir at the top is a very useful design feature. It gives smoke a place to collect away from occupied zones and provides a location for side exhaust vents, which are more trouble-free than vents in the roof (Figure 5-2).

All model building codes require an effective means of both smoke control and smoke exhaust. When fire or smoke is detected, the air supply to the fire floor shall be automatically shut down, thus helping to suppress the fire (1984 BOCA 620.3.1.2). Likewise the return air to nonfire floors shall be shut down, and dampers closed, creating a positive pressure to keep smoke out. Where the atrium is not fully enclosed, a draftstop at the perimeter extending at least 18 inches down from the ceiling of each open floor will help to keep smoke from spreading to that floor along the ceiling.

Provisions for a required smoke exhaust system are identical for each of the three model building codes. (The 1981 Life Safety Code does not specify these design requirements.) For atria smaller than 600,000 cubic feet in volume, the system shall be located at the ceiling and provide six air changes per hour, or 40,000 cubic feet per minute, whichever is greater. For atria larger than 600,000 cubic feet, only four air changes per hour are required. Mechanically introduced supply air, directed at the ceiling, is required at the atrium floor if its height is greater than 55 feet. For lower atria, supply air may be introduced by gravity, since natural stack effect will suffice. The amount of supply air varies between 50 and 75 percent of exhaust capacity. This kind of system can be effectively used in conjunction with the atrium as return-air plenum. The mechanism required to activate the smoke exhaust system varies between the three model codes. A fire suppression system, smoke detectors, manual alarms, and/or manual controls may be used. Emergency power is uniformly required for these systems and activating devices.

Limiting the spread of fire through enclosure and suppression gives fire fighters the time to extinguish the blaze. Of course this assumes that effective fire prevention measures were already in place. It is interesting to note that the fire safety measures for atria are basically the same for all occupancies of the parent building.

An electrically supervised automatic fire suppression system is required in all floor areas directly connected to the atrium — including the atrium itself — which are not separated from it by two-hour fire-rated construction. The Life Safety and Southern Building codes do not require sprinklers in atria with ceilings over 55 feet high, since they are not effective. In these cases, sprinklers should be located in side walls or other atrium features such as canopies. At the Erie County Community College (Design Study 18), they are housed in special floor-mounted units which also contain supply-air grilles.

Atrium enclosure remains an effective means of limiting fire and smoke spread. Thus, each model code requires a one-hour fire-rated enclosure for all but three floors. A glass wall may be utilized for smoke control only if it is protected by a deluge system of sprinklers spaced 6 feet on center, not more than 1 foot from the glass. This is required on both sides of the glass in the case of a gallery walkway. The 1984 BOCA Basic Building Code expands this provision to require tempered, wired, or laminated glass mounted in gasketed frames and without any curtains or drapes to keep the water from wetting the entire surface. At the Yale Center for British Art (Design Study 23), automatic fire shutters within the windowlike openings overlooking the atrium create another method of fire separation.

The final and ultimate concern is the safety of the occupants. They need a readily available, easily understood, protected route from almost anywhere in the building to the outside. The use of the atrium as part of this route is not wise, because of the smoke problems previously mentioned. This is particularly problematic on circulation galleries, although the 1984 BOCA Basic Building Code seemingly allows up to 150 feet of travel distance including this route (1984 BOCA 620.2.4). In an atrium hotel served by galleries, the galleries must be pressurized. Use of the atrium floor for egress is safer. The BOCA Code is the only model code permitting use of an unenclosed stair of up to three levels as part of the exitway (1984 BOCA 620.1.3).

For all intents and purposes, the required exitway should be separated from the atrium by protected corridors leading to enclosed stairs with fire doors. The stairs should be mechanically pressurized to remain free from smoke. This route should be thoroughly thought out by the designer so as to be easily executed by all people. The tendency may be to seek the atrium if it is commonly used as the means of entry and exit. When this route is unprotected, its use should be discouraged by signs and obstacles. At 1201 Pennsylvania Avenue (Figure 5-3), fire exiting is routed through the office space, averting the atrium gallery.

Detection of fire and smoke is necessary before escape or suppression can be undertaken. Of course, the sprinklers have their own heat or smoke detection mechanism for automatic activation, with the smoke detecting type being the most useful in an atrium building. Smoke detectors to alert occupants are also required by all the model codes. They should be located at the atrium ceiling. Locations on the underside of floors projecting into the atrium are also required by all but the Life Safety Code. The 1984 BOCA Basic Building Code adds a provision for a fire alarm system to be activated by either the fire suppression system or at least two smoke detectors located in the atrium (1984 BOCA 620.2.3).

The Philadelphia Stock Exchange Building (Design Study 1) can be used to illustrate how these fire safety requirements have been resolved into an integrated scheme.[2] The atrium has a smoke exhaust system with individual exhaust fans at the roof level. When they are activated, the supply-air system at the street level shuts down. Of course, the atrium itself presents no fire hazard since it is paved in brick and used as a garden. Separation of the tenant areas from the atrium by a drywall and glass enclosure with a water curtain of

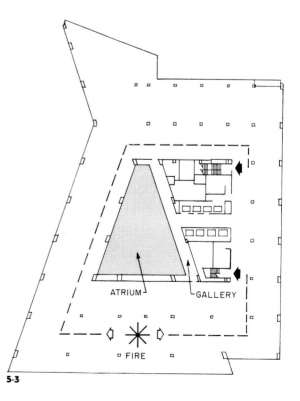

FIGURE 5-3 Fire exit scheme, 1201 Pennsylvania Avenue, Washington, D. C. (Architects: Skidmore, Owings & Merrill—Washington. (Delineator: Michael Bednar)

ATRIUM GALLERY

FIRE

5-3

sprinklers on the tenant side affords fire and smoke protection. Egress from the office floors directly to the street is provided by six fireproof stairways which are mechanically pressurized. The balconies and terraces which open onto the atrium are not protected, because they are not considered as continuously occupied zones.

A rather sophisticated fire safety system has been provided at the Trump Tower (Design Study 47) commercial atrium, which has a 1200-person public occupancy capacity.[3] The major escape route is through this public space via two fire stairs. The smoke detection system is the key to the operation. Smoke detectors in the return-air ducts at each floor level, or any sprinkler flow switch, can shut down the central air system. Simultaneously, the 60,000 cubic feet per minute (cfm) smoke exhaust fans at the atrium ceiling and the 45,000 cfm outdoor air supply fans are energized for operation at the Fire Command Station in the lobby. This provides six air changes per hour at a 75 percent negative pressure. All ductwork and plenums for this system are encased in fire-rated materials. Smoke detectors at each atrium floor and in the basement will activate the visual and audible fire alarm system. When signaled by a smoke detector or sprinkler flow switch, all elevators are recalled to street level for use by the firemen. Smoke detectors will also automatically open the skylight vents (1:150 vent-to-floor-area ratio). Atrium floors are fully sprinklered except below the skylight and between balconies. Water curtains with sprinkler heads on 6-foot centers are installed at each wall opening between the atrium and adjoining buildings, along edges of floor balconies, and along the inside walls of all store frontages.

The execution of modern-day atrium buildings has come to rely upon complex electronic and mechanical solutions to fire safety problems. Hopefully these systems have enough built-in redundancy and/or back-up measures to render them effective when an emergency situation occurs. Many atrium buildings could not be constructed were it not for the availability of these safeguards.

Fire safety design in atrium buildings is a rapidly evolving field. The American Institute of Architects' Codes and Standards Committee recently studied the issue and developed the following position statement:

> Present codes relating to treatment of atrium space lack an extensive history and/or background and should be looked to as the best interim solution presently available to the designer. Some atrium designs are presently being penalized by code regulations directed towards the maximum design solution. The need for more research, testing, and applied engineering design relative to the fire and smoke effects is therefore necessary to provide the designers with the best possible design regulations without undue economic and aesthetic restrictions.[4]

This is a prudent position which itself needs constant reevaluation as experience and research continue to develop.

VERTICAL TRANSPORTATION

The resurgence of the atrium concept, along with its high-rise development, has given architects new opportunities to exploit the experiential potential of this space. Viewing an atrium from the top is more dramatic than viewing it from below. Viewing it while in motion on elevators or escalators makes the experience even more dynamic and exciting. This potential has been actualized in many atrium buildings through innovative elevator and escalator designs, which have extended the technology of these systems.

The invention of the passenger elevator by Elisha Graves Otis in 1851 approximately coincided with the development of the enclosed atrium. As such, many of these early atrium buildings took advantage of the elevator for functional, spatial, and aesthetic purposes. An excellent late nineteenth-century example is seen at the Bradbury Building in Los Angeles, where two open-cage, counterweighted traction elevators, located on opposite sides of the atrium, are the feature attraction (see page 14). They serve a functional circulation purpose by being centrally located in the five-story building, while their transparency allows dynamic views. The elevator cage, its shaft enclosure, and the lifting mechanism — all made of iron — are an intrinsic form of kinetic sculpture (Figure 5-4). In 1967 John Portman designed the elevators at the Hyatt Regency Hotel in Atlanta with these same purposes in mind. His intention to pull the elevators out of the walls and make them an experience harks back to these nineteenth-century origins (Figure 5-5).

FIGURE 5-4 Cage elevators, Bradbury Building, Los Angeles, California. (Architect: George Wyman. Photographer: Michael Bednar)

FIGURE 5-5 Observation elevator cars, Hyatt Regency San Francisco, San Francisco, California. (Architects: John Portman & Associates. Photographer: Michael Bednar)

5-4

5-5

FIGURE 5-6 Observation elevator car, Hyatt
Regency San Antonio, San Antonio, Texas.
Thompson, Ventulett, Stainback & Associates
with Ford, Powell & Carson. (Photographer:
Michael Bednar)

FIGURE 5-7 Elevator hoistway, Hyatt Regency
Indianapolis, Indianapolis, Indiana.
(Architects: 3D/International. Photographer:
Alexandre Georges)

5-7

5-6

Relating the elevators to the atrium reinforces the atrium's centroidal role as the organizing space. The elevators are the crucial circulation link between the atrium, or point of arrival, and an occupied zone,
or destination. Their location in plan establishes this relationship by
being within, alongside, or proximate to the atrium. The elevators in
Portman's early Hyatt hotels, such as O'Hare (Design Study 28) and
Atlanta (Design Study 27), are freestanding towers with the observation cars riding the perimeter and the lobby on the inside. In other
buildings, such as the Hyatt Regency Dallas (Design Study 31), the
elevator bank is positioned so that only a few cars are of the glazed,
observation type and the remainder are conventional cars in an enclosed shaft. This scheme not only reduces costs but also affords an
option for those passengers who suffer from vertigo. A third scheme
has no observation cars; only the elevator lobby overlooks the atrium,
as at One West Loop Plaza in Houston (Design Study 9).

Ideally, from the viewpoint of construction economy and user orientation, there should be only one elevator bank. Although there is an
economic advantage to serving a large floor area from a single building
core, a disadvantage may arise in lengthy circulation. In buildings
such as Boise Cascade (Design Study 2) and Irving Trust (Design
Study 12), the elevators, encased in a solid core, have been placed in

FIGURE 5-8 Planting bed barrier at elevator hoistway, Hyatt Regency Dallas, Dallas, Texas. (Architects: Welton Becket Associates. Photographer: Michael Bednar)

the geometric center of the plan, thereby occupying the center of the atrium and detracting from its spatial integrity. In other buildings, the elevator core has been split in two, with some diseconomy and potential orientation confusion, but with increased convenience. Good examples of this arrangement are found at 1300 New York Avenue (Design Study 7) and at Hercules Plaza (Design Study 8). At the Philadelphia Stock Exchange, the elevator core has been split to serve two entrances at opposite corners of the block-long building. This building also has two observation elevators in a third location along the south side.

The ultimate means for kinetic exploitation of the atrium is found in the observation car. The ascending ride in one of these glazed capsules gives the impression of being catapulted through the vast interior space. Descending is like landing in a parachute. In the atrium hotels, these elevators have been utilized with great fanfare to add excitement to one's stay. They often ascend through the roof to arrive at revolving restaurants. In office buildings, their role is less glamorous and more pragmatic, but still provocative.

The design of the observation car has given architects an outlet for imaginative expression. In plan shape, the glazed cars have been circular, square, octagonal, and rectangular. The exterior expression has varied from space capsules to amusement rides to elegant modern vehicles (Figure 5-6). Interior and exterior lighting in colors or twinkling patterns has added to the chosen image. Although it appears that the entire cab is cantilevered from the hoistway, in reality the guide rails are along the sides, along with the counterweights, making only half the car cantilevered. A disturbing visual problem appears when these cars are placed in a linear bank in that the collective hoistways present a large, black, mechanistic area within the interior elevation (Figure 5-7). Arranging the cars in groups around a lobby space minimizes this problem. One final concern is in how the elevator meets the floor. Both water pools and planting beds have been used to great effect in keeping people away from this zone of hazard (Figure 5-8).

Observation cars do cost considerably more than standard elevator cabs. When they were within an enclosed shaft, cab exteriors were unfinished. Now the complex geometry, customized shapes, and sleek appearance all add considerable cost, as does the redesigned hoistway mechanism. With the addition of glazing, the car structure must be stiffened. The decision to use observation elevators requires a difficult trade-off between increased marketability and equipment cost. A compromise solution providing some observation cars and some standard cars reduces cost without reducing advantages.

Escalators serve an entirely different purpose from elevators. They are a very good economic and functional solution to high-volume situations with a limited vertical rise. Their relatively slow speed is compensated by little waiting time. Recent developments have provided additional passenger safeguards against injury and accidents. Stop buttons, skirt switches, warning stickers, and improved balustrade designs will help to reduce pedestrian accidents. Research concerning escalator width, location, and length will aid in designing more efficient systems.[5]

Multifloor escalator systems are most useful for commercial and retail applications. If located so as to form a continuous circulation scheme in combination with walkways, they can be used to encourage movement from floor to floor. This causes people to stay longer and shop more, which is one of the goals of commercial centers. At the

5-8

5-9

retail levels of the Philadelphia Bourse (Design Study 42) the escalators are discontinuous, causing shoppers to move to the opposite end of the atrium to continue their ride. At the Trump Tower the paired (up and down) escalators are the featured kinetic attraction, occupying a prominent place in the atrium. Their pink mirrored-glass surfaces and clear-glass balustrades project an image of graceful movement, and the views from them are spectacular (Figure 5-9). Escalators may also be located along one side of the atrium. In this way they contribute dynamism to the space without reducing valuable commercial frontage (see Citicorp Center, Design Study 46).

Escalators work well in atrium buildings when teamed with elevators, each serving their respective role. Escalators are best for connecting the lower retail, public, or assembly floors. Elevators are best for reaching the upper floors quickly. They can also serve to provide access to the lower floors for the elderly and physically handicapped. Using both is the most reasonable scheme for office buildings with a retail base, for hotels, and for other mixed-use complexes. Escalators can also be used to make high-peak-load connections with subway systems.

Another way of using escalators and elevators together is to create a transfer floor. If this floor is the atrium floor, it establishes an orientation datum. The transfer floor can also be used to sort out user circulation and destinations. Architect John Portman has used this scheme in many of his hotels (see Hyatt Regency San Francisco, Design Study 26). An added advantage of the transfer floor is a sense of arrival on coming up into the atrium via an escalator from a lower-level entry. The transfer floor can also be used to separate public and private circulation for security purposes, as is done at Hercules Plaza. Escalators are better than hydraulic elevators for reaching the transfer floor because they can carry a higher passenger volume while remaining a contiguous part of the pedestrian system.

Floor openings for escalators fall under a separate category in the 1984 BOCA Basic Building Code (620.3). If the building has an automatic fire suppression system, escalator openings through more than one floor require an additional draft curtain and sprinkler water curtain. An automatic exhaust system and smoke control method is required in the absence of a complete sprinkler system.

Elevators and escalators can be creatively designed to serve the vertical circulation needs of atrium buildings. In this new context, they become architectonic elements which define space and add visual interest. Most important, they are means to experience the space, to exploit it in a dynamic mode. Their design potential will surely continue to be recognized and explored.

GLAZING SYSTEMS

The modern enclosed atrium was born of the glass and metal glazing systems invented in the nineteenth century. These systems permitted the enclosure of space while retaining desirable light and view but prohibiting the undesirable effects of climate. The development of glazing systems has progressed very rapidly in recent years, expanding design possibilities while solving difficult technical problems. The large-scale glazed surfaces used in contemporary atria are significant design components which create spatial drama and exciting views.

The design criteria for glazing systems have grown more stringent as the design possibilities have continued to expand. Whereas the primary function of skylights in the nineteenth century was to keep the climate out, contemporary glazing systems must meet a number of design requirements:

Climate Protection Resistance to rain, snow, and wind infiltration

Safety Resistance to wind and snow loads; resistance to breakage and/or safety to occupants when broken; resistance to fire

Cleaning Self-cleaning exterior; means for cleaning interior

Economy Balance of cost and value in materials; reasonable installation cost

Energy Control of solar heat gain and radiant heat loss; optimal daylight availability; view opportunities; glare control

Appearance Compatibility with building image, aesthetics, and geometry

Balancing these requirements in choosing a glazing system is among the most difficult problems in completing an atrium building.

There are three basic configurations of glazing systems: horizontal, sloped, and vertical. The horizontal types (commonly known as skylights) must resist snow loads in cold climates and must have some means for effectively draining water. Vertical systems have grown in use, since they maximize views while shedding water easily. Sloped systems have the advantages of both skylights and glazed walls, but they also have the problems of both. Although they shed water well, they require both wind and snow load resistance and safety protection from breakage or falling. However, they are architecturally dramatic and afford optimal daylight penetration.

These three configurations can be further delineated as form types which have specific geometrical and structural characteristics. Seven such form types are described and illustrated below.

Vault Skylight The most natural form since it mimics the sky-dome; logical structural shape; economical use of standard repetitive elements; can be smooth curve with plastic as at the Bourse (Design Study 42), or segmented curve with glass as at AT&T Long Lines (see Figure 5-10).

Ridge Skylight An economical gable form that can span wide distances; sheds water well to each side of roof; made of a minimum of repetitive elements; roof pitch can vary (see Hercules Plaza, Design Study 8; Philadelphia Stock Exchange, Design Study 1; Old Post Office, Design Study 39; see also Figure 5-11).

Multiple Linear Skylights Can either be vaulted as at the International Monetary Fund, ridged (also called *ridge-and-furrow*) as at the Ford

5-10

5-11

5-12

5-13

Foundation (Design Study 6), or saw-toothed as at Lockheed (Design Study 10), Gregory Bateson (Design Study 3), or Enerplex South (Design Study 5); saw-toothed is best for solar control through selective orientation; all require an independent, long-span structural system; natural drainage gutters are formed in the valleys of all three types (see Figures 5-12, 5-13, and 5-14).

Multiple Unit Skylight Can be either pyramidal or domed, of either plastic or glass; requires an independent, long-span, two-way structural system; gutters formed in each valley (see World Trade Center, Design Study 40; see also Figure 5-15).

Pyramid/Dome Domes were the traditional nineteenth-century form over circular rotunda spaces; pyramidal forms are adjustable to differ-

5-14

5-15

FIGURE 5-16 Pyramid skylight, Loew's Anatole Dallas, Dallas, Texas. (Architects: Beran & Shelmire. Photographer: Michael Bednar)

FIGURE 5-17 Vertical glazed wall, One West Loop Plaza, Houston, Texas. (Architects: I. M. Pei & Partners. Photographer: Michael Bednar)

ent spans and geometries; glazing is integrated with the structural system; sheds water well to adjacent roof; strong visual exterior form (see Erie County Community College, Design Study 18; Loews Anatole Hotel, Design Study 37; see also Figure 5-16).

Glazed Walls. Entirely glazed walls as at John F. Kennedy Library (Design Study 20); treated as a structural diaphragm braced against the building; can incorporate sunshades as at San Antonio Hyatt Regency (Design Study 34); usually treated as flat planes; can also be designed as facade with infill glazing as at Hercules Plaza; (see Figure 5-17).

Sloped Systems Considered a sloping skylight when it spans an opening as at State of Illinois Center (Design Study 4); considered a sloping wall when it is braced against other building elements as at Pennzoil or 1300 New York Avenue (Design Study 7); usually treated as a flat plane with structure and glazing integrated; sheds water and possibly snow, depending on slope; (see Figures 5-18 and 5-19).

There are many design variations upon these seven basic glazing form types. These may be geometric variations, such as the trihedron space frame at the National Gallery of Art East Building (Design Study 25), or they may be combinations, such as the vertical and sloped systems at the Dallas Hyatt Regency (Design Study 31). There are also unique examples of special designs. Philip Johnson's crystalline-cubed space frame over the Crystal Court at IDS Center has no counterpart. Another variation is to make an opaque roof only partially skylit in order to control solar gain as at the Hyatt Regency West Houston (Design Study 30). Clerestories are sometimes used in lieu of skylights but are not discussed here since they present no unique glazing considerations.

Glazing systems are integrated assemblies of structure, metal frames, and glazing materials. Since the performance of this constructional subsystem is based upon integrated functioning, it should be designed and detailed as an integrated unit.

5-16

5-17

A basic glazing form type must be selected before a structural system can be designed. Linear forms span one way across the space, bearing upon columns or walls which surround the atrium. These systems are flat, gabled, or arched trusses, sometimes joined together to form space trusses. Skylight purlins then span in the other direction to support the glazing frames. Two-way truss systems are economical when the opening is square and support is available on all sides. Space frame systems made of lightweight members are both economical and visually elegant. I. M. Pei & Partners have favored a system made of tubular members joined to connectors for horizontal and vertical glazing, as at Wilson Commons (Design Study 21), the John F. Kennedy Library (Design Study 20), and One West Loop Plaza (Design Study 9). Flexibility to accommodate varied geometries is inherent in this system. They can either bear upon the surrounding walls or be supported independently. At Chevron Geosciences in Houston, designed by the firm of Caudill Rowlett Scott, the triangular space frame rests upon three large round columns (Figure 5-20).

Structural supports are usually more complex for horizontal and sloped systems than they are for vertical assemblies. The degree of complexity very much depends upon the spans involved and the loads to be carried (snow, wind, mechanical equipment, walkways, washing equipment, lights). Steel is almost always the material of choice for its strength, ease of fabrication, and "visual lightness." To maintain this visual quality, structural tubes and beams are not often used. Since structural depth is not a great concern, systems which rely upon geometry and configuration for strength are more appropriate. Letting daylight freely penetrate, they are also more visually interesting. The steel is often painted white to reflect light and to soften its appearance against the sky. However, at the Loews Anatole Hotel in Dallas, the long-span pyramidal skylight structure is painted black, forming an interesting geometric tracery.

Glazing frames are supported by the structure and join the glazing panes together. They are usually made of aluminum extrusions with

FIGURE 5-18 Sloping skylight, Rust-Oleum Corporate Headquarters, Vernon Hills, Illinois. (Architects: Murphy/Jahn. Photographer: James R. Steinkamp)

FIGURE 5-19 Sloped glazed wall, Pennzoil Place, Houston, Texas. (Architects: Philip Johnson & John Burgee. Photographer: Michael Bednar)

5-18

5-19

5-20

integrated gaskets. The need for structural value depends upon the distances between secondary structural members. However, the main role of glazing frames is to provide waterproof seals. In previous eras, this was the weak point in the glazing system. Now, because of advanced neoprene gaskets and silicone sealants, moisture integrity can be assured with confidence. Care in fabrication and installation is very necessary. There are many proprietary glazing systems available which have been developed and tested over many years to be reliable. They have adjustments for thermal expansion as well as built-in condensate and leakage gutters which drain to the outside. The sash is rarely operable, relying upon fixed seals to ensure watertightness. The large majority of projects should utilize and/or modify one of these systems, relying faithfully upon manufacturers' recommendations (Figure 5-21).

Choice of glazing material has greatly expanded in recent years owing to the rapidly developing glazing industry. The basic choice is between glass and plastic. Choices regarding tinting and coatings, thickness, strength, and insulating properties follow.

Glass is now available in an unprecedented variety of tints, colors, and reflecting properties. Most atrium skylights in northern climates use clear glass to maximize daylighting while reducing material cost. Tinted glass is often used in vertical systems where optimal viewing is

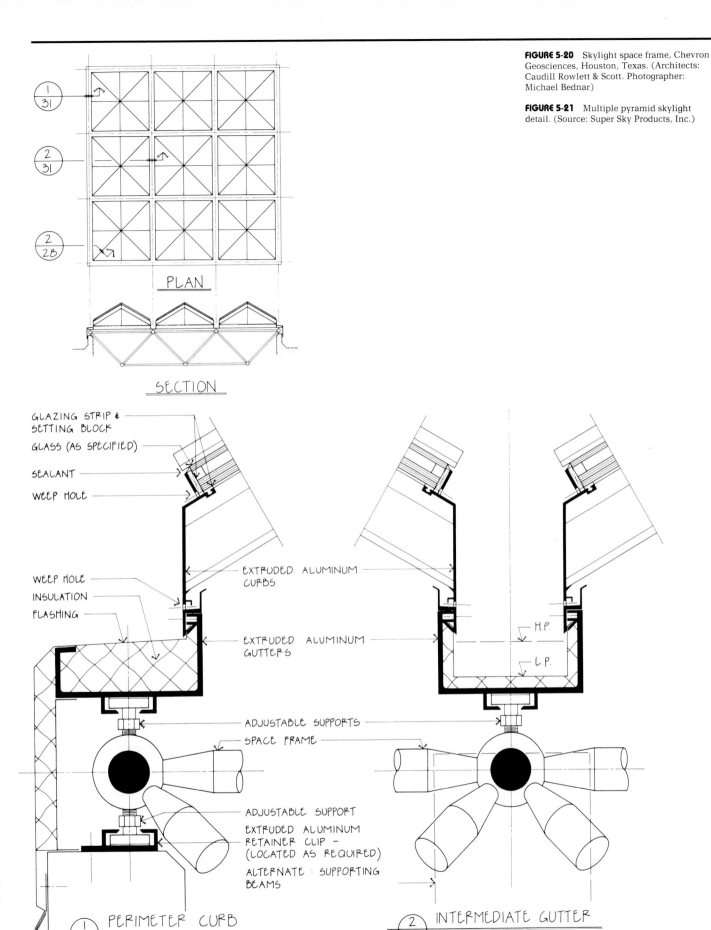

FIGURE 5-20 Skylight space frame, Chevron Geosciences, Houston, Texas. (Architects: Caudill Rowlett & Scott. Photographer: Michael Bednar)

FIGURE 5-21 Multiple pyramid skylight detail. (Source: Super Sky Products, Inc.)

PLAN

SECTION

GLAZING STRIP & SETTING BLOCK

GLASS (AS SPECIFIED)

SEALANT

WEEP HOLE

WEEP HOLE

INSULATION

FLASHING

EXTRUDED ALUMINUM CURBS

EXTRUDED ALUMINUM GUTTERS

H.P.

L.P.

ADJUSTABLE SUPPORTS

SPACE FRAME

ADJUSTABLE SUPPORT

EXTRUDED ALUMINUM RETAINER CLIP — (LOCATED AS REQUIRED)

ALTERNATE : SUPPORTING BEAMS

PERIMETER CURB
1/31   3" = 1'- 0"

INTERMEDIATE GUTTER
2/31

5-21

a concern and glare is a problem. In hot climates, reflective glass is the choice to reduce solar heat gain while providing views.

A great concern in regard to large-scale skylights is safety for the people below when the glazing breaks and/or falls. In the past, wired glass was used, but it is not as resistant to breakage or fire as annealed, heat-strengthened, or tempered glass. Heat-strengthened glass is twice as strong and tempered glass four times as strong as annealed glass. The additional advantage of tempered glass is its fracturing into crystals rather than shards. The safest skylight is laminated glass formed by two layers of tempered, annealed, or heat-strengthened glass bonded to a polyvinyl butyral interlayer which keeps the pieces from falling when broken. Manufacturers' recommendations vary as to thickness and type of laminated glass, depending upon span, loading, and impact hazard.[6] The Architectural Aluminum Manufacturers' Association recommends the use of laminated safety glass for all skylights.

The problem becomes even more complicated in the case of insulating glass, which may be required as part of the energy strategy. The outer layer should be heat-strengthened or tempered with reflective coatings as necessary. The inner layer should remain as a laminated safety glass.[7] Various low-emissivity and high-transmittance coatings are now available for the inside surfaces of insulating units. Condensation on the outside surfaces is not a problem as long as air movement over the surfaces can be maintained.

Acrylic or polycarbonate plastic as a glazing material has the advantage of great resistance to breakage but the disadvantage of combustibility and deformation under heat. When there is a sprinkler system, this may not be a problem. Acrylic has fifteen to thirty times the impact strength of normal glass, and polycarbonate is even stronger. Plastics are subject to discoloration with aging, abrasion, and reaction to certain chemical compounds. Plastic does have the advantage of light weight and can easily be formed into bubbles, pyramids or curves.[8] At the Philadelphia Bourse, these latter advantages led to the choice of clear acrylic domes on a vaulted structure located high above occupied zones, where the fire risk was low. Skylight bubbles are usually made of two layers of plastic, either clear or translucent, so as to have insulating value.

Plastics can also be formed into various kinds of translucent panels, which have greater spanning capability and insulating value. Acrylics and polycarbonates can be extruded in cored sections with internal ribs which entrap tubes of air. A new manufacturing process creates a honeycomb material by heating the plastic sheets and pulling the surfaces apart. A third method uses sheets of reinforced polyester bonded to a structural frame of aluminum, producing a lightweight, translucent, Class-A, fire-resistant panel of remarkable strength. The oldest (thirty years) manufactured version of this system is Kalwall, which is 2¾ inches thick and weighs less than 2 pounds per square foot. Different-colored face-sheets can be used, and the voids between the aluminum grid can be filled with translucent fiberglass insulation of different densities. The result is a highly flexible system yielding U values of 0.40, 0.24, and 0.15, light transmission from 3 to 83 percent, and shading coefficients from 0.06 to 0.94.[9] The 5-foot-wide panels will span 9 feet 2 inches with a 30-pound live load and 8 feet with a 40-pound live load. This system has been incorporated on the 20,000 square foot renovated skylight at the Erie County Community

FIGURE 5-22 Kalwall skylight, Erie County Community College, Buffalo, New York. (Designer: Cannon Design. Photographer: Barbara Elliott Martin)

5-22

College (Design Study 18; Figure 5-22), utilizing panels with a U-value of 0.24 and a shading coefficient of 0.38.

The value of glazing systems designed with solar controls will continue to increase, as mentioned in Chapter 4, "Energy Performance." In seasonal climates, there must be a means for restricting or admitting solar energy to the interior. A few atria presented in this book (Enerplex, Yale Center for British Art, and Hyatt Regency San Antonio) have fixed shading controls. Only the Gregory Bateson Building has an automatic system of motorized louvers. Systems of external and internal shading of skylights and glazed walls are now being developed and marketed for ready application in the coming decade.

A final concern is the method for cleaning the glazing. Exterior surfaces are detailed to be as self-cleaning as possible; flush surfaces with minimal projections are used so that dust and debris will wash off easily. Interior surfaces require periodic manual cleaning. Glazed vertical walls are the easiest to accommodate using available exterior window washing rigs. Safety harnesses can be used when there are ledges for footholds. When there is a space truss, the window washer can climb up and down using safety hooks. The same is true for skylights which have an open structure. Otherwise, built-in tracks are needed to suspend individuals or rigs. With a linear skylight, a window-washing rig which rolls on tracks can be utilized as at the Philadelphia Bourse (Design Study 42) and The Park in Houston Center (Design Study 44). At the Bourse, the rolling crane used for construction is now used for skylight and interior window washing. It is stored out of sight above a bridge.

The problems of leaking and safety have been greatly reduced through advanced materials and installation experience. This frees the architect to concentrate on making decisions which balance the many other design requirements. Developing a glazing system is far more complicated than it would seem to be. Glazing design horizons have been greatly expanded, making this one of the most exciting aspects of atrium buildings.

DETAILS AND FINISHES

Development of architectural details and choice of finish materials are very important to the final design of an atrium. Well-designed atria have received careful and coordinated consideration through each stage of design development. This section will deal with the nonmechanical elements of circulation, the design of interior facades, and the treatment of interior surfaces.

A fundamental decision is the design of circulation from entry to destination, including horizontal and vertical movement. This system must be continuous, safe, and efficient, and above all easy to use and understand. Relating it to the atrium to maintain constant orientation is invaluable. Positioning of elevators, escalators, and stairs relative to horizontal circulation is important in reducing travel distances. The choice of gallery circulation versus interior corridors is fundamental to the interior facade development. Programmatic need for access and control will aid in this decision. Some buildings combine both circulation types to advantage, creating varied atrium facades. This occurs at 1201 Pennsylvania Avenue (see Figure 5-3), where orientation is maintained with a gallery along only one side of the triangular atrium, leaving the other two sides available for office windows to overlook the skylit space.

The interior facades of traditional atrium buildings were sur-

5-23

5-24

rounded with galleries which formed a part of the continuous circulation system. The galleries were often joined together by stairs placed in the atrium as freestanding, figural objects. The Bradbury Building (see page 15) once again serves as an excellent example with its elegant tiled galleries and two wrought-iron stairs at opposite ends of the skylit space. Sculptural stairs to connect galleries are used at the Hyatt Regency West Houston (Design Study 30) as an alternative means of vertical movement. The State of Illinois Center (Design Study 4) has stairways between upper floors suspended at dizzying heights.

Historically, the stairs were sometimes placed away from the atrium, leaving a space defined on all sides by continuous arcaded galleries. At the Pension Building in Washington, D.C. (see page 13), the interior facades are composed of galleries in front of walls or partitions which separate the occupied zones from the atrium. Because of the visual prominence of these galleries, the balustrade or guardrail is one of the most significant architectural elements in the atrium. It is often repeated on all sides on all floors. A series of solid guardrails in the plane of the gallery spandrel forms a virtual facade plane with the openings reading as strip windows. With open balustrades or guardrails, the occupied zone wall assumes greater importance as a facade element. The decision between solid and open guardrails must come early in the interior design. Of course, the two can be combined, often to great visual effect. This was done at the Hyatt Regency Cambridge (Design Study 33), where brick, concrete, and iron guardrails were combined to achieve a better sense of scale.

Beyond visual appearance, the guardrail detail must provide the required safety to pedestrians. Most building codes require a 42-inch height with no horizontal or vertical openings exceeding 6 inches. Providing a handrail along the top is desirable for elderly and handicapped users. Psychological safety is a concern above and beyond physical safety. Tempered-glass guardrails have become very popular among architects for their reduction of gallery mass and minimalist aesthetic (Figure 5-23). However, they do frighten many people who need something which appears to be substantial for looking over or leaning against. John Portman solved this problem at the Hyatt Regency Atlanta (Design Study 27), by extending a concrete grid to hold planting pots level with the floor. These permit a clear line of vision downward as well as a sense of safety for those leaning against the iron guardrails (Figure 5-24). At the Children's Hospital of Philadelphia (Design Study 19), safety glass screens on top of the solid guardrails keep children from climbing. One can overdo the safety aspect by making the guardrail too high. At the Houston Hyatt Hotel, where this occurred, the experience of overlooking the focal space was essentially cancelled. It is improbable that anyone has ever fallen over or through a gallery guardrail; however, many people are afraid of heights, making this psychological issue a real design concern.

The key to a successful guardrail design is to use it to shape a series of gallery spaces for movement and pausing. Using the guardrail in this way has a reciprocal effect from the atrium side, breaking up the relentless visual linearity. Galleries at the Dallas Hyatt Regency Hotel (Design Study 31) are a rather banal plastered plane topped with a metal handrail. However, there are intermittent semicircular balconies festooned with vines which create special overlook places (Figure 5-25). This scheme of creating balconies off of galleries is also used at the Hyatt Regency Atlanta, the Children's Hospital of Philadelphia,

5-25

FIGURE 5-26 Guardrails, Hercules Plaza, Wilmington, Delaware. (Architects: Kohn Pederson Fox Associates. Photograph: Public Relations Department, Hercules Incorporated)

and the Dallas World Trade Center. Changing from a solid to an open guardrail, as was done at the Hyatt Regency Cambridge, is another way to achieve spatial articulation within the gallery and between gallery and atrium.

The gallery guardrail contributes to tectonic expression. Its design can be an extension of the detailing scheme for the whole building. At Hercules Plaza, visually open steel balustrades with natural wood handrails match the exposed steel structure of the same color (Figure 5-26). A juxtaposition of plaster, concrete, and tempered glass is used at the Hyatt Regency San Antonio to heighten the contrast between solid and void. Many designers like to use plants in conjunction with guardrails to let the trailing vines soften their appearance. This can be seen, as previously mentioned, at the Dallas Hyatt Regency Hotel. Designs which allow the planting boxes to be removed for servicing of the plants are the most practical.

In recent years, bridges have been incorporated into gallery circulation, crossing the atrium in order to reach elevator towers, for shortcuts, or simply to provide daring outlooks. At the Boise Cascade Home Office (Design Study 2) and the Hyatt Regency O'Hare (Design Study 28), bridges connect the centrally positioned elevator towers to surrounding galleries. In buildings with linear atria, such as Lockheed Missiles and Space (Design Study 10), bridges in the center of each floor reduce circulation distances. In buildings with U-shaped plans, bridges are used to close the circulation loop. At Hercules Plaza (Design Study 8), this bridge type, with balcony projections for seating, is positioned along the glazed wall, with spectacular views over Brandywine Creek. Similar bridges are used as lounges at the Hennepin County Government Center (Design Study 11). One of the most spectacular bridges occurs at Irving Trust (Design Study 12), where a single bridge crosses the atrium at the seventeenth floor, joining a cafeteria serving line to a corporate dining room.

A serious tragedy involving an atrium bridge collapse remains in the consciousness of many U.S. architects. In July 1981, two walkways

5-26

5-27

FIGURE 5-27 Atrium facades, Ford Foundation Headquarters, New York, New York. (Architects: Kevin Roche John Dinkeloo and Associates. Photographer: Michael Bednar)

FIGURE 5-28 Atrium fenestration, Park Avenue Atrium, New York, New York. (Architects: Edward Durrell Stone Associates. Photographer: Michael Bednar)

5-28

collapsed at the Kansas City Hyatt Regency Hotel causing 111 deaths and nearly 200 injuries.[10] The two skybridges were 8.7 feet wide and 120 feet long, suspended over each other at the second and fourth levels. Guests dancing on these bridges exceeded the 100 pounds per square foot design load causing failure in the suspension connections. In the ensuing investigation the fault was ambiguous. Building codes which treat skybridges as corridors must be reviewed in light of this tragedy. Designers of pedestrian bridges in atria must indeed heed the warning raised by this event.

In atria without gallery circulation, the walls are the interior facades. There are two attitudes to be taken with respect to their design. One harks back to the atrium's origin as an open-air courtyard. The atrium facades in this case are part of the building exterior relating to the other exterior facades. This can be seen quite clearly at One West Loop Plaza (Design Study 9) where the exterior curtain wall is wrapped around the atrium interior. A similar scheme is used at the Ford Foundation Headquarters with its interior facades of weathering steel and tinted-glass sliding doors, which open for ventilation (Figure 5-27). Early enclosed atrium buildings used the same materials for exterior and interior facades. Contemporary examples more often take the opportunity to economize, since interior facades do not need to withstand the climate. At 1300 New York Avenue (Design Study 7) and Enerplex South (Design Study 5), scored drywall is used in lieu of concrete and stone respectively.

The opposite attitude acknowledges the interiorness of atrium facades and the need to maximize daylight distribution and views. The result is usually lightweight, planar walls with a one-hour fire rating and a sprinkler deluge system. This requires the sash to be fixed in most cases. Clear or lightly tinted glass is most effective. Reflective glass not only restricts daylight but sets up reflections across the space, which are visually disturbing (Figure 5-28).

One of the most intriguing interior facades is seen at Hercules Plaza, (Design Study 8) where it is articulated as three screens: a planting support frame painted rose, the structural frame painted dark blue, and the glass and stucco curtain wall painted powder blue (Figure 5-29). The layering of these vertical grids forms de Stijl visual patterns and articulates tall, thin slots of space.

5-29

5-30

FIGURE 5-29   Atrium facades, Hercules Plaza, Wilmington, Delaware. (Architects: Kohn Pederson Fox Associates. Photographer: Norman McGrath)

FIGURE 5-30   Cantilevered balconies, Galleria II, Houston, Texas. (Architects: Hellmuth, Obata & Kassabaum. Photographer: Kiku Obata)

FIGURE 5-31   Paving detail, Citicorp Center, New York, New York. (Architects: Hugh Stubbins & Associates. Photographer: Norman McGrath)

The interior facades can be articulated with balconies, terraces, or bay windows. These create special transitional spaces between the atrium and the occupied zones. Projecting or recessed balconies or terraces provide ways of being in the atrium without destroying the fire separation of the facade. Semicircular, cantilevered balconies with iron railings form a rhythmic pattern on the facades of Galleria II in Houston (Design Study 43; Figure 5-30). Many guest rooms at the Vista International Hotel (Design Study 32) have bay windows to increase viewing opportunities.

The fundamental design attitude regarding exterior versus interior space extends to the floor treatment. If the atrium facades are considered as extensions of the exterior, then the floor should be treated similarly. This position also fits with the notion of the atrium as an urban space, that the floor should be an extension of the surface of the city. Brick pavers are commonly used for their color, texture, and durability (Figure 5-31). John Portman often uses off-white paving tiles in a distinct concentric pattern. The atrium floor at 1300 New York Avenue has a formal geometric pattern utilizing three kinds of marble, reminiscent of Renaissance pallazzo courtyards. Floors of atria which are treated as interior spaces should still use hard-surfaced materials for durability, although more highly finished marbles and tiles are appropriate. Floors and the water wall at Trump Tower (Design Study 47) are of a rose, peach, and orange breccia perniche marble from Verona, Italy, lending a sumptuous aura to this sophisticated retail center (Figure 5-32). The plush monochromatic carpet throughout the main floor of the Dallas City Hall atrium, on the other hand, seems highly incongruous in such a monumental public space.

Ceilings in atria are not usually a design issue since they are predominantly skylights. For those designers desiring a less high-tech appearance, the nineteenth-century laylight should be considered. This is a second layer of glazing, usually translucent, applied to the underside of the skylight structure to obscure it and also to reduce sky

5-31

5-32

5-33

glare. The Hyatt Regency Atlanta is one of the few buildings to employ this feature, utilizing a translucent white plastic laylight. The ceiling in a clerestory scheme is usually an exposed steel structure with a painted metal deck, which can be visually acceptable if well detailed.

There are, of course, many other concerns during design development, most notably the coordination of HVAC systems and lighting. However, only those which are unique to the atrium have been discussed here in an effort to make architects and engineers aware of those special issues.

ART, WATER, AND PLANTS

Art, water, and plants were often included in ancient atria and courtyards because the settings were conducive to these elements. The defined context of an atrium was appropriate to viewing artwork, particularly sculpture. Water produced actual or symbolic refreshment; trees provided shade; and plants the enjoyment of close inspection. Similarly, the enclosed atrium is reciprocally enhanced by and conducive to these elements. The architecturally defined grand space, bathed in daylight, is perfect for their enjoyment.

Having created this wonderful space in the center of a building, the designer is impelled to put something in it. If done with discretion, so as to enhance the space, this motivation is worthwhile. The fear is that the atrium may become compromised in the process, that is, that the artwork, fountains, or landscaping will overwhelm it, destroying its very essence. The answer lies in designing the space with art, water, and plants rather than adding them later. These enhancements will then serve to enrich the space rather than detract from it.

Coordinated design is the other concern. Successful integration of all three elements is difficult and rare. Architect John Portman achieves this at the Hyatt Regency San Francisco (Design Study 26) by limiting the size and quantity of each element. There is one reflecting pool running the length of the space, lined with banyan trees and bird cages (Figure 5-33). Tubs of chrysanthemums are used as embellishments, and trailing vines line the gallery balustrades near the skylight. The sculptural focus, poised above a pentagonal fountain, is a transparent form of gold-anodized aluminum 35 feet in diameter, by Charles O. Perry. These elements do not compete with each other, but rather form a mutually supportive ensemble.

An approach which is easier to execute, and is equally or more effective, is to feature one element and use the others to support it. The Hercules Plaza atrium has a terraced garden with 4000 plants varying from fig trees to exotic shrubs and ground cover. A 90-foot-long metaphorical creek — formed of brick — runs down its center in the direction of Brandywine Creek to the north. The water feature enhances the garden through the integrated design of both elements (Figure 5-34).

Traditional painting and sculpture are usually inappropriate to an atrium, since the scale and viewing distances are quite different from those of an art gallery. Only in Louis I. Kahn's Yale Center for British Art (Design Study 23) is an atrium designed and scaled as a painting gallery. In comparison, the atrium of the National Gallery of Art East Building is scaled for large sculpture and large wall hangings. In fact, unless an atrium has been specifically designed for the purpose, two-dimensional art does not fit well, because there are few blank surfaces on which to hang it. At the Hyatt Regency Cambridge (Design Study

FIGURE 5-34 Water course, Hercules Plaza, Wilmington, Delaware. (Architects: Kohn Pederson Fox Associates. Photograph: Public Relations Department, Hercules Incorporated)

FIGURE 5-35 Atrium hanging by Larry Kirkland, Shell Woodcreek Offices, Houston, Texas. (Architects: Caudill Rowlett & Scott. Photographer: Michael Bednar)

5-34

5-35

33), a wall was set aside high in the space to receive a 21-foot by 38-foot trompe l'oeil painting by Richard Haas entitled "Venetian Facade." Similarly, 12-foot-high display walls were set aside in four of the seven atria at the Shell Woodcreek offices in Houston to receive a display, two murals, and a tapestry representative of the division housed in each building unit. The remaining three atria have three-dimensional, suspended pieces including Larry Kirkland's unique woven nylon and porcelain hanging which depicts seismic sound waves bouncing from geological formations (Figure 5-35).

Suspended, nonrepresentational pieces are best suited for atria because they exploit the volume of the space, are revealed by the play of

FIGURE 5-36 Mobile by Alexander Calder, National Gallery of Art, East Building, Washington, D. C. (Architects: I. M. Pei & Partners. Photographer: Michael Bednar)

daylight, and can be viewed from all sides and below. Floor-mounted and/or representational sculpture can also be suitable if chosen or commissioned with discretion. Actually there is a very interesting representational work by George Segal at Butler Square Phase II (Design Study 45), depicting two trapeze artists and a safety net. One of the most compelling sculptural installations is Alexander Calder's untitled mobile (1976) in the National Gallery of Art East Building (Design Study 25; Figure 5-36). Here is a work enveloping a vast volume of space, kept in motion by air currents from supply registers. The 86-foot-wide kinetic sculpture is made of aluminum plates painted red, blue, and black. It mesmerizes the observer with its gentle motion and free forms dappled in daylight.

Banners of various kinds have been suspended in many large interior spaces—with varying degrees of success. When they are positioned and scaled to articulate or modulate the atrium space, the result is usually successful. The banner at the Hyatt Regency O'Hare (Design Study 28) is 90 feet tall and 16 feet in diameter and is composed of 700 brightly colored Japanese silk kites (Figure 5-37). It is artificially lit from the inside and gives identity to one of the atrium quadrants. The tall, thin, baronial banners at the Loews Anatole Hotel (Design Study 37), on the other hand, are seemingly placed at random. A very subtle minimalist work of banners by Robert Irwin has been installed

5-36

FIGURE 5-37 Cylindrical banner, Hyatt Regency O'Hare, Rosemont, Illinois. (Architects: John Portman & Associates. Photographer: Alexandre Georges)

5-37

in the upper part of the Old Post Office atrium in Washington, D.C. (Design Study 39).[11] It is a simple grid of translucent white cotton panels, suspended on the north-south axis where it may interact with the changing daylight.

The most intriguing atrium sculptures might be termed "environmental," for their sole purpose is to interact with the characteristics of the space. At the Tampa Electric Company Building, artist William Severson has created a kinetic sculpture out of 32 brass tubes, each 3 inches in diameter and 60 feet long. Each tube is attached to a solar collector which generates electricity that is transmitted to a geared apparatus, causing the tubes to move in a pattern depending on the sun.[12] Utilizing computer-aided design, artist Bob Fisher has created a work entitled "Galaxy" for an atrium at One Heritage Place, a corporate office building in Quincy, Massachusetts. Its purpose is to interact with the daylight through reflection from 1000 brass rods, 6 inches long and suspended on silver hang-gliding cable. The effect is that of a shimmering curtain hovering in space.[13] A third example, devised by Charles Ross for the atrium of the Spectrum Building in Denver, is an ethereal sculpture of rainbow-colored light created by sixteen acrylic prisms, each 8 feet long and 14 inches to a side.[14] The prisms are positioned to project rainbows on the atrium surfaces, creating magical effects of colored light in motion.

5-38

FIGURE 5-38 Manmade river, Hyatt Regency San Antonio, San Antonio, Texas. (Architects: Thompson, Ventulett, Stainback & Associates with Ford, Powell & Carson. Photographer: Michael Bednar)

FIGURE 5-39 Atrium lake, Hyatt Regency West Houston, Houston, Texas. (Architects: Lockwood, Andrews & Newnam. Photographer: Michael Bednar)

Water is an intrinsically compelling element which finds its place in atria in many manifestations and for many purposes. There are countless examples of small fountains used to embellish planting areas — for instance, the Philadelphia Stock Exchange — or to provide visual sparkle, as at the Dallas Hyatt Regency. Other, somewhat larger fountains are used to provide an acoustic presence of water, as at the Hyatt Regency Atlanta, or to serve as a dark reflecting surface in which to mirror the surrounding space (see the Hennepin County Government Center, Design Study 11). When these purposes are combined, the water feature becomes focal, as at the Atrium on the Bayshore in Tampa, Florida (Design Study 29), with its group of spouts at one end of a reflecting pool surrounded by landscaping. All of these uses of water are somewhat traditional.

Of particular interest are those instances where an atrium has been designed which takes special advantage of naturally occurring water features. These cases have no real precedent within enclosed spaces, thus adding a new dimension to the genre. Such is the case at the well-known Hyatt Regency San Antonio (Design Study 34), where a man-made spur of the San Antonio River literally flows through the atrium to join its natural counterpart. As the water enters the atrium, its natural forms are disciplined to the geometry of the architecture, producing, among other things, the controlled spillway shown in Figure 5-38. At the Hyatt Regency West Houston (Design Study 30) the design concept was to place the hotel in an artificial lake, with the water surface extending through the atrium, being interrupted only by a glass wall. Much of the atrium floor is water, filled with plants and goldfish, creating a refreshing reflective quality throughout (Figure 5-39). The water spills into a basin from which it is filtered and recirculated. John Portman uses large water surfaces at his Peachtree Plaza Hotel in Atlanta and Bonaventure Hotel in Los Angeles for their romantic and sensual qualities. He places people close to the water in seating areas, drinking booths, and walkways, and exploits its reflective properties through artificial lighting. In the San Antonio and Houston examples, the water assumes a naturalistic form, whereas in

5-39

Portman's Atlanta and Los Angeles hotels it becomes an architectural surface.

Among the most daring uses of water in atria are large waterfalls which dramatize the verticality of the space. The focal point of the Trump Tower atrium (Design Study 47) is a six-story water wall beginning at the skylight and extending to a garden concourse one level below the street (Figure 5-40). The water flows down an articulated wall composed of 1000 pieces of breccia perniche marble 1⅝ inches thick and of varying sizes. Visual drama is enhanced by spotlights and lights recessed in the water wall itself. An actual six-story waterfall is the focal point of 1300 New York Avenue in Washington, D.C. (Design Study 7). Inspired by the Boboli Gardens in Italy, this water feature cascades in sections, forming a cylindrical sheet before reaching a semicircular, ground-level pool. Because of the excitement generated by these two schemes, more vertical water features are sure to follow.

The technical problems to be solved with any water feature are made complicated indoors by the fear of leakage. Thorough architectural detailing and specification must be carried out so as to prevent the completed fountain from being an inoperable eyesore. The operation of the mechanical system, including pumps and piping, must be thoroughly studied. The subject of interior fountains is quite new, but guidelines related to exterior fountains can be utilized as discussed in "Decorative Pools and Fountains" by M. Paul Friedberg and Cynthia Rice.[15]

The notion of atrium as interior garden had its origin in the nineteenth-century involvement with greenhouses and conservatories. To have a garden in a building available for year-round enjoyment is both a highly romantic and a fundamentally humane intention. People respond to plants as living things with rich visual, tactile, and olfactory qualities. The interior garden as a metaphor for nature is a longstanding architectural concept.

The design and execution of interior gardens is among the most complex aspects of an atrium building. An architect without direct experience in this regard should not attempt this task without the aid of a qualified landscape consultant. Those with experience will already realize the value of such professional aid. This section will outline the considerations regarding atrium landscaping, including relevant examples. The conditions for planting will be discussed first, followed by considerations of planting design, execution, and maintenance.

Most planting in atria is thought of as an enhancement for the space. Planting beds or raised planters define seating areas or walkways at the floor level. Trees are often used to provide shade and scale and to define places to sit. Hanging plants are often used to soften balcony edges or to otherwise embellish interior facades. Pots of flowers or seasonal plants bring changing areas of color and visual enrichment to selected locations.

The most natural location for planting is on the ground floor, although placement on terraces and along balconies can be integrated with the architecture. It is sometimes disconcerting to see plants in awkward, isolated locations as if they were artificial. Planting should be placed in groups to develop enough critical mass to make an impact upon the space. Exceptions are pots of flowers or sculptural trees on the ground floor.

5-40

In several contemporary atrium buildings, the designer has given over the entire ground floor area to the creation of an interior garden. These are among the most memorable spaces known, since they have strong design concepts which have been consistently executed. Three such schemes are presented as design studies in this book:

Ford Foundation An 8500 square foot, brick-terraced public garden, including seasonal plantings (Design Study 6)

Philadelphia Stock Exchange Thirty-six species of plants and trees in a 16,000 square foot brick-terraced public garden (Design Study 1)

Hercules Plaza An 8100 square foot, brick-terraced public garden with 4000 plants and a waterway (Design Study 8)

5-41

These gardens are a joy to behold, providing an attractive amenity for office workers and the public alike.

In all cases of interior planting, the architecture of the atrium establishes the basic conditions of size, access, natural light, and climate. Raised planters create defined planting areas with given depths for soil and drainage. Even atrium floor planters have limited depths due to structural capacity and spaces below. The weight of a garden averages 400 to 500 pounds per square foot. Large trees can weigh up to 4 tons, requiring heavy structural support or locations at or near column points.[16] Access for maintenance and/or replacement is another concern, particularly in elevated locations. At Hercules Plaza, a separate system of catwalks is provided to service plants along the freestanding structural frame (Figure 5-41). Mechanical lifting devices or scaffolding should not be necessary.

The most critical landscaping limitation imposed by the architecture is the availability of natural light. Most plants require a minimum intensity of 50 to 75 footcandles while others, such as ficus trees, require up to 200 footcandles. An atrium designed according to sound principles of daylighting can supply this intensity of diffused daylight. Artificial lights can be used as supplements to compensate for cloudy days or extreme seasonal variation. In some cases, artificial lights can be a safety factor to offset errors in daylight prediction or other unforeseen circumstances. The high-intensity discharge, white mercury, or metal halide lamps have proven to be the most effective in high spaces, for both intensity and energy efficiency.[17] At the Hyatt Regency O'Hare, a 1000-watt metal halide fixture is suspended from the skylight over each silk oak to compensate for the low light levels in the winter. Duration is also a concern, with twelve hours of light recommended for most species and a corresponding period of relative darkness. This need for a dark period is open to debate; some plant physiologists claim that it is unnecessary for interior foliage plants. Richard Gaines recommends that landscapers specify footcandle hours rather than levels of footcandles or hours.[18] Natural daylight provides the correct color spectrum whereas researchers continue to explore the relationship between plant growth and color of light relative to different lamps. Direction of light affects plant shape, since plants are light-seeking. Toplight is the most evenly distributed, producing balanced plant shapes, whereas natural sidelight needs to be balanced by artificial lighting from the opposite direction.

The architecture also establishes the climatic conditions. Interior plants can accept a wide variation in air temperature as long as it does

FIGURE 5-42 Planting plan, Philadelphia Stock Exchange, Philadelphia, Pennsylvania. (Architects: Cope/Linder Associates—redrawn)

TREES: Weeping Fig, Indian Laurel, Jacaranda, Alexander Palm
GROUNDCOVERS: Kangaroo Ivy, Holly Fern, English Ivy, Green Prayer Plant, Boston Fern, Dwarf Boston Fern, Velvet Lear Vine, Golden Pothos, Peace Lily
SHRUBS: Ardesia, Cast Iron Plant, Weeping Bottlebrush, Camellia, Narrow Leaf Pleomele, Warnecki Dracaena, Janet Craig Dracaena, Japanese Aralia, Weeping Fig, Gardenia, Hibiscus, Waxleaf Privet, Pittosporum, Selloum, Parsley Aralia, Arboricola

not get much below 40 degrees Fahrenheit. Rapid temperature changes, as may occur when the HVAC systems are shut down during weekends, can also be a problem. Each atrium has climatic variations due to stratification, heat buildup due to the greenhouse effect, cold zones near entrances, and drafts from supply registers. Any of these may affect certain plant species adversely. Although foliage plants desire high relative humidity levels of 70 to 90 percent, minimum levels of 30 percent are tolerable. Various forms of indoor air pollution, such as fumes, smoke, or gases, can also affect the health of interior plants.

Planting design requires a sensitivity to scale, texture, form, and color; the composition created must relate to the architectural context. Architect and landscape architect need to work together during schematic and final design stages.

At the Philadelphia Stock Exchange (Design Study 1), Gerald M. Cope, AIA, partner in charge for Cope/Linder Associates, was both architect and landscape architect, unifying the design of atrium and garden (Figure 5-42). The scheme, conceived as a green oasis within a commercial district, steps down in a series of terraces to the level of the Stock Exchange trading room, 19 feet below street level. The result is a densely planted grotto surrounded by pedestrian traffic. The entire ground plane and vertical garden walls are covered in brick to give a uniformity of color and texture. Bollards and piperails are an unobtrusive forest green, as is the tile border. The wide variety of landscape materials (thirty-six species of trees, shrubs, ground cover, flowers, and vines) are arranged to form small-scale garden spaces with abundant shade. A watercourse flows throughout with pools, falls, and streams adding acoustic ambience.

Plants for interior gardens are predominantly semitropical or tropical to match the relatively constant interior climate for humans. They are propagated in Florida, Texas, and California for shipment throughout the United States. Procedures for acclimatization have been developed whereby plants are grown in reduced sunlight under soil, water, and root conditions similar to those in the interior. This reduces the trauma and adjustment for these plants, resulting in less replacement and better growth. A list of trees and plants suitable for interior use, information on growing conditions, and photographs are provided in the books *Handbook of Specialty Elements in Architecture*[19] and *Interior Plantscaping*.[20]

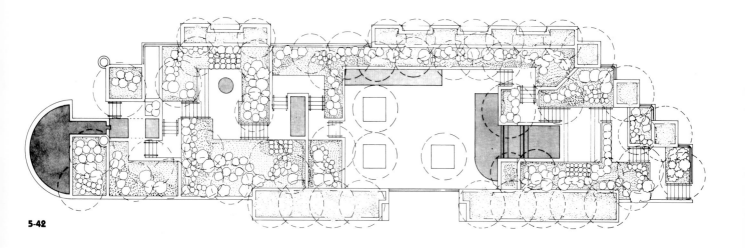

5-42

After plant species have been selected, the growing medium can be determined. Many types of soils are available. Constant experimentation will reveal the best mixture for a given plant. All interior soils are lighter in weight than exterior soils, thereby reducing structural loads, while allowing better water and air circulation to the roots. Heavier, compost-based soils are needed to give firm support to trees and large plants. Another concern is whether to leave the plants in their nursery containers or remove them for direct planting, which is generally healthier for the plants since root growth is unrestricted. On the other hand, plants in containers can be replaced more easily. Soilless hydroponic growth media are also available with a constant irrigation system for supplying nutrients.

Watering and feeding can be done by hand or through automatic irrigation systems. Hand watering is actually considered more reliable, since automatic systems can fail. It is an issue of labor cost versus capital cost. Most existing atrium gardens have been successfully hand watered. Spray heads, misters, bubblers, and various automatic means of drip irrigation are available, with attendant advantages and disadvantages. Self-watering planters are a new solution. These have a reservoir of water in the planter which is drawn to the plant through the capillary action of a wick. A tube in each planter provides a means for measuring the water level for refilling.

The presence of water for plants creates the problem of waterproofing and drainage. Undoubtedly, planters should be waterproof or contain drains to handle overflows and reduce root rotting. Spaces surrounding plants may be subject to water damage from spraying, misting, or maintenance, not to mention potential leakage from planters.

Maintenance is the last area of concern. Plants must be fertilized, sprayed to prevent insects, and pruned as necessary. Sometimes they need to be replaced altogether. Keeping them in their original planters aids this process. Planting beds must be cleared of debris and new mulch or soil added. The plants also get dusty, requiring periodic leaf washing by hand or thorough spraying. Direct access to all of the plants for these purposes is absolutely necessary. It is estimated that annual costs for plant maintenance average 25 percent of the initial installation cost.[21] It is for this reason that maintenance guarantee contracts with landscape contractors are quite prudent.

In any interior landscaping scheme, there are a multiplicity of design variables to be considered, not all of which are completely understood or predictable. Although basic arrangements and conditions can be planned, a certain amount of fine-tuning and adjustment will inevitably be necessary. Some plants will die, others will suffer a lack of growth. Plant species may need to be changed. The use and type of artificial lighting can be modified, as can watering schedules and fertilizing. A well-designed interior garden will accommodate these adjustments. The atrium garden is after all a miniature ecosystem requiring a level of stasis between the needs of the plants and the environment of humans.

NOTES

[1] BOCA Basic Building Code/1981, Building Officials and Code Administrators International, Chicago, 1980, pp. 137.
[2] Personal letter to author from Steven W. Henkelman, Partner, Cope/Linder Associates, October 20, 1983.

[3] Personal letter to author from John Peter Barrie, AIA, Swanke Hayden Connell Architects, April 20, 1984.

[4] "Issue: Atrium Code Requirements," Codes and Standards Committee, American Institute of Architects, January 6, 1983.

[5] Richard Rush, "Designing the Moving Experience," *Progressive Architecture,* December 1979, pp. 92–99.

[6] "Skylights: Better Technical Performance for an Architectural Favorite," *Architectural Record,* June 1979, pp. 143–148.

[7] "Dimensions Unlimited 1983," Super Sky Products, Meguon, Wisconsin, 1982, p. 35.

[8] Richard Rush, "The Light Heavyweights," *Progressive Architecture,* October 1981, pp. 125–133.

[9] Kalwall, Kalwall Corporation, Manchester, N.H., 1983.

[10] "The Skywalk Collapse," *Progressive Architecture,* October 1981, pp. 33–36.

[11] Benjamin Forgey, "Old Post Office: Brilliant Rebirth," *The Washington Post,* September 13, 1983, pp. B1, B14.

[12] Robert Martin, "TECO Building's Moving Sculpture Gets a Charge out of Solar Cells," *The Tampa Times,* August 6, 1981, p. 2B.

[13] Roberta Walton, "CAD-Sculpture Is New Trend for Atrium Art," *Contract,* January 1984, pp. 166–169.

[14] "Prisms," *Architectural Record,* Mid-August 1981, pp. 60–61.

[15] M. P. Friedberg and C. Rice, "Decorative Pools and Fountains," in Andrew Alpern, (ed.) *Handbook of Specialty Elements in Architecture,* McGraw-Hill, New York, 1982, pp. 265–304.

[16] "Green Stuff," *Progressive Architecture,* May 1981, pp. 167–171.

[17] M. C. Cunningham, M. P. Friedberg, and M. K. Morrison, "Gardens on the Inside," *Landscape Architecture,* January 1980, pp. 33–38.

[18] R. L. Gaines, *Interior Plantscaping,* Architecture Record Books, New York, 1977, p. 69.

[19] E. Conklin and S. Korner, "Trees and Plants for Interior Design," in Andrew Alpern, (ed.), *Handbook of Specialty Elements in Architecture,* McGraw-Hill, New York, 1982, pp. 65–128.

[20] Gaines, op. cit., pp. 79–121.

[21] "Green Stuff," op. cit., p. 171.

PART II Design Studies

Much can be learned from the comparative study of atrium buildings. To see how other architects have approached this design problem is to learn from their experience. To evaluate the successes and failures in these buildings in order to develop design guidance is one of the primary purposes of this book. It is in this spirit that the buildings in Part II are presented.

There are now a significant number of recently constructed atrium buildings (approximately 200 in number) available for documentation and analysis. Moreover, they represent a broad range of spatial subtypes, of differing contexts, scales, and functional purposes. All of the buildings presented as design studies in Part II are in the United States and have been completed (a couple are in the final stages of construction) in the last two decades. Some are quite well known as examples of this building form and have been included because of their historical and design significance. Others have been included because they are particularly well designed or they are exemplary with regard to a design feature (garden, fountain, materials) or design approach (daylighting, urban design). The final selection was made to provide a balanced representation of the five spatial subtypes (closed, open, linear, multiple lateral, and partial) and the four programmatic categories (office, institutional-civic, housing-hotels, and retail–mixed-use). The presentation is organized according to a two-way matrix with each programmatic category presented as a group (see Design Studies Chart below). Plaza atria or strictly retail shopping atria have not

DESIGN STUDIES CHART

	CLOSED	OPEN
OFFICE	**1** Philadelphia Stock Exchange Building	**5** Enerplex
	2 Boise Cascade Home Office	**6** Ford Foundation
	3 Gregory Bateson Building	**7** 1300 New York Avenue
	4 State of Illinois Center	**8** Hercules Plaza
		9 One West Loop Plaza
INSTITUTIONAL & CIVIC	**17** Phillips Exeter Academy Library	**19** Children's Hospital of Philadelphia
	18 Erie County Community College	**20** John F. Kennedy Library
HOUSING & HOTELS	**26** Hyatt Regency San Francisco	**30** Hyatt Regency West Houston
	27 Hyatt Regency Atlanta	**31** Hyatt Regency Dallas
	28 Hyatt Regency O'Hare	**32** Vista International Hotel
	29 The Atrium on the Bayshore	**33** Hyatt Regency Cambridge
		34 Hyatt Regency San Antonio
RETAIL & MIXED USE	**39** Old Post Office Building	
	40 World Trade Center, Dallas	
	41 Atlanta Apparel Mart	

been included. Several historic preservation projects have been included. Perusal of the chart indicates which spatial subtypes and programs have been the most widely used, since the twenty matrix boxes are not equally represented.

The intention throughout Part II has been to present each atrium building in the same manner to maximize the opportunity for comparative analysis. Each design study includes a written evaluation, site plan, ground floor plan, typical floor plan, building section, exterior photograph, and interior photograph (there are some exceptions due to lack of availability and/or relevance). All studies except the partial atrium examples are presented in a two-page format (partial atria are presented on one page). Each written evaluation concentrates upon an analysis of the atrium and includes a statement of the project concept, a description of the parent building, a description of the atrium, an evaluation of its design significance, and a discussion of any specific technical features.

The atrium concept has multifarious possibilities. The design studies certainly demonstrate its wide range of adaptability to different contexts and programs. Moreover, it is an architectural concept which can be expressed in a variety of styles and materials. If the following design studies open the reader's mind to these possibilities and challenge his or her creative response, then they have fulfilled their purpose.

	LINEAR	MULTIPLE LATERAL	PARTIAL
	10 Lockheed Missiles & Space Company **11** Hennepin County Government Center **12** Irving Trust Operations Center **13** Tennessee Valley Authority — Chattanooga Office Complex	**14** Intelsat	**15** Chicago Board of Trade Addition **16** 875 Third Avenue
	21 University of Rochester-Wilson Commons **22** Dallas City Hall	**23** Yale Center for British Art **24** New Thomas Jefferson University Hospital **25** National Gallery of Art East Building	
	35 Mercantile Wharf Building **36** Constitution Quarters **37** Loews Anatole Dallas	**38** Antoine Graves Homes	
	42 The Philadelphia Bourse **43** Galleria II **44** The Park in Houston Center	**45** Butler Square	**46** Citicorp Center **47** Trump Tower

Design Study 1

PHILADELPHIA STOCK EXCHANGE BUILDING
Philadelphia, Pennsylvania

ARCHITECT: *Cope/Linder Associates*
CONSTRUCTED: *1981*
ATRIUM: *80 feet by 190 feet by 8 stories*

Why would the developer of a speculative office building build an eight-story building containing a huge atrium when the zoning would have permitted a building with a site area ratio of 12? The reasons are several and upon analysis yield the design scheme for this project.

The site context was one of the primary determinants of this building form. The location along Market Street in center city Philadelphia between 19th and 20th streets was capable of drawing prime rental rates. Across an alley establishing the southern property line was a high-rise co-operative apartment building with exposed parking decks at street level. The residents of this building had already defeated a high-rise hotel scheme, since it would block their views. The atrium design scheme would achieve a high-quality office environment with a strong image, capable of attracting prime tenants willing to pay premium rents, thus justifying a lower building. Offices along the alley could obtain daylight and views from the atrium. The lower building would take less time to build, reducing financing costs and allowing earlier entry into the rental market. Compared to the small floors of a high-rise building, the large floors of the lower atrium building would provide more flexibility in accommodating a variety of tenants. Interestingly, developer William Rouse had envisioned an atrium solution before he embarked on the project.

The result is not only a successful real estate venture but one which contributes to the life of the city. The atrium is designed as a park, complete with trees, flowers, waterfalls, and pools—a welcome relief within this hard, dense cityscape. Although the atrium park is provided for the tenants and office workers, it is also available to the public. Pedestrians are drawn in through two recessed entrances, three stories high, at the street corners, to either pass through or pause and enjoy. The trading room of the Philadelphia Stock Exchange is located on a level 19 feet below the atrium floor, which steps down in a series of terraces, to afford visitors a view of the action through a large window.

The shape of the atrium is highly modulated in both plan and section to reduce the scale and create special spaces within the surrounding office floors. Offices are glazed with ¼-inch green-tinted glass on the atrium side. On the west end, there are a series of terraces which project into the atrium. This sectional stepping is reversed on the east end, forming a series of recesses. Along the sides, there are occasional projected or recessed balconies

Lawrence S. Williams

and projecting bay windows, glazed on all sides including the sloping roof. All of these balconies and terraces are festooned with overhanging vines, which are growing long and lush, forming leafy screens in front of office windows. Elevator banks and service cores are provided at each end of the building. Two additional elevators on the south side have observation cars, which provide dynamic views of the atrium while they ascend. The entire array of shapes reaches a point of resolution at the simple, gable-framed, rectangular skylight.

The ambience of this atrium contributes significantly toward creating a very

humane office environment. The lush garden with its splashing water and wide variety of plants strikes a sympathetic chord in the building's users. It is a place of relief from the surrounding intense work space. The uncluttered detailing of the architecture, with strip windows set flush in smooth white walls, forms an effective backdrop for the landscape materials. The developer wanted to create a unique office environment of high quality. In achieving this goal, he also created a financial success which is a worthy contribution to the architecture of this great city. (See Figure 5-42.)

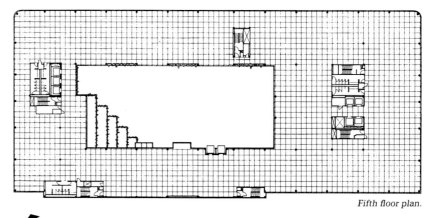

Fifth floor plan.

MARKET STREET

N

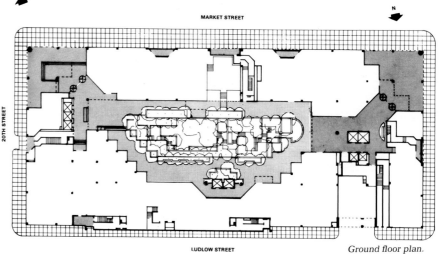

LUDLOW STREET

Ground floor plan.

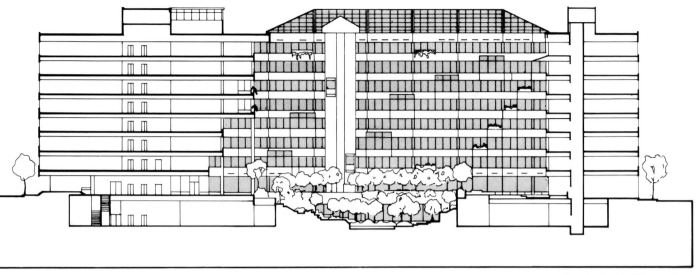

Longitudinal building section.

Lawrence S. Williams

BOISE CASCADE HOME OFFICE
Boise, Idaho

ARCHITECT: *Skidmore, Owings & Merrill — San Francisco*
CONSTRUCTED: *1971*
ATRIUM: *106 feet by 106 feet by 6 stories*

The primary rationale for this atrium building form was the client's need to promote communication among the employees. The architects responded by designing a low building with large (56,000 square feet) office floors surrounding a square atrium. This scheme maximizes the opportunity for visual contact and spontaneous exchange of information. Placing the elevators in the center of the atrium with four bridges connecting them to the offices maximized access between and within floors, with the bridges serving as shortcuts. The central presence of the atrium symbolically represents the corporation, spatially binding all employees together to serve a common purpose.

This is the Boise Cascade Corporation headquarters, accommodating some 1200 employees. The building occupies an entire block in downtown Boise, Idaho. The first floor is raised 40 feet above the street, creating deep pedestrian loggias on all four sides and a landscaped reception area within the enclosed ground floor of the atrium. The basement contains a computer center, mechanical rooms, and shipping-receiving accessible by a ramp. The second, third, fourth, and sixth floors are semi-open plan offices with a toilet, mechanical, and stair core in each corner. The fifth floor has a 250-seat cafeteria and an auditorium.

The atrium is an elegant space, pure in its geometry, with minimalist detailing and taut surfaces. This is in keeping with the Miesian character of the building exterior. Atrium facades are clear-glazed from floor to ceiling. An aluminum space frame with acrylic skylight domes covers the entire atrium roof. The atrium floor has entrances on all four sides, planting in each corner, and a surface of square brick pavers which extends to the street curb. The four freestanding round elevator shafts, encased in painted steel, are a wel-

Jeremiah O. Bragstad

come counterpoint to the rigid orthogonal geometry.

This is the prototypical expression of an urban corporate headquarters: a square building occupying its own block, an entity unto itself. The square atrium, a prism of space from floor to roof, gives the building an inward focus and thus supports the corporate image. All aspects of the plan are based upon a 5-foot 2-inch by 5-foot 2-inch module with 36-foot 2-inch by 72-foot 4-inch structural bays. Perhaps the weakest aspects of this scheme are the 72-foot-wide loggias with a thin exterior band of landscaping and interior band of paving. They serve little purpose in this cold, wind-swept climate and offer little pedestrian amenity. It would have been better to widen the atrium floor to increase the interior garden or provide exhibition space. Otherwise, the building is extremely successful for the rational clarity of its execution and its satisfaction of both the explicit and implicit client program.

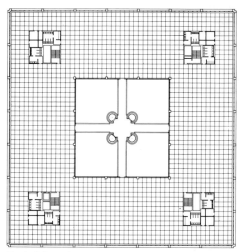

Typical floor plan.

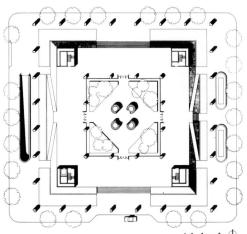

Site and ground floor plan.

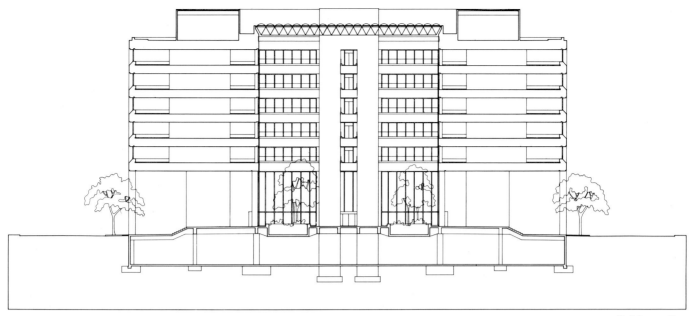

Building section.

Design Study 3

GREGORY BATESON BUILDING
Sacramento, California

ARCHITECT: *Office of the State Architect (Sim Van der Ryn)*
CONSTRUCTED: *1981*
ATRIUM: *150 feet by 144 feet by 4 stories*

This was the first completed office building of a series developed under the leadership of State Architect Sim Van der Ryn. The two primary programmatic objectives were to create a humane work environment and to make advances in conserving operating energy. These two objectives have been successfully unified in a design scheme based upon the atrium plan.

The atrium in this scheme has the simultaneous role of being a public plaza and an employee lounge. As a public space it occupies a position between the park on the east and an outdoor plaza on the west. The atrium joins these two existing urban spaces with generous entrances opposite each, thus encouraging the public to pass through or to stop and rest. Since this atrium is surrounded by government offices, it naturally becomes an employee lounge, a place where employees and public can meet and mingle for coffee breaks and lunch. Staff meetings, discussions, and conference sessions are also held in the atrium, where the informal atmosphere may be conducive to more effective communication. The presence of a snack bar as an amenity aids these activities. The employee cafeteria, however, is on the second floor with a deck overlooking the park. It is interesting to conjecture whether this function should have been more directly related to the atrium.

The atrium here also serves as a place of orientation and center of circulation. Both entrances lead to the atrium after a transitional lobby. An open stair is adjacent to each entrance to encourage pedestrian use in lieu of elevators, another way to save operating energy. All galleries and office access points face onto the atrium, creating a spatial focus, a natural place of orientation where there is a constant ebb and flow of people.

The atrium plays a crucial role in the overall energy strategy for the building. It is topped by large, south-facing, angled clerestories with automatically operating vertical louvers. These close on summer afternoons to reduce heat gain and open in the winter to allow the concrete structure to store heat. Smaller, north-facing clerestories admit year-round daylight. Thus, the offices receive daylight from both exterior facades and interior fenestration, although the deep (92 to104 feet) bays cause a dark zone in the center.

One of the primary energy strategies of this building is to use cool night air to

Ben Shook

Michael Bednar

flush heat from the building, to cool the concrete structure, and to store coolness in the rock bed. Night air is drawn through the office bays and exhausted through the atrium roof. It is also brought in through the two vertical shafts located in the atrium to cool the rock bed underneath it. Although the atrium is not air-conditioned, it remains comfortable both winter and summer. Four large yellow canvas tubes hanging from the atrium roof have fans inside which aid in reducing air stratification. (See Figure 4-12.)

The atmosphere in the atrium is appropriately bright and colorful. The brick paving adds to the sense of continuity with exterior spaces, as do the trees and plants. Furnishings are informal: natural wood

tables and red-painted wooden chairs. Natural redwood gallery railings and roof trusses complement the gray concrete structure. Elevator and duct shafts are encased in blue metal panels. The yellow canvas tubes are the most prominent visual feature because of their color and position. The color could have been softened to make them less obtrusive. However, in scale and overall effect, the setting is conducive to its activities.

This project sets a high standard of design innovation and quality for state government office buildings. The performance of its many features will require careful study and evaluation. But it does show that state office buildings need not be mundane.

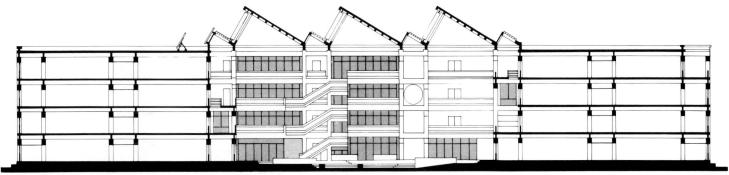

Building section.

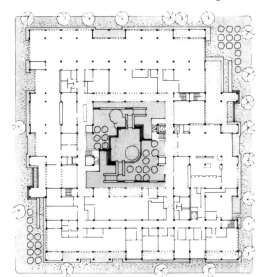

Second floor plan.

Michael Bednar

Design Study 4

STATE OF ILLINOIS CENTER
Chicago, Illinois

ARCHITECT: *Joint Venture: Murphy/Jahn and Lester B. Knight & Associates*
CONSTRUCTED: *1984*
ATRIUM: *175 feet in diameter by 18 stories*

This is one of the more spectacular atria to be built in the present era. In scale alone it is awe-inspiring, rising as a cylindrical space through the entire building to project above the roof, where it is capped by a continuous circular skylight sloped towards the southeast. The atrium is here termed a ''rotunda,'' to be placed among all of the other domed rotunda spaces found in important governmental and civic buildings. This historical association is quite direct, owing to the clarity and power of the cylindrical atrium form. However, few historical rotundas can match the technological bravura or spatial intensity of this space.

The building occupies the block bounded by La Salle, Randolph, Clark, and Lake streets in downtown Chicago. It is defined by these streets except at the corner of Randolph and Clark where the curved facade steps back in three tiers, forming a paved plaza with a piece of monumental sculpture by Jean Dubuffet. A two-story arcade at the base of this facade (which continues around the La Salle and Clark sides) forms a transition between the plaza and the rotunda. An important difference between this and historic rotundas is the way in which the atrium is connected to the exterior of the building with a full-height transition space. This enables the rotunda to be viewed from the plaza as a form of literal transparency.

Circulation within the rotunda is a significant attribute of its dynamic character. In addition to the ceremonial entrance, there is a vehicular drop-off entrance from La Salle Street and an overhead train and underground subway entrance on Lake Street. Escalators connect the lower commercial floors. Two banks of elevators with observation cars rise as architectural towers on either side of a radial axis running from the plaza through the rotunda. They discharge passengers onto curved galleries which bound the space. The most dizzying feature is a pair of stairways which cascade down the sides of the rotunda on either side of the radial axis. They are suspended within this majestic space to offer a spectacular spatial experience, while serving as convenient interfloor circulation. (See rendering, page 61.) A 20-foot-wide band around each office floor is open plan, separated from the gallery by a low storage wall. There is no intervening glazing.

This 1,150,000 gross square foot building does much more than accommodate a variety of state agencies. It makes a symbolic statement about the central role of state government through the use of the

Keith Palmer & James Steinkamp

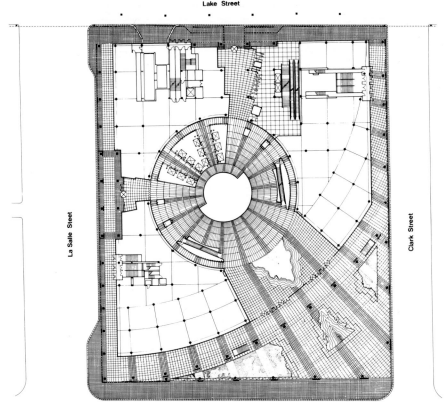

Lake Street

La Salle Street

Clark Street

Randolph Street

Site and ground floor plan.

historically significant circular rotunda. This space forms a central place of orientation and figuratively represents the state as the common purpose of the employees. The truncated top of this cylinder makes a statement on the skyline and serves as a lighted beacon at night. The

building also makes a civic gesture with its plaza oriented towards the civic center of Chicago. The center of the rotunda, on the lower floor, is a public forum—a place to meet, talk, eat, and drink—a public place in a public building, available to all.

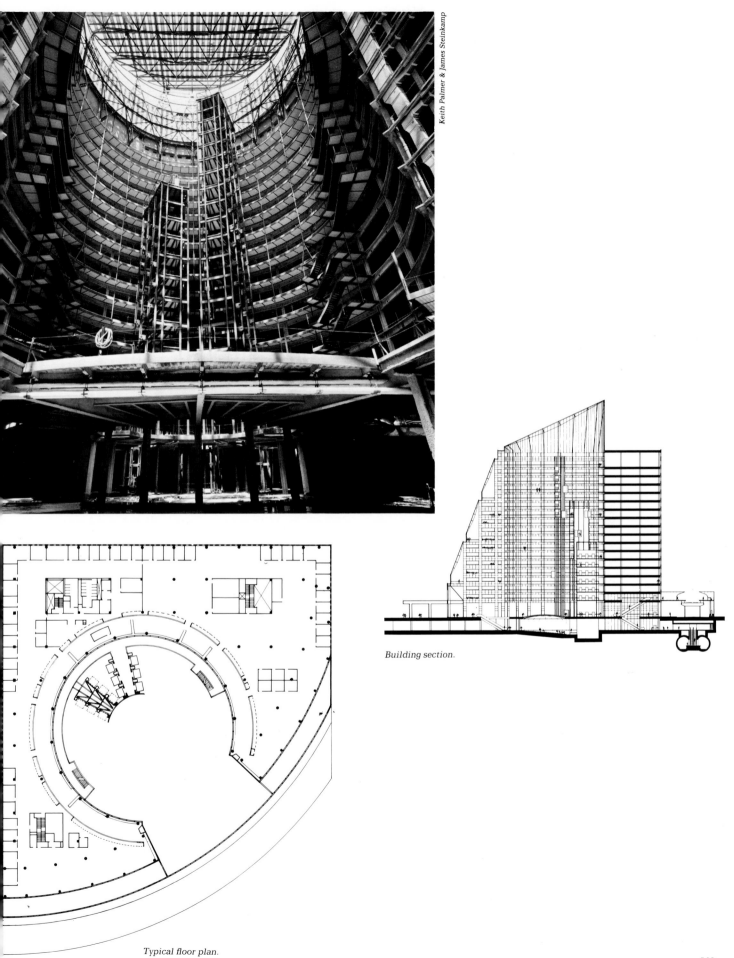

Keith Palmer & James Steinkamp

Building section.

Typical floor plan.

149

Design Study 5

ENERPLEX

Plainsboro, New Jersey

ARCHITECT: *North Building: Skidmore, Owings & Merrill— New York. South Building: Princeton University School of Architecture (Alan Chimacoff)*
CONSTRUCTED: *1984*
ATRIUM: *North— Irregular Plan, 3 stories; South— 100 feet by 60 feet by 3 stories*

This pair of speculative office buildings at Princeton Forrestal Center is the result of a fruitful collaboration between the Princeton University School of Architecture; Skidmore, Owings & Merrill of New York; and the Prudential Insurance Company. The latter had been sponsoring research at Princeton's Center for Energy and Environmental Studies and decided to implement the research results in this low-energy-consumption office complex. The intention was to offer cost inducements to tenants in a competitive office rental market. A pair of equal-sized three-story office buildings were proposed, with atria facing each other across a shared courtyard.

The North Building has its atrium facing south, occupying the full southern elevation. It is topped by a sophisticated skylight system. Here the energy role of the atrium is that of a giant solar collector with the heat being gathered and stored underneath the building. In the summer the atrium is vented, and sunshades on the facade and skylights prohibit direct sun. Since daylighting is one of the major energy components, this building has facades with an inner and an outer layer of continuous single-sheet glazing. The 18-inch space in between has insulating value and is used as a plenum for circulating warm air from the mass storage and cool air from the summer night. Daylighting is also introduced via a skylighted, three-story, U-shaped circulation zone.

The South Building has its atrium facing north and is smaller in area, with south-facing roof monitors to introduce sunlight, and no mechanical conditioning. Facade glazing area is limited to that needed for effective daylighting, and green-tinted sunshades on the south elevation keep out unwanted heat. A three-story U-shaped circulation zone is also incorporated here, with roof monitors that bring in equal components of north and south daylight. The three daylight sources (atrium, circulation zone, and exterior wall) provide balanced lighting to the 40-foot-deep office bays, insuring considerable electrical energy savings. (See Figures 4-6 and 4-15.)

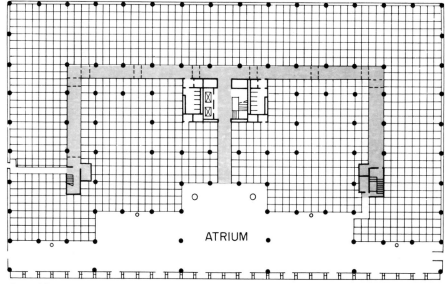

Ground floor plan, North Building.

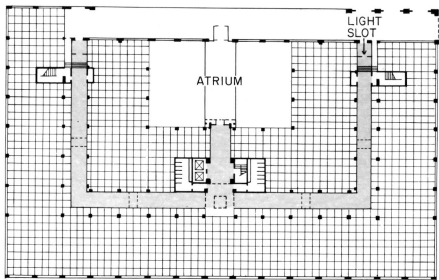

Ground floor plan, South Building.

Atrium view, South Building.

150

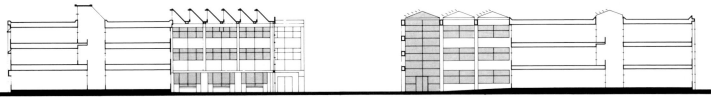

Atrium view, North Building.

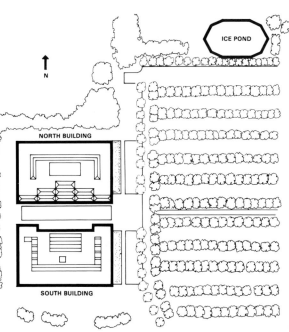

Site plan.

The design strategy for each of these buildings and their atria is quite different. Both atria are to be used as employee lounges, and both buildings have the same office area. However, the North Building takes a very active approach toward the use of solar energy, whereas the South Building takes a passive or defensive approach, concentrating on energy conservation. Both of them maximize the use of daylighting, resulting in well-lighted office interiors. Both buildings are also very handsomely designed, demonstrating that energy conservation and aesthetic sensitivity are not mutually exclusive intentions.

Design Study 6

FORD FOUNDATION
New York, New York

ARCHITECT: *Kevin Roche John Dinkeloo & Associates*
CONSTRUCTED: *1967*
ATRIUM: *approximately 120 feet by 95 feet by 12 stories*

As with all buildings of excellence, the Ford Foundation can be evaluated at many levels with equal success. As an urban building, it exploits the fortuitous site on 42nd Street at Tudor City by using the atrium as the transitional zone between public and private worlds. As the headquarters for an important institution, it symbolizes this entity through a memorable building image. As a working environment, it offers the 350 employees views, daylight, fresh air, and the garden as amenities while engendering a sense of common purpose by promoting visual and social communication. As a work of architecture, it gives the corporate office building a new design interpretation, which has been executed here with the utmost sophistication and thoughtfulness.

As the dominant spatial element in this scheme, the atrium imbues the building with a powerful sense of place. Its form, with two sides of glass facing the city and two sides surrounded by offices, establishes a transitional equality between public and private, inside and outside. Thus the atrium can be simultaneously interpreted as an extension of the urban landscape, a plaza or park, and as the common space for the institution, a courtyard or lobby. The brick pavement of the city forms the ground-level plaza, with street trees, flowers, and landscaping forming the park. Like a courtyard, it is a place protected from the elements and outside influences by its enclosure. Visual contact (all workers see each other) and the sharing of a common space foster a sense of institutional cohesion. (See Figure 1-28.)

The building is essentially a twelve-story corporate office building with one below-grade parking level and one below-grade semipublic auditorium level. Total floor area is 287,400 square feet with 8500 square feet in the garden. The eleventh floor contains dining, with seating capacity for each employee. The president's office is also on this level, within direct view of all employees and visitors. The offices of the board chairman occupy the top floor, the only suite which does not overlook the atrium. These top two floors surround the atrium on all four sides, give definition to the top of this space, and form a large-scale cornice for the building.

The architectural execution here is superb with regard to craftsmanship, detailing, and quality of materials. The bearing structure is concrete, faced with mahogany-colored granite, and the spanning structure is all *COR-TEN* steel. The skylight is a unique alternating ridge-and-furrow system with exposed

Keven Roche John Dinkeloo & Associates

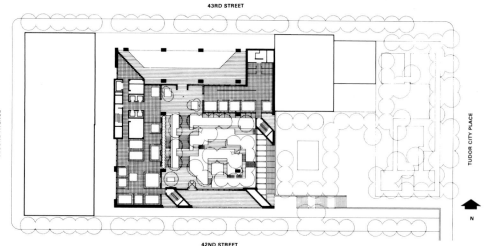

(Above) Ground floor building plan (with surrounding site conditions).

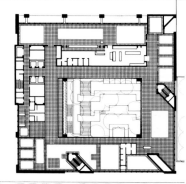

(Left) Top floor plan.

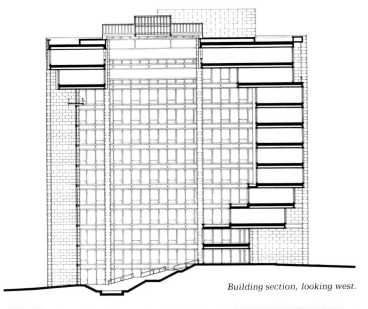

Building section, looking west.

steel trusses and $\frac{1}{4}$-inch wire glass. All interior facades are made of sliding windows, allowing offices to be opened to the atrium garden. Heating is a forced air system with supplementary fin-tube radiation at exterior glass walls and at horizontal beams of the garden wall. Air conditioning is a high-pressure double duct system which uses the atrium as a return-air plenum. The sliding windows allow access for interior window washing with spandrel beams offering footing positions.

The atrium is the idyllic garden in the city. Landscape architect Dan Kiley has developed a paradise of trees, shrubs, vines, flowers, and ground cover around a small sunken pool. The terraced ground level extends to three elevated terraces along the north side of the atrium, with some additional planting on the tenth floor. The ground-level garden is provided with a zoned automatic irrigation system and liquid fertilizer injection pumps. Irrigation water is collected from rainfall on the roof, stored, and used as needed. These services and the abundant natural light have caused the garden to prosper and mature. It is a serene oasis in the hard urban landscape, a place for respite shared by the public and employees.

Michael Bednar

153

1300 NEW YORK AVENUE
Washington, D.C.

ARCHITECT: *Skidmore, Owings & Merrill —
Washington*
CONSTRUCTED: *1984*
ATRIUM: *Square plan with slanted stepped section*

Michael Bednar

The design of this building is a sophisticated response to complex contextual conditions. The five-sided site fronts on New York Avenue, NW, one of the broad radial avenues of L'Enfant's 1791 urban plan. A soon-to-be-improved civic space in front of a church is formed where New York Avenue, H Street, and 13th Street intersect. In order to better define this space, the new 600-foot-long, curved building facade forms an abstracted neoclassical plane at the street edge. An arched, recessed entrance at the center leads to an exedra-shaped lobby and thus to the square atrium. The sequence continues via a peripheral colonnade to separate domed elevator lobbies on the cross axis. Located on the entrance axis is a six-story waterfall beginning at an upper terrace which itself overlooks the historic Church of the Epiphany on G Street.

The atrium parti for this speculative office building was chosen for several reasons. The urban design decision to build up to the street edges resulted in a very deep, dark floor plan, which the atrium resolved by bringing daylight and view to the center. Without the atrium, the 76,000 square foot floors were too large both for rental flexibility and to be served by one vertical core. An atrium could be placed in the building to resolve these design problems without reducing rentable floor area, resulting in a twelve-story building on a floor-to-area ratio (FAR) 10 site. Moreover, the atrium would enhance the prestige image of the building, provide additional office perimeter, and offer a gracious user amentiy, all in the interest of rental marketability. The resulting 1 million square foot building includes one office level and three parking levels below grade (for 600 cars). The ground floor is available for commercial tenants with access from both the street and the atrium colonnade. (See rendering, page 101.)

The atrium design owes its inspiration to certain Italian pallazzo cortiles and the terraced gardens of the Italian Renaissance. The ground level has a strict formal geometry with its cross-axial concept, square plan, and regular colonnade. The square, diagonal-grid marble floor, recessed below the colonnade, reinforces this formality. The six-story terraced office element with its landscaping and cascading waterfall is the most dramatic feature. Daylight and view are provided by a stepped, glazed southern wall supported by a space frame. The reverse-stepped building section is structured with two-story-high steel transfer trusses spanning the atrium.

Perhaps the most intriguing aspect of this atrium design is the visual richness

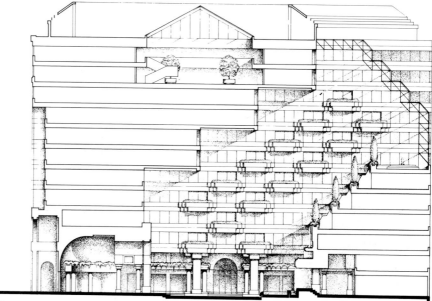

Transverse building section.

created by the juxtaposition of varied elements. The ground floor is distinctly neoclassical with its arched entrance, round columns, domed ceilings, exedra lobby, and patterned marble floors. It is furnished only with tall pyramidal forms covered with ivy. The glazed, space-framed south wall and steel transfer trusses are, in contrast, high-tech elements. Added to this are typical strip window office facades with scored gypsum board spandrels. Fortunately, these are relieved by a series of projecting planters. The marble-faced fountain is the culminating sculptural element. The entire assemblage leaves one slightly uneasy though extremely interested. It is a provocative scheme executed without timidity, one which adds a most significant interior space to a city rich in this regard.

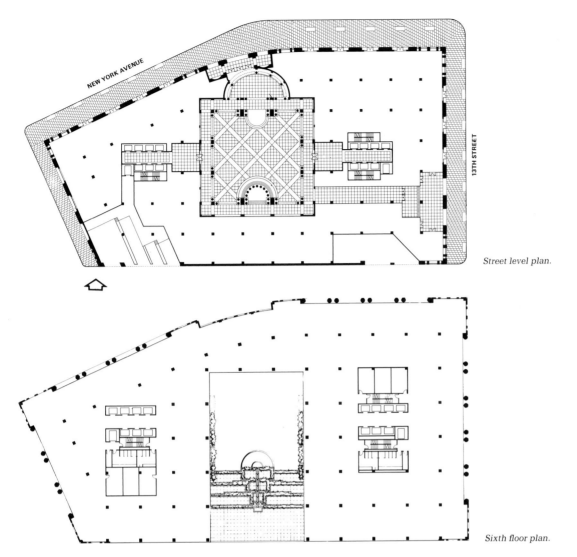

Street level plan.

Sixth floor plan.

Michael Bednar

Design Study 8

HERCULES PLAZA
Wilmington, Delaware

ARCHITECT: *Kohn Pedersen Fox Associates*
CONSTRUCTED: *1983*
ATRIUM: *nominally 90 feet by 110 feet by 13 stories*

This atrium scheme was devised to serve as a connection between the downtown core and Brandywine Creek, which forms the city's edge. A civic plaza gathers the public, shoppers, and employees before they proceed through an arcaded entrance to the lobby. From this point, shoppers continue along the arcaded sides of the space, crossing a bridge at the end to form a pedestrian loop. Employees take an escalator up to the control point on a bridge from which they cross to elevator banks on either the east or the west side. The most splendid procession is saved for the public, who move via terraced stairs through the atrium garden to emerge at a smaller civic plaza and park overlooking the Brandywine Creek. A watercourse, which begins at the lobby, cascades down the building's central axis as a symbolic connection to the creek. (See Figure 2-2.)

The 45,000 square foot office floors are basically U-shaped with glazed galleries along the sides and offices facing the view of the state capitol to the south. Bridges cross each floor at the north end of the atrium, providing places to pause suspended between the interior garden and exterior park.

The most compelling aspect of this atrium is the design of the space itself: the choice of materials, explicitness of details, and sensitivity of colors. The lobby and terraced garden are paved in an orange-brown brick similar to that used for exterior paving, creating a sense of civic continuity. The commercial arcades along the atrium sides are defined as a twelve-story slot of space by the building's steel structural frame, which is painted a deep blue. The beams at each level support planters. Catwalks to service each planter are in turn supported by another steel frame, painted rosy red and resting upon brick piers which rise from brick walls defining the sides of the garden. Interior glazing mullions are painted a powder blue. The result is like a de Stijl painting with lines of color overlaying each other and forming shifting compositions, all bathed in abundant daylight from the fully glazed north facade and gable-framed skylight. (See Figure 5-29.)

This is one of the most successful office building atria of recent years. Within the atrium section it is able to reconcile the program intentions of a corporate enclave with those of the larger community. Moreover, the atrium interior is designed as a series of visual screens, pathways, and bridges, giving it spatial richness. The superb detailing creates scale and interest which makes the space memorable. The exterior form of this building is notable in its own right, although in contrast to the provocative interior.

Norman McGrath

Longitudinal section, looking west.

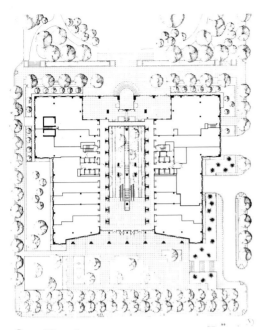

Ground floor plan.

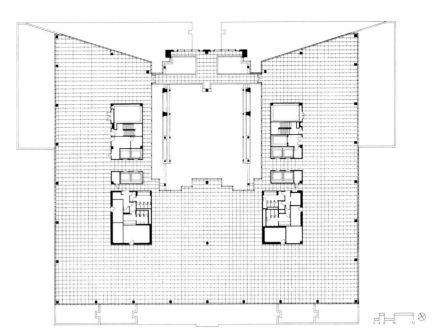

Ninth floor plan.

157

Design Study 9

ONE WEST LOOP PLAZA
Houston, Texas

ARCHITECT: *I. M. Pei & Partners*
CONSTRUCTED: *1980*
ATRIUM: *64 feet by 62 feet by 134 feet high*

This is a classic atrium office building design with an essentially square atrium plan within an essentially square building plan. The atrium rises the full eleven stories to be capped by a reflective glass skylight supported by a unitized aluminum space frame. The uniqueness of this design occurs on the north side, where the office floors terminate in diagonal 45 degree walls, thus forming a recessed entrance plaza and exposing the full side of the atrium. The offices facing the atrium have views out through this fully glazed wall. The wall also makes the atrium an extremely successful transition space between plaza and office, between outside and inside. The symmetrical building plan is designed around an entrance axis which leads to the centrally placed elevator lobby.

The design execution is superb in all respects. The motif of the exterior curtain wall made of taupe-painted aluminum spandrels and dark reflective glass bands, set in a taut plane, is repeated around the atrium. However, the materials change to plaster panels and clear glass windows with vertical shades to maximize office daylight and its control. The skylight is reflective glass to reduce heat gain, except for a clear glass band around its edge. The north atrium wall is clear glass to admit glare-free daylight without solar radiation. These glazed surfaces are carefully detailed as exercises in high-tech geometry. The elevator lobby is a double-height balcony, with alternating recessed semicircular balconies which overlook the atrium.

In keeping with its transitional role, the atrium, like the 7200 square foot plaza, is paved with black-brown bricks and carnelian granite trim. The space is simply treated with large ficus trees, ivy ground cover, and granite benches. Ground-floor lease space is utilized by nonprofit organizations.

This building, within the highly competitive West Houston office rental market, sets a high standard for speculative office development. Although the atrium floor represents only 1.5 percent of the gross building area, its volume is 13.8 percent of the total building volume. More significant is the fact that the entrance plaza, which represents nearly one-quarter of the site, was not built upon. Economically, the value of these amenities to the developer must have been justified by the prestige of the design and the unique building image. Also included in this Phase I was a 980-car parking garage; two 30-story office towers are projected for Phase II.

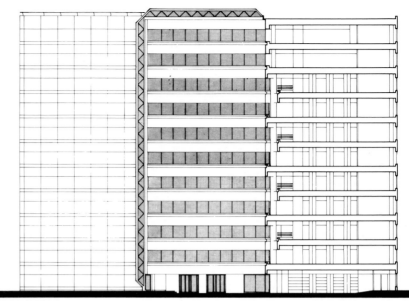

Building section.

Richard Payne, AIA

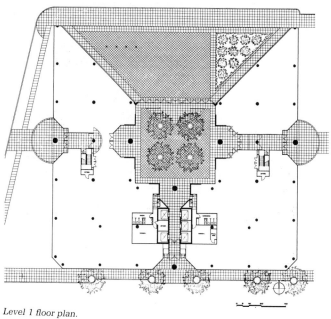

Level 1 floor plan.

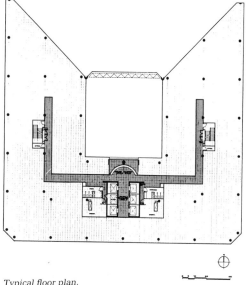

Typical floor plan.

LOCKHEED MISSILES & SPACE COMPANY
Sunnyvale, California

ARCHITECT: *Leo A. Daly*
CONSTRUCTED: *1983*
ATRIUM: *300 feet by 60 feet by 5 stories*

The primary design objective for this office building was to create a high-quality environment with minimal energy use. Optimizing the use of daylight became the primary means to achieve this objective. The building form itself was devised to effectively collect and distribute daylight. Its elongated plan maximizes north and south exposures, while locating core elements on the east and west ends in order to block low-angled morning and evening sun. In the center is a 60-foot-wide atrium, here termed a "litetrium," which balances the daylighting for the 90-foot-deep office bays and at the same time provides a social space. Offices directly overlook the atrium without intervening glazing or galleries.

The innovative building section was designed to control and distribute the daylight throughout the office areas. A ceiling which slopes from a 15-foot height at the perimeters to 10 feet at the center of the bay provides low-brightness ambient illumination with reduced shadowing and veiling reflections. On the north and south sides, daylight enters through clear glass and is reflected against this ceiling from light shelves 13 feet deep. A specially shaped 4-foot 10-inch projection on the south elevation gathers additional daylight while shading the reflectively coated glazing (17 percent transmission) below it. On the north side, tinted glazing (41 percent transmission) is used as vision glass. Continuous saw-toothed skylights span the atrium with their slopes facing south. A special glass diffuses the direct sun rays, thereby reducing glare from this source. An intricate artificial lighting system and sophisticated HVAC distribution network complete the overall energy strategy. (See Figure 4-10.)

The 600,000 gross square feet in this building have been planned with flexibility and efficiency in mind. A central bay is used for entry and vertical circulation via escalators. Circulation on the office floors is located in the middle of the bay, where the ceiling and the lighting are both at their lowest. Over 90 percent of the offices are open plan; conference rooms and closed offices abut the core areas at each end. A computer room is located on the east end of each floor. The ground floor accommodates a conference center, an auditorium, and executive conference rooms. The 900-seat dining room, which is also located there, looks out on the landscaped atrium.

This building projects an image of rationality and efficiency befitting its cor-

porate function. The white structural surfaces of the atrium are embellished only by planters along the balcony edges and sparse landscaping on the ground floor. Placement of escalators and bridges at the center of the atrium improves its linear proportions while concentrating circulation. The projected energy use of

19,600 Btus per square foot per year is 55 percent below the stringent California energy standards. The life cycle energy savings of this building will eventually exceed the initial building cost. This level of energy performance in a high-quality work environment is a noteworthy and admirable achievement.

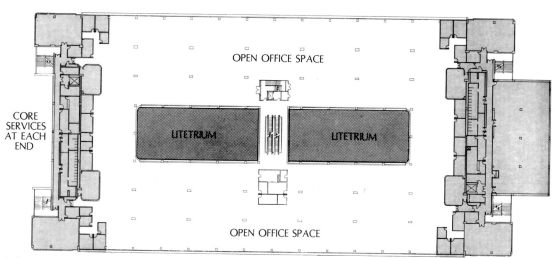

Typical floor plan.

OPEN OFFICE SPACE

CORE
SERVICES
AT EACH
END

LITETRIUM

LITETRIUM

OPEN OFFICE SPACE

TRUE
NORTH

REFERENCE
NORTH

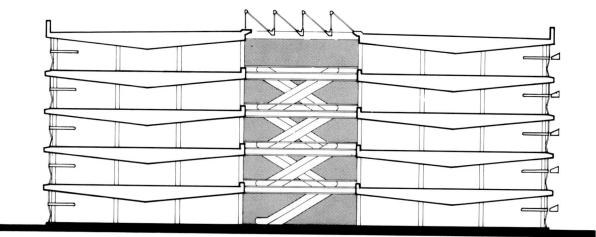

Transverse section.

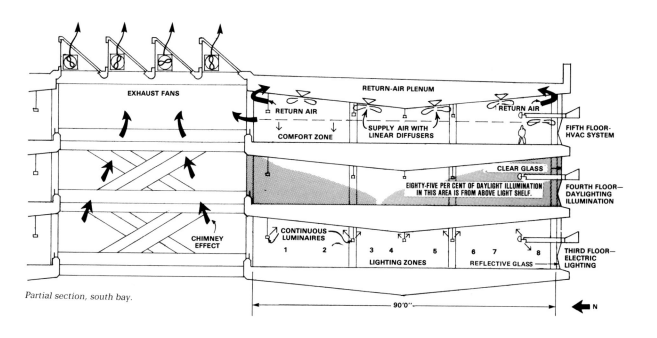

Partial section, south bay.

EXHAUST FANS

RETURN-AIR PLENUM

RETURN AIR

COMFORT ZONE

SUPPLY AIR WITH
LINEAR DIFFUSERS

RETURN AIR

FIFTH FLOOR-
HVAC SYSTEM

CLEAR GLASS

EIGHTY-FIVE PER CENT OF DAYLIGHT ILLUMINATION
IN THIS AREA IS FROM ABOVE LIGHT SHELF.

FOURTH FLOOR-
DAYLIGHTING
ILLUMINATION

CHIMNEY
EFFECT

CONTINUOUS
LUMINAIRES

1   2   3   4   5   6   7   8

LIGHTING ZONES   REFLECTIVE GLASS

THIRD FLOOR-
ELECTRIC
LIGHTING

90'0"

N

HENNEPIN COUNTY GOVERNMENT CENTER

Minneapolis, Minnesota

ARCHITECT: *John Carl Warnecke & Associates*
CONSTRUCTED: *1974*
ATRIUM: *60 feet by 175 feet by 350 feet high*

The design concept for this project was based upon a programming study which recommended the separation of county offices from the district and municipal courts. The result was a pair of twenty-four-story towers, functionally distinct and joined together by an atrium. The atrium floor is treated as a public plaza, with a fountain, trees, and brick paving. Services requiring a high level of public access are located on the ground level of each tower. The basement of the new county building contains a cafeteria and printing, computer, mail, and other support facilities, and is connected underground to the 1906 Municipal Building on the adjoining block. The two towers (which have separate vertical cores) are otherwise independent, except for seven bridges, spaced three levels apart, which serve as employee lounges.

This complex is considered the focal point of a future civic center encompassing an eighteen-block area. Pedestrian bridges will eventually connect the towers to the other elements of the master plan. The two towers establish an urban design direction by straddling a street and creating two pedestrian plazas on the remainder of the two-block site. The axial relationship of the atrium and tower of the Municipal Building is visually powerful. As one ascends the towers, the twenty-four-story glazed end wall of the atrium affords breathtaking and continuously changing views of this old building and the city beyond. Unfortunately, the south wall avails no similar view, although the lounge bridges in the atrium endeavor to define this end of the grand space. With its circular fountain, the plaza between the new and old government buildings is a potentially strong spatial focus for the total civic center. (See Figure 2-5.)

The atrium's structural design is a tour de force in both conception and execution. The atrium space frame is a structural cage with steel cross bracing on all four sides. This enables the towers, braced against each other, to absorb lateral wind forces through the diaphragm action of the floors. The result is less steel and fewer complex connections in the tower framing. The skylight is framed with large steel tetrahedrons which continue the tower bracing concept but reduce the skylight width. Since the structural framing is exposed on the atrium interior, it yields the predominant visual expression. Carefully detailed geometric tracery of the white steel gives visual enrichment to this dramatic space.

Phillip MacMillan James

Daylighting is an aspect of the atrium design which has been reasonably considered. The north end wall is completely glazed with clear glass, affording maximum daylight. The south end wall is treated similarly, but the placement of bridges one bay in from the end allows a measure of control over the amount of direct sunlight to reach the atrium and offices, although the bridges themselves are very bright. The skylight is not the full 60-foot width, thus reducing direct sun penetration to the topmost offices. Tinted glazing on the offices reduces glare and is recessed on the court tower to create a circulation gallery and control potential acoustic reverberation across the atrium. However, the depth of the towers (85 feet) is too great to permit effective daylight penetration except for the perimeter zones.

For its sheer scale and audacity, this atrium deserves notice. The atrium volume of 4.3 million cubic feet is 27.6 percent of the enclosed tower volumes, a large ratio indeed. The atrium's height of 350 feet, with completely glazed ends, gives the space an awesome vertical emphasis and strong transparency in regard to exterior space. The exhilaration of being on a lounge bridge poised between inside and outside and suspended in the midst of this vast space must be experienced to be fully appreciated. Moreover, this experience is varied, since there are seven bridges to cross. The 60-foot distance between towers is sufficient to separate them without impairing the visual associations between employees in either tower. It is this visual dialogue across the atrium at each floor level which establishes a sense of common governmental purpose. Thus, this atrium takes its place in the tradition of monumental spaces in which the public and the public servants are spatially united.

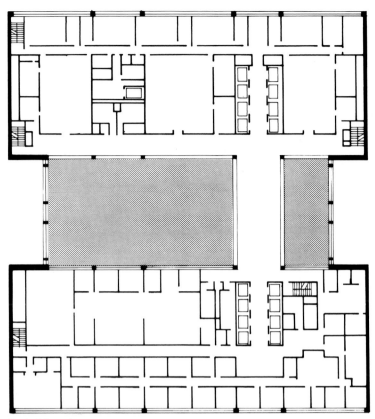

Typical floor plan.

Transverse section.

Phillip MacMillan James

Michael Bednar

Design Study 12

IRVING TRUST
OPERATIONS CENTER
New York, New York

ARCHITECT: *Skidmore, Owings & Merrill — New York*
CONSTRUCTED: *1983*
ATRIUM: *60 feet wide by approximately 280 feet long by 23 stories*

Wolfgang Hoyt ESTO

The rationale for this building parti grew out of the circumstances of the site and the demands of the program. The site in lower Manhattan, one block north of the World Trade Center, was divided by Washington Street, with an existing building on its southwest corner. The only efficient way to build a high-rise building was to close this street. However, the architects chose to incorporate the street in the design as a 60-foot-wide atrium, an interior street running through the entire building. This scheme resulted in a sixteen-story tower for the client's needs and a twenty-three-story tower for rental purposes. As client operations expand, they can utilize additional floors in the higher tower, since bridges connect it to the lower one. An enormous employee cafeteria is located on the seventeenth floor of the lower tower, under the stepped roof. Shops may be located along Greenwich Street in the future.

The circulation sequence begins at the formal entry on Barclay Street or the staff entry on Greenwich Street. The interior street, paved in slate, is used to reach the elevator core positioned on its axis. Bridges connect the elevator lobby to the two towers. The most spectacular sequence occurs on the seventeenth floor: the cafeteria serving line is in the west tower, with a bridge crossing the atrium to arrive at the dining garden in the sky.

Much design effort has been expended to maximize the daylighting distribution. The 3-bay, 90-foot-deep towers effectively limit daylight penetration to the outer bays, but the office landscape furnishings permit distant views in all directions. The exterior skin has horizontal bands of glass: opaque white glass to cover spandrels and heating units, partially reflective glass for upper windows, and clear vision glass at eye level. All surfaces in the atrium are white, and glazing is clear and single-sheet from floor to ceiling. Nevertheless, the high S.A.R. (height-to-width ratio) of the atrium will delimit the amount of available daylight reaching many of the offices facing it. The highly glazed end bays of the

atrium will help, as will the clerestories of the stepped roof. Skylights over the atrium would have been more effective. Though daylight should be quite perceptible throughout, its availability in sufficient quantity to be useful, in all but perimeter zones, is doubtful.

This is a powerful urban building which incorporates its context into its form. The interior street is a grand gesture which is unfortunately marred by the central position of the elevator tower, as well as

by security issues which prohibit its public use. The four-story dining garden at the top is a spectacular space with sweeping views to the east, north, and south. It is furnished as a roof terrace with huge bamboo plants, green carpet, and white garden furniture. The pipe truss spanning the atrium relates these two dramatic spaces through the continuity of the stepped roof. This is probably the most spectacular corporate cafeteria to be found in any American urban office building.

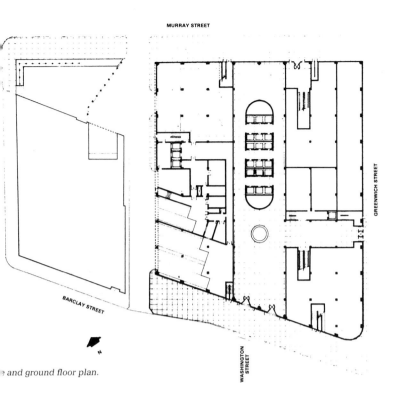

e and ground floor plan.

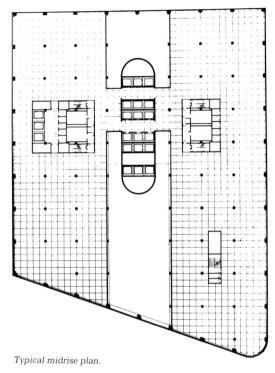

Typical midrise plan.

Michael Bednar

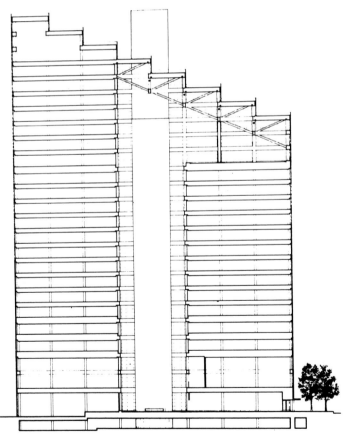

West-east section.

Design Study 13

TENNESSEE VALLEY AUTHORITY OFFICE COMPLEX
Chattanooga, Tennessee

ARCHITECT: *The Architects Collaborative; Caudill Rowlett Scott; Van der Ryn/Calthorpe & Partners; TVA Architectural Design Branch*
CONSTRUCTED: *1984*
ATRIA: *4 linear atria of different lengths, all 6 stories high with a stepped section*

The Architects Collaborative

The primary design objective established by the client for this project was to advance the state of the art in energy-conscious office building design while being sensitive to user needs and the urban context. A highly innovative team was assembled in 1979 to undertake this 1 million square foot project, which is now being completed.

After initial investigations, daylighting emerged as the central design strategy to both conserve energy and achieve environmental quality. A series of linear atria running east-west would maximize the availability of north-south daylight while providing a user amenity. An added benefit of the linear atria scheme was the reduction of building scale to fit the context. Parametric studies conducted to arrive at the proper balance between the exterior thermal load and the glazed area necessary to make daylight available to the offices showed that enclosing the open courts of the initial scheme to form atria would result in a 23 percent energy reduction.*

The office complex occupies a prominent four-block downtown site bisected by a major street. Glazed third-level pedestrian bridges join all building elements together, including the five-story computer center. The two primary buildings span Broad Street and have entrances into the atria on either side under these bridges. The atria themselves do not span the street. Areas between buildings are treated as landscaped pedestrian plazas; the amphitheater at the northeast corner is a major civic amenity, integrated with and adjacent to an information center and auditorium at the ground-floor level.

The sophisticated development of the atrium section is the true innovation of this project. Twelve-foot-high ceilings are used to distribute ambient daylight to the offices. In the atrium, a light scoop for reflecting light against the ceiling is attached to each floor, which projects beyond the floor above. On the northern exterior, shading is eliminated by sloped glazing. On the southern exterior, shading and daylight projection are achieved with a light shelf. The sloped plane skylight is inclined towards the south to receive direct solar heating in the winter, while maximizing daylight availability from the mostly overcast sky. The most innovative aspect of this scheme was the motorized

* S. Matthews and P. Calthorpe, ''Daylight as a Central Determinant of Design,'' *AIA Journal*, September 1979, pp. 86–93.

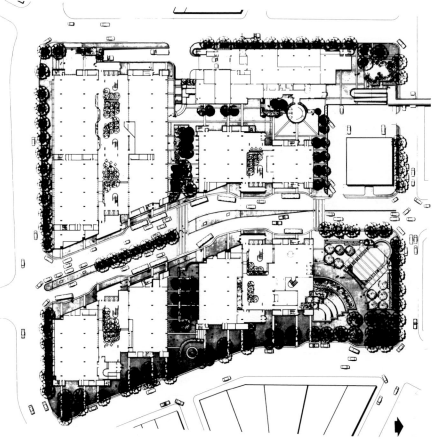

Site plan and ground level plan.

skylight louver system intended to provide a dynamic mechanism for projecting daylight and controlling solar loads. (See page 87.) Unfortunately it had to be eliminated due to its high cost, and reflective glass has been installed instead of the original clear glass. Model analysis of the original scheme predicted an ambient daylighting level of 30 footcandles throughout most of the offices and 70 footcandles in about 50 percent of the building during most working hours. What daylighting levels will actually be achieved without the skylight louver system remains to be seen.

The atria serve primarily as entrance areas, circulation spines, and employee lounges. Entrances are at the ends, where elevators are located, with sculptural stairs along the circulation spine. The landscaped lounge areas are all on the entry level. The horizontality of the solid gallery guardrails and the curved forms of the light scoops dominate the interior image. Overall, a bright, cheerful, and efficient ambience prevails. Through this building, the Tennessee Valley Authority has once again made a significant contribution to both its region and the nation.

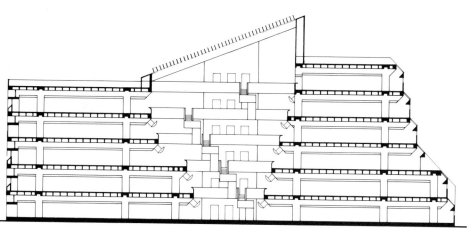

Transverse section.

INTELSAT
Washington, D.C.

ARCHITECT: *John Andrews International with Anderson Notter Finegold*
CONSTRUCTED: *1985*
ATRIA: *5 octagonal atria nominally 90 feet by 90 feet by 5 stories*

The International Telecommunications Satellite Organization (INTELSAT) has 109 member nations and owns and operates a global satellite system for public telecommunication services. The building program requirements for this organization included spaces for administration, satellite control, operations, simulation, maintenance, and conferences in several phases of staged growth. The program also required maximum exposure of offices to daylight and views, a high degree of space efficiency, and a minimum of energy utilization. The 12-acre site along Connecticut Avenue in northwest Washington, D.C., would in the future be surrounded by new chanceries and the University of the District of Columbia.

The competition-winning scheme by John Andrews brilliantly accommodates the program requirements while simultaneously utilizing the site to advantage. The design parti is a spine composed of linked octagonal atria which step with the site contours. An urban plaza entrance occurs at the Connecticut and Van Ness intersection, with a landscaped ceremonial entrance where the spine intersects the access road on the west side of the site. The remainder of the site is retained as a park with mature tree groups. There are actually five linked atria, although Atrium 4 at the ceremonial entrance is not full height like the others. Atrium 5 is the most spectacular at this time, since it has two open sides with magnificent views of downtown Washington. The modular scheme with octagonal pods of offices surrounding the atria allows for staged construction while maintaining access control and a 76 percent spatial efficiency. The repetitive structural units provide construction economy, and the atria maximize the opportunities for daylight and view.

Among the most innovative aspects of this project are its energy conservation features. To begin with, the space-framed skylights form a flat-topped pyramid with reflective and clear glazing located judiciously to control solar gain while admitting maximum daylight. Glazing at the atrium facades is full-height clear glass with automatic drapery controls (subsequently deleted); only 26 percent of the pod area at the center requires artificial lighting. As a result, the enclosed atria reduce the thermal loads on 40 percent of the total building facade by 80 percent. Fresh air admitted to the atria is spray-washed by the water in the extensive ponding, while exhaust air is vented by means of the natural stack effect and prevailing winds. The HVAC system is modularized, with separate air-handling

Sisson Studios

Michael Bednar

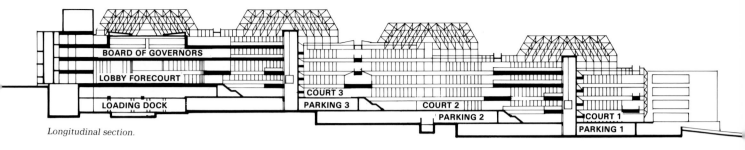

Longitudinal section.

Labels in section: BOARD OF GOVERNORS / LOBBY FORECOURT / LOADING DOCK / COURT 3 / PARKING 3 / COURT 2 / PARKING 2 / COURT 1 / PARKING 1

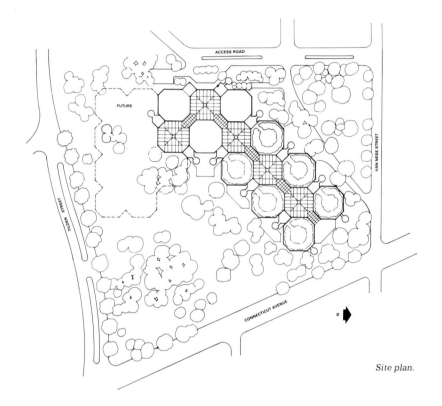

Site plan.

Labels in site plan: ACCESS ROAD / FUTURE / TILDEN STREET / VAN NESS STREET / CONNECTICUT AVENUE

units for the areas surrounding each atrium and separate thermal water storage tanks to offset peak energy demands. Temperatures in the unconditioned atria are maintained between 60 and 80 degrees Fahrenheit during occupied hours. Night ventilation will be utilized during summer months when possible. The result is a projected operating energy budget of 29,242 Btus per square foot per year.

The atria in this building maintain the character of glass-enclosed, landscaped courtyards, with water ponds which penetrate from outside to inside. The high-domed skylights extend the space skyward with a high degree of transparency. Visual connections between atria extend the space horizontally. The processional circulation sequence is among the most significant aspects of this project. The atria floors step up the site with connecting stairs at the links between them. A single elevator tower surrounded by a spiral stair is located at the center of each atrium along the spine. Bridges connect this vertical element to the access point for each office pod. The result is a spatially exhilarating sequence through a series of space-age atria set in a verdant landscape.

Level 5 plan.

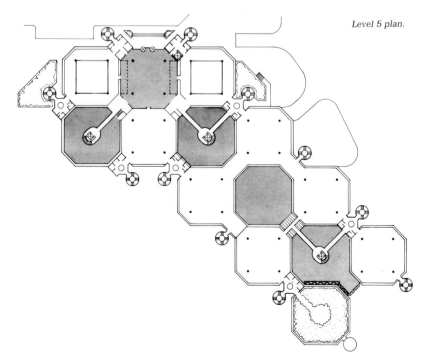

Design Study 15

CHICAGO BOARD OF TRADE ADDITION
Chicago, Illinois

ARCHITECT: *Murphy/Jahn; Shaw and Associates; Swanke Hayden Connell Architects*
CONSTRUCTED: *1982*
ATRIUM: *105 feet by 125 feet by 11 stories*

In designing this addition to the 1930 Holabird and Root Board of Trade Building, one of Helmut Jahn's primary concerns was to sympathetically relate the two buildings in exterior, expression and spatial form. The massing of the addition reflects that of its predecessor, including a pyramidal roof, although the primary facade material is a uniformly gridded glass curtain wall. An eleven-story atrium which utilizes a portion of the south facade of the preexisting building as one of its interior facades forges the spatial relationship between old and new. The glazed roof of this atrium offers an impressive view of the soaring tower of the parent building.

The main programmatic reason for the new addition was to create a large trading floor and support spaces for the Chicago Commodities Exchange. This 35,000 square foot, column-free, three-story space occurs on the third floor of the base building. A two-story-high trussed floor was needed to span the trading floor and to support the eleven floors of offices and the atrium above. A separate bank of express elevators runs to the new sky lobby. Unfortunately, these elevators protrude clumsily into the atrium, covering part of the old facade. The office space surrounding the atrium is U-shaped in plan, similar in configuration to the original building. A separate bank of six observation elevators serves the atrium floors, standing within the space as a piece of mechanistic sculpture.

The art deco motif of the scalloped echelon is used throughout the addition building as it was in the original. In the atrium, this motif forms the building section on the east and west sides. It is also used in the boldly patterned floor and for the shape of the express elevator bank. The east and west facades rise in alternating vertical bands of clear and reflective glass, a pattern which continues across the pyramidal skylight. Exposed steel trusswork, painted blue-green, supports the skylight, the north and south facets of which are completely clear-glazed. In contrast, open circulation galleries with glass guardrails give a horizontal emphasis to the south side of this space.

No atrium has been similarly placed in a high-rise office building with the purpose of spatially relating an old and a new structure. This atrium is a space full of contrasts: an old, buff-colored limestone facade and a new glazed curtain wall; clear as well as reflective glazing; horizontal and vertical emphases. It is a hard-surfaced space full of reflections, strong colors, and patterned daylight.

Building sectional perspective.

Keith Palmer & James Steinkamp

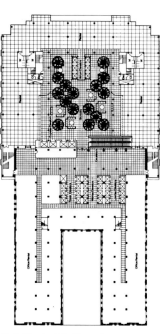

Skylobby twelfth floor plan.

Design Study 16

875 THIRD AVENUE
New York, New York

ARCHITECT: *Skidmore, Owings & Merrill — Chicago*
CONSTRUCTED: *1982*
ATRIUM: *4 partial, vertically stacked atria*

The architectural firm of Skidmore, Owings & Merrill has pioneered the concept of stacking several atria vertically in a high-rise building. The intention is to reduce the scale of these large buildings by organizing several floors around a focal atrium space for orientation, identity, daylight, and views. In this twenty-nine-story, multitenant office building, three atria, each four stories in height, have been created at the tenth, eighteenth, and twenty-fifth floors. A fourth atrium at street level extends one level below (to the subway concourse) and five stories above. Escalator circulation connects several office floors with the three retail levels they overlook.

This building is unusual in its plan geometry due to contextual circumstances. Commercial structures built prior to World War II occupy the corner of Third Avenue and east 53rd Street. The typical 24,000 square foot floor has a 45 degree geometry, resulting in a fourteen-sided plan. The present entrance sequence is organized around a diagonal pedestrian passage extending from the corner of Third Avenue and east 52nd Street to east 53rd Street, with entrances at both ends. The building core, with twelve passenger elevators, is located along this pedestrian passage and will be on a diagonal axis from the primary (the northwest) building corner once the old structures are removed and a new retail pavilion is added. This pavilion will indeed be splendid with abundant daylight and a landscaped rooftop terrace.

The upper atria provide a rental advantage for attracting prestige tenants. The four floors surrounding each atrium are rented together to a single tenant who may use the atrium floor as an in-house library or reception area. The stepped-back atrium section allows daylight to penetrate deep into these floor areas. The tenants pay a premium for the atrium since their rental agreements are based upon full rather than reduced floor areas. Each upper atrium has a four-story clear glass wall which affords spectacular views northward, the length of Third Avenue.

This is truly a design scheme which has created advantages out of circumstantial disadvantages. Although project phasing and site geometry created obstacles, a superb design effort created a unique building which reconciles these contextual forces. The four stacked atria are an additional measure of design innovation, giving this building a distinctive image.

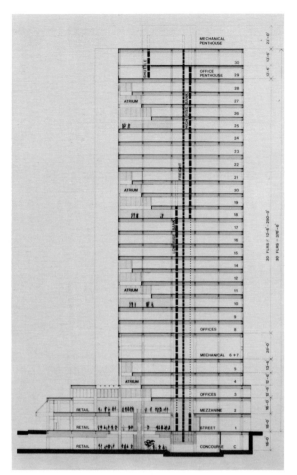

Building section.

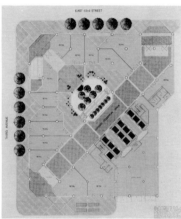

Street level plan.

Michael Bednar

Design Study 17

PHILLIPS EXETER ACADEMY LIBRARY

Exeter, New Hampshire

ARCHITECT: *Louis I. Kahn*
CONSTRUCTED: *1972*
ATRIUM: *40 feet by 40 feet by 7 stories*

This is in most respects a classical atrium building. The square plan atrium occupies the center of a square plan building, serving as the focal space. Galleries surround the atrium on all levels, giving access to the programmed spaces. There are, however, several anticlassical variations in this scheme. Building entrances are at the corners and lead to an open, curving stair extending up into the atrium. Although the atrium is top-lit in the classical sense, this is achieved by means of clerestories rather than skylights. The clerestory openings are small and the natural concrete beams diagonally supporting the atrium roof act as daylight baffles. The result is a subdued, nonglaring light which softens and reveals the texture of the enclosing concrete planes, with their large-scale circular cutouts.

The form of this building is truly centroidal. The plan is composed of two interlocking square doughnuts with the atrium common to both. The outer doughnut is made of brick walls and accommodates readers at window carrels. The inner doughnut is made of concrete and keeps the books out of the way of strong daylight, utilizing a muscular structure to support the great concentrated weight. The atrium is simultaneously the resultant space in the center and the pure geometric space which generated the square doughnut configuration.

The atrium is the antithesis of the building it occupies. It has no programmed purpose—not even circulation—in contrast to the surrounding, highly programmed spaces. Thus, the center of the plan is unoccupied. It is a place of repose. Symbolically, the atrium represents the place of human beings, where there are no books. It is the space where the totality of the surrounding books and their contained knowledge can be comprehended. Interestingly, it is now being used as a place where the community gathers for concerts, with the audience lining the galleries.

Louis I. Kahn thought of the atrium as a great entrance hall, a place where the books are visible all around to create a feeling of invitation. In many great libraries throughout history the reading room has been the hierarchically important space, with the walls lined with books accessed by galleries. In this building, however, reading is regarded as a private affair, a relationship between the person and the book, in a quiet place with good daylight and view. This newly constituted set of relationships has been expressed here without compromise. The building speaks of these relationships truthfully and with clarity, yielding a great work of architecture.

(Drawings courtesy of the Louis I. Kahn Collection, University of Pennsylvania; photos courtesy of the Library, Phillips Exeter Academy)

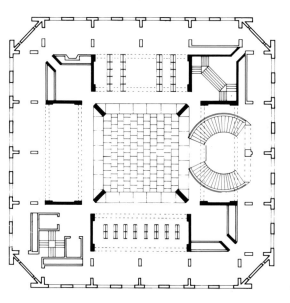

Ground floor plan.

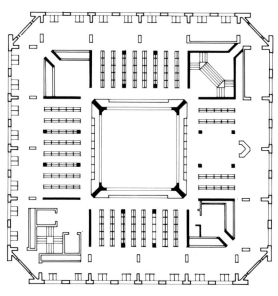

Third floor plan.

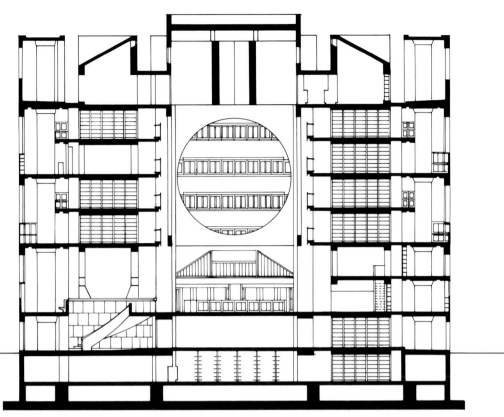

Building section.

Bradford F. Herzog

Cervin Robinson

Design Study 18

ERIE COUNTY COMMUNITY COLLEGE
Buffalo, New York

ARCHITECT: *Cannon Design*
CONSTRUCTED: *1982*
ATRIUM: *137 feet by 114 feet by 4 stories*

This is an excellent example of adaptive reuse — the matching of the characteristics of a landmark structure with the needs of a new community facility. The existing post office and federal building by O'Rourke, Aiken and Taylor, built in 1900, contained a one-story skylit court used as a mail sorting room. When it was vacated in 1975, feasibility studies deemed it to be a "white elephant" until the idea of housing the community college was recognized. Precedent for this can be found in the Wilson Brothers' 1890 Drexel Institute Building in Philadelphia, where the atrium now serves as a student commons. The same scheme was utilized in Buffalo where a new library and 400-seat auditorium were built in the courtyard, with a student commons area on top of these spaces. The floor level is stepped to reduce the scale and enrich the space. A new skylight was built at the roof level, creating a four-story atrium. Faculty offices and galleries were placed on each floor facing the atrium, and classrooms were located in the perimeter zone facing the city.

The integrity of the historic structure was not disturbed by this adaptive reuse. New spaces constructed in the old courtyard were provided with new footings, columns, and structure. The exterior and interior facades were completely restored. Woodwork, oak doors, mahogany paneling, stained glass, and plaster were restored. A new sprinkler system had to be installed throughout. In the new commons area, the sprinklers are installed in floor-mounted columns which also supply fresh air. In historic areas, bronze sprinklers were installed on the walls.

The reconstruction reduced energy expenditures by almost 50 percent. Double-wall fiberglass panels were used for the new skylight (0.24 U-value) and double glazing was installed in all exterior windows. (See Figure 5-22.) The closed-loop heat pump system which replaced the steam radiators permits transfer of heat to classrooms where it is needed. The heavy masonry mass of the structure also helps to mediate temperature fluctuations. Drawing air from the top of the atrium and reintroducing it at lower floor corridors reduces stratification.

Economics completes the success story of this project. Not only was a landmark structure preserved and facilities provided for 2000 students, but this was accomplished at an estimated savings of 25 percent over new construction, not including the cost of the land. The commons area is still somewhat sterile, but it will mellow with use. The great communal space, surrounded by classrooms and protected from the harsh northern climate, is highly appropriate for a community college setting.

Patricia Layman Bazelon

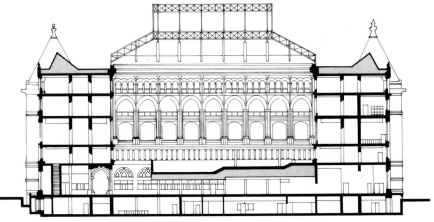

East-west building section.

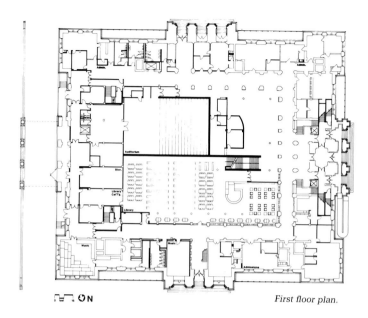

First floor plan.

Third floor plan.

Patricia Layman Bazelon

Design Study 19

CHILDREN'S HOSPITAL OF PHILADELPHIA
Philadelphia, Pennsylvania

ARCHITECT: *H2L2 Architects/Planners*
CONSTRUCTED: *1974*
ATRIUM: *96 feet by 96 feet by 8 stories*

It is unusual to find an atrium in a hospital, because it might be viewed as a waste of space or an unnecessary luxury. Yet the value of an atrium in a hospital is truly demonstrated in this precedent-setting example.

Children's Hospital is a 259-bed teaching, research, and referral center for chronically ill children, 55 percent of whom are under two years of age. The hospital has two levels of parking below grade and nine levels of services above. Eight of these levels surround and give form to the atrium. The ground level of the hospital is the most public area, with a bank, a gift shop, an auditorium, waiting lounges, and a gymnasium, along with administrative offices, the emergency room, and outpatient clinics. The atrium floor assumes the role of a park within this public area and is filled with fig trees, benches, a fountain, and even a McDonald's restaurant.

The seven upper floors which surround the atrium have inpatient rooms and clinics on the east and west sides and waiting areas and circulation on the north side. The first three floors on the south side are clinic spaces, but the upper floors are open to the sun. This upper area of the south side is traversed by bridges which serve both as play areas and as sunshades, admitting winter sun but shading the atrium in the summer. (See Figure 4-3.)

The unique U-shaped hospital plan formed around the atrium provides constant orientation for both users and staff, a commodity in short supply in most labyrinthine hospitals. The elevator lobby relates directly to the atrium, as does the main transverse corridor. Many inpatient rooms overlook the parklike setting, offering patients vicarious participation. The atrium provides an unprogrammed space in contrast to the hospital's crowded and highly programmed floor areas.

The atrium is also a part of the overall energy strategy. It is roughly cubic in proportion to fit into the similarly cube-shaped building. The upper part of the south side and the roof have been designed to let in the winter sun as direct-gain heating while blocking the summer sun through shading. The saw-toothed clear glass skylight is sloped to reflect the summer sun while admitting northern daylight. The ground floor is air-conditioned in a normal manner, while the remaining height of the atrium is used as a return-air plenum. Return air is discharged through slots in the galleries, thus eliminating the need for large return-air ducts. The atrium serves as a heat sink, and the constant-volume, terminal reheat system

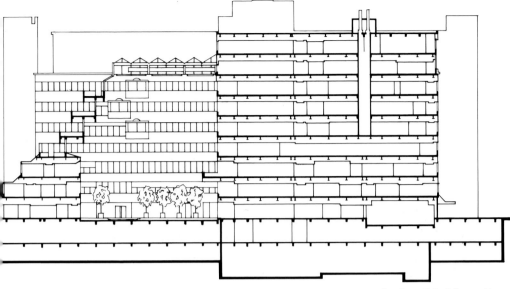

South-north building section.

Ground floor plan.

utilizes the rejected heat to temper air and to heat domestic hot water.

The result is perhaps the most architecturally humane and spatially pleasant hospital in existence. It is just what the doctor ordered for kids who must go there. Gone are the winding corridors, the confusion and disorientation. In the center is the ever-present, friendly atrium with sunshine, a terrace, and a park on the ground floor. To top it off, there is a McDonald's close at hand.

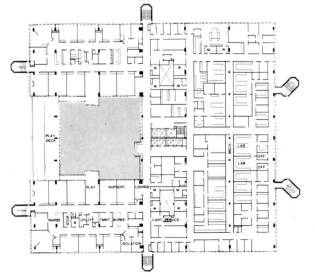

Typical floor plan.

Design Study 20

JOHN F. KENNEDY LIBRARY
Boston, Massachusetts

ARCHITECT: *I. M. Pei & Partners*
CONSTRUCTED: *1979*
ATRIUM: *80 feet by 80 feet by 110 feet high*

The design of this building is as unique as the man whom it was designed to honor. The atrium, as a space, has little if any precedent. In form, it is similar to Pei's Wilson Commons and One West Loop Plaza, with walls and roof entirely of glass, supported by space frames. As at Wilson Commons, this is an atrium which unites the elements of the parent building.

The program for this project, which includes a library, archives, and a museum commemorating President Kennedy, was in large part determined by the Presidential Libraries Act of 1955. It has been interpreted here in discrete elements: a low, curved form housing two theaters, a square base building for exhibition, and a nine-story triangular tower, the upper seven floors of which house the library and archives. These disparate elements are spatially and geometrically united by the prismatic atrium, which satisfies the condition that an atrium be a centroidal space which brings the other spaces or elements of a building into relationship. The white triangular tower gives the library function prominence, and it engages the gray-glazed atrium of similar height. This wedding of forms may symbolically connote yin and yang, solid and void, positive and negative, or white and black.

The choreographed sequence of movement to and through the building reveals the relationships among the program elements and exemplifies the unifying role of the atrium, here termed a "pavilion." The entry lobby, at the balcony level, overlooks the atrium to provide orientation to it and the ocean. After viewing a film, visitors proceed downstairs to the below-grade exhibition spaces, which have no exterior views or light. The exhibit engagingly depicts the life of President Kennedy and the history of an era. One then emerges into the soaring glass atrium, which offers compelling views of the sea and the distant Boston skyline. Kennedy's favorite sailboat, the *Victura*, is below on the lawn, which meets the granite sea wall. The atrium is a profound space, a place to gather one's thoughts and contemplate, for it is devoid of furnishings save for an enormous American flag hung from the roof. Its monumental scale is juxtaposed with the grandeur of the sea. The walls of the library tower rise above, with strip windows in an apsoidal recess providing overlooks for the researchers. A granite stair under the tower's corner takes one back to the lobby level.

The atrium, or pavilion, is a pure but symbolically charged space. Its material

Nathaniel Lieberman

Nathaniel Lieberman

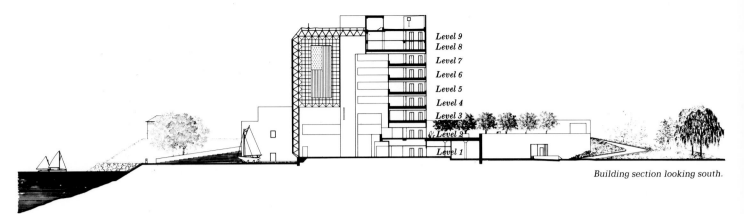

Level 9
Level 8
Level 7
Level 6
Level 5
Level 4
Level 3
Level 2
Level 1

Building section looking south.

components are minimal: a space frame of gray steel struts with aluminum hubs, gray glass, and granite floor. Its true components are natural light and views of the sky and the ocean beyond. The atrium's emptiness, except for the visitors, is intended perhaps to symbolize the void created by President Kennedy's assassination. The Kennedy Library is an inspiring public place where one can contemplate the meaning of this man's life and one's own role in the nation's future.

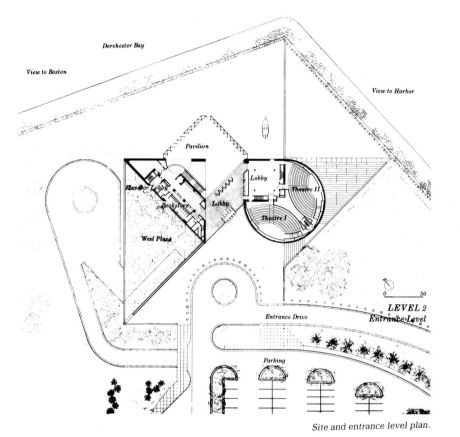

Dorchester Bay

View to Boston

View to Harbor

Pavilion

Elevator Lobby

Lobby

Bookstore

Lobby

Theatre II

West Plaza

Theatre I

0   50

LEVEL 2
Entrance Level

Entrance Drive

Parking

Site and entrance level plan.

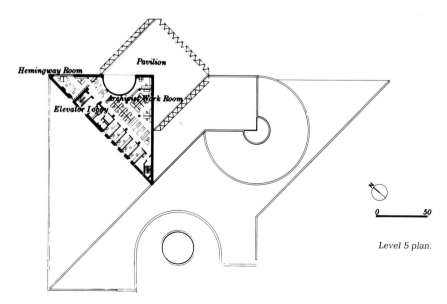

Hemingway Room

Pavilion

Elevator Lobby

Archivist Work Room

0   50

Level 5 plan.

UNIVERSITY OF ROCHESTER — WILSON COMMONS
Rochester, New York

ARCHITECT: *I. M. Pei & Partners*
CONSTRUCTED: *1976*
ATRIUM: *48 feet wide by 150 feet long by 86 feet high*

This building spatially expresses the essence of a student commons as both a public space and the nexus of campus pathways. The public place is in this case a linear atrium glazed on all exterior surfaces. The nexus is formed by external bridges from the library and main dining hall converging with a tunnel and two other ground-level pathways. This sense of connection is continued within the atrium via three bridges which cross the space and three public staircases which connect the five levels. This system of movement not only maximizes access to the various facilities but also provides a multitude of opportunities for social encounters among the university community.

The building form was generated by diagonally slicing a square plan, forming a long rectangular atrium and two five-story triangular towers. These towers are then joined by bridges, thus classifying this building as a linear atrium type. All spaces intentionally focus inward, since the building has no exterior fenestration. The large glazed atrium creates the illusion of being an exterior space without the negative consequences of the harsh northern climate. In fact, the atrium also serves as a passive solar heating source by taking the superheated air from below the skylight and ducting it to areas of the building which require heating. Although the main building entrance is at ground level, the atrium floor level is 9 feet below grade.

Programmatically, this is a student union building for a small but prestigious upstate New York university. The atrium accommodates two primary activity areas: a dining space for 100 people and a main lounge which visually opens onto the campus green. The first level (below grade) also houses a 125-person rathskeller and student activities rooms. A lecture hall and gallery are on the entrance level, with a 400-person multipurpose room on the third level. The fourth and fifth levels accommodate additional lounges and music rooms.

The architecture clearly expresses the parti by opposing the visual transparency of the atrium with the solid masses of the two triangular towers. The latter are surfaced with brick inside and out. These large planar exterior surfaces without fenestration, and the flat roof, are quite in contrast to the surrounding small-scale colonial revival buildings. Balconies and bridges in the atrium are surfaced with white gypsum board. Atrium floors are done in brick pavers, with minimal planting in movable, cylindrical tubs.

Ezra Stoller ESTO

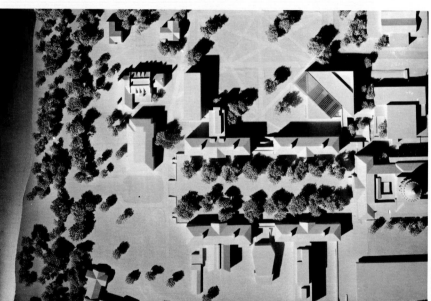

I.M. Pei & Partners

Furnishings are brightly colored and also movable to allow flexibility in arrangement. The main architectural feature is the triodetic space frame of white galvanized steel tubing, which braces the glazed walls and supports the low-pitch ridge-and-furrow skylight. Tempered clear glass is used for these walls, reflective tempered laminated glass for the skylight. The glazing is held on a 6-foot-square grid by dark, anodized aluminum frames which contrast with the white structure. Overall, there are many design similarities between this building and the John F. Kennedy Library, which was built a few years later.

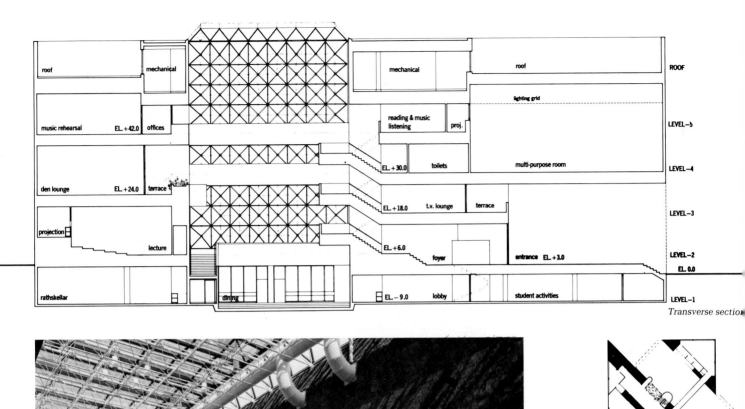

					ROOF
roof	mechanical		mechanical	roof	
				lighting grid	LEVEL—5
music rehearsal EL.+42.0	offices		reading & music listening	proj.	
			EL.+30.0	toilets	multi-purpose room	LEVEL—4
den lounge EL.+24.0	terrace					
			EL.+18.0	t.v. lounge	terrace	LEVEL—3
projection	lecture		EL.+6.0	foyer	entrance EL.+3.0	LEVEL—2
					EL. 0.0	
rathskellar	dining	EL.−9.0	lobby	student activities	LEVEL—1

Transverse section

Ezra Stoller ESTO

5

4

3

2

Floor plan

Design Study 22

DALLAS CITY HALL
Dallas, Texas

ARCHITECT: *I. M. Pei & Partners*
CONSTRUCTED: *1978*
ATRIUM: *223 feet long, varying width, by 6 stories high*

A city hall must simultaneously serve as a representative symbol for the city and as a functioning building housing the city administration. In a city the size of Dallas, these roles become enlarged, yielding a building of monumental scale and significant programmatic complexity. The scheme for this building is grand in conception — a linear monolith some 550 feet long and 8 stories high, facing a 7-acre civic plaza. The building section is truly unique, with its entire north facade facing the plaza and canted inward at a 34 degree angle — a statement of engagement between building and urban space. The linear atrium, which occupies half of the building's length, extends the public space of the plaza into the interior as a complementary gesture.

In a building of this scale, complexity, and level of public usage, circulation and directional orientation are of paramount concern. The main lobby is articulated as the unique bay along the six-bay facade, with the mayor's office and the council chamber above it. Escalators reach up to the atrium floor, one level above the plaza. Open lounge areas 30 feet high relate the atrium to the plaza. Primary public service functions are located on this floor. Elevator banks at either end of the atrium serve the open galleries along the south side. Upon entering the atrium, the citizen or visitor has a sense of the totality of the city administration and how to reach a particular department. In this regard, the floor at the plaza level below is unfortunately dissociated from the rest of the building.

The sectional characteristics of the building serve two other design objectives. The stepped atrium and sloped north side yield floors of varying areas, a characteristic which is useful in programming these office spaces for the various-sized departments of the city. This variation in depth means that the deeper floors receive less daylight in the middle. The atrium is skylit by three semivaulted clerestories which face north and yield a constant glare-free light. The stepped section gives each gallery direct daylight, and the solid concrete guardrails help to reflect light to the offices across the atrium, which are glazed. Vines overhanging the galleries and carpet underfoot help to soften the otherwise hard-surfaced space.

The conceptual and visual relationship of atrium to plaza makes a grand civic statement which is very appropriate for a city hall. The consistent use of unarticulated, poured-in-place concrete on the interior and exterior enhances the large-scale monolithic quality of the building. This, combined with a certain structural bravura, yields a powerful civic monument, a heroic symbol for Dallas, Texas.

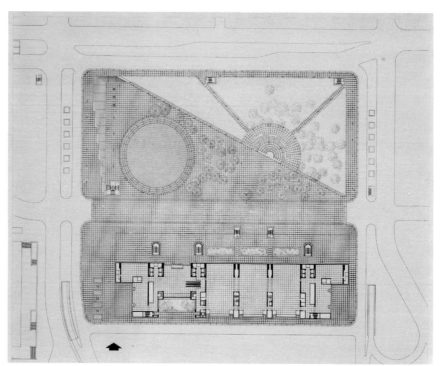

Site and first floor plan.

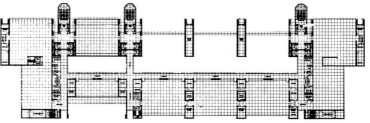

Third floor plan.

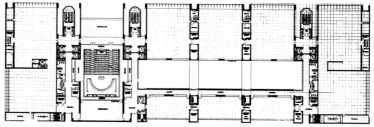

Sixth floor plan.

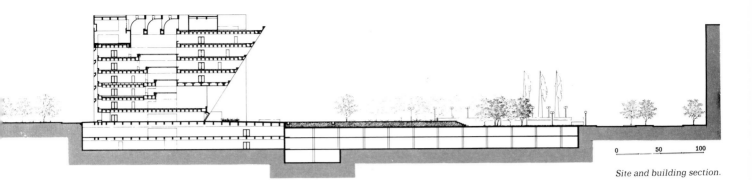

Site and building section.

YALE CENTER FOR BRITISH ART
New Haven, Connecticut

ARCHITECT: *Louis I. Kahn (completed by Pellecchia and Meyers Architects, after his death)*
CONSTRUCTED: *1977*
ATRIA: *40 feet by 40 feet by 4 stories, and 40 feet by 60 feet by 3 stories*

Tom Brown

This building is probably the ultimate expression of Louis I. Kahn's idealistic, life-long search for order in space and construction. The rigorous adherence to a 20-foot square bay yields a building six bays wide (120 feet) by ten bays long (200 feet) with the long side abutting the sidewalk of Chapel Street, across from Kahn's 1953 Yale Art Gallery Building. Within this rectangular box, two atria are formed to yield an interior spatial order. One serves as an entry court, the other as a picture gallery. Both are formed by the omission of the structural elements which create the surrounding bays. The highly complex program of exhibition galleries, study spaces, library, archives, offices, and lecture hall, with a series of shops along the street, has been accommodated within this disciplined container with ingenuity and deftness. The building section is used to advantage to yield a variety of spaces with varying conditions of daylighting and orientation.

The processional sequence of spaces, with the two atria as the focal points, is intriguing. The atria are each two bays wide in plan, yet they are starkly different in section. The building entrance is distinctly anticlassical, beginning at the northeast building corner with a low, dark exterior void. The four-story entry atrium, with its travertine marble floor, is surrounded by galleries with overlooking windows. The circulation through these galleries is room-to-room, recalling an eighteenth-century British manor house. The rooms are formed by movable partitions which do not disrupt the overall integrity of the spatial zoning. The visual transparencies across the atrium and down into it enrich the spatial experience.

The picture gallery atrium or grand hall is one level up from the entry atrium and is reached by the public stair, which is encased in a concrete drum. This concrete object, without openings, stands within the grand hall as a silent intruder. It violates the integrity of this beautiful hall. The disorienting vertical stairwell is starkly juxtaposed with the orienting focal space of the building. Along the sides are two-story library and research spaces. At the top floor, the spatial sequence is completed with public galleries which surround all sides of both atria. The great hall, with its oak floors, oak-paneled walls, and overlooking gallery windows, is a serene room meant for receptions or chamber music concerts.

The entire building is capped by a

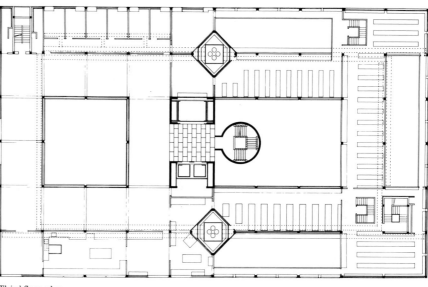

Third floor plan.

coffered skylight system which occurs in each of the sixty bays except for the two over the elevator lobby. The square coffers are formed by V-shaped concrete beams which contain ducts and provide splayed surfaces to receive and reflect the entering daylight. Skylights in the entry court are clear domes. All others are fitted with uniquely designed baffles on the outside and refracting glass panels inside. The result is a diffuse, glare-free light which bathes the galleries and brings out the true colors in the paintings. (See Figure 4-5.)

The interiors of this building have a serenity and dignity which bespeaks their role as spaces in which to contemplate the

history of British art. The palette of materials—travertine marble floors and borders, beige wool carpets, silky gray exposed concrete, white oak paneling, and natural linen wall covering—is rich but not ostentatious. The joints between materials, surfaces, and elements are of such clarity and directness as to make one marvel at the intelligence and craftsmanship which created them. Everything is under control; there is order everywhere. Container and contained, building and art are supportive rather than competitive. This is pure architecture born of the belief in the power of space and its architectonic expression.

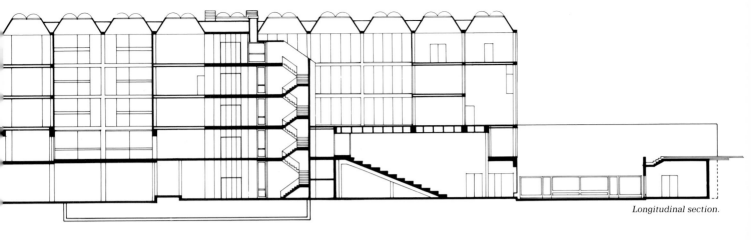

Longitudinal section.

Entry atrium view.

Picture gallery atrium view.

NEW THOMAS JEFFERSON UNIVERSITY HOSPITAL
Philadelphia, Pennsylvania

ARCHITECT: *H2L2 Architects/Planners*
CONSTRUCTED: *1978*
ATRIA: *two atria, each 56 feet by 120 feet by 8 stories*

The spatial organization of this new teaching hospital is exemplary in many ways. The structure occupies half a city block in center city Philadelphia along Chestnut Street, between 10th and 11th streets. The building plan is organized around a circulation spine, connecting entrances and lobbies on the two side streets. Two identical atria extend from the second level to the skylit roof. On the north side of the two atria, physician's offices are located on floors four, six, and eight with single-patient rooms on floors three, five, seven, and nine. Diagnostic and treatment facilities are located on the south side of the building on odd-numbered floors, with interstitial mechanical floors in between. The first floor accommodates commercial space along Chestnut Street and a loading dock along Sansom Street. The second floor (atrium level) accommodates administrative and central support services. Thus, the hospital is organized horizontally into four minihospitals with the physicians' offices only one floor removed from their patients' rooms.

The two atria serve very important spatial roles within this building scheme. They provide orientation, their elevator lobbies serving as balconies, with curved glass enclosures, which overlook the atria. They also provide daylight and views to the patient rooms, which face either the atria or the streets. The atrium floors function as dining and lounge spaces served by a centrally located cafeteria serving line. These floors are one level up from the two entrance lobbies in order to maintain security.

The two atria are well-proportioned rectangular volumes defined by planar white facades, with tinted-glass strip windows, and topped by clear-glass ridge-and-furrow skylights. Freestanding stairs within well openings extend down to the entrance level. There is a linear planting bed along the north side of both atria with ficus trees that are underscaled. Huge rainbow-colored banners are hung within the space to bring color relief to the otherwise bland interior. Colored canvas umbrellas over the dining tables bring additional color and scale. The presence of these two bright and cheerful social spaces within the megastructure of a contemporary hospital does a great deal to make this a humane place.

H2L2 Architects/Planners

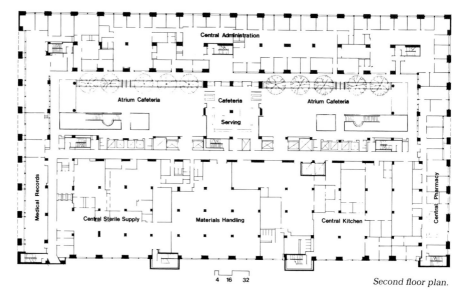

Second floor plan.

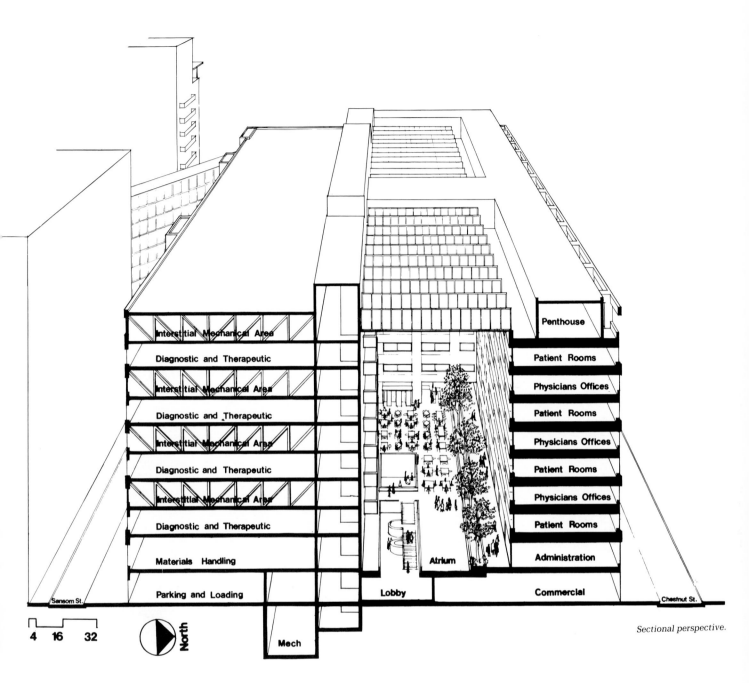

Interstitial Mechanical Area
Diagnostic and Therapeutic
Interstitial Mechanical Area
Diagnostic and Therapeutic
Interstitial Mechanical Area
Diagnostic and Therapeutic
Interstitial Mechanical Area
Diagnostic and Therapeutic
Materials Handling
Parking and Loading

Penthouse
Patient Rooms
Physicians Offices
Patient Rooms
Physicians Offices
Patient Rooms
Physicians Offices
Patient Rooms
Administration
Commercial

Atrium
Lobby
Mech

Sansom St.
Chestnut St.

4 16 32

North

Sectional perspective.

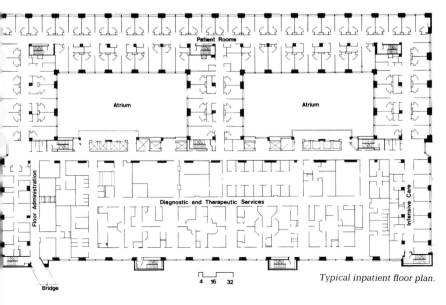

Patient Rooms

Atrium   Atrium

Floor Administration

Diagnostic and Therapeutic Services

Intensive Care

Bridge

4 16 32

Typical inpatient floor plan.

H2L2 Architects/Planners

NATIONAL GALLERY OF ART
EAST BUILDING
Washington, D.C.

ARCHITECT: *I. M. Pei & Partners*
CONSTRUCTED: *1978*
ATRIA: *no. 1—an isosceles triangle 225 feet on two sides and 150 feet on the other, 70 feet high; no. 2—angular plan, 70 feet high*

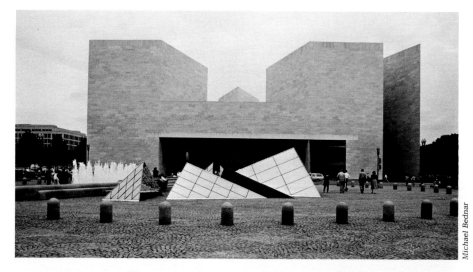

Michael Bednar

On June 1, 1978, President Carter opened the new East Building and stated that it symbolized the connection between art and public life in the United States. Indeed it does, for this magnificent building invites the public into its presence to enjoy and appreciate art. This is accomplished through a sequence of public spaces beginning with the Mall, leading to the Fourth Street Plaza, and proceeding through a large-scale covered entrance into the grand triangular atrium. (See Figure 2-6.)

The atrium's position and geometry are a result of the contextual forces and building parti. The building entrance is on axis with the main building to the west, but is off-center on its own facade. The triangular atrium plan is derived from the angle of Pennsylvania Avenue and the need to divide the building into two distinct components: a symmetrical isosceles triangle to house the gallery, formally related to the main building, and a right triangle to house the Center for Advanced Study in the Visual Arts, with its main facade facing the Mall.

The atrium itself is a three-level space above the plaza entrance level, 16,000 square feet in area. It has a fourth level below grade. The processional sequence can begin at the plaza, continuing past the Henry Moore sculpture in the recessed entry and through a 10-foot-high lobby into the atrium. A more dramatic spatial sequence follows the long, low tunnel from the main building into a light well at the southwest corner of the atrium and up a flight of marble stairs to the main floor. Another grand flight of stairs sweeps up to the mezzanine level, from which a graceful escalator reaches the top level. A "flying" bridge at the back of the atrium leads to the main gallery. The descending sequence occurs via a balconied stair and a bridge at the mezzanine level back to the main stair. The entire assemblage of stairs, bridges, escalators, and balconies has been organized to choreograph movement and to imbue the place with dynamism and excitement.

Natural light is as important as concrete and marble as a material which gives shape to this place. The steel and aluminum skylight/space frame covers the entire atrium and is supported by its enclosing walls. Daylight is ever-present and generally uncontrolled, except for sunscreens in the skylight which diffuse and filter it to reduce glare and harshness. The quality of daylight changes throughout the course of every day and as days change

View of gallery atrium.

Leonard Jacobson

between seasons. The moods of climate and cloud cover are also revealed: the shadows change and the light levels vary. These natural phenomena are in counterpoint to the building's otherwise highly controlled man-made characteristics. As it falls on the Tennessee marble surfaces, the light brings out the subtle shadings of pink and brown, casting an iridescent aura.

Alexander Calder's last work, a red and black mobile of aluminum, spanning up to 70 feet, is hung from the skylight. It is a constant source of fascination as it undulates, kept in motion by the building's air supply issuing forth from air scoops at the skylight perimeter. (See Figure 5-36.)

The other major section of the East Building, the Center for Advanced Study in the Visual Arts, also has an atrium space, although there is no skylight. Daylight enters from two 6-story vertical bands of glazing on the south side, resulting in uneven distribution. The skylight would have aided this circumstance. The role of

this space is as a reference and reading hall, surrounded by book stacks and research offices. It is sedate and subdued in materials and furnishings. Entry is either from a deeply recessed space off of the plaza or directly from the main atrium.

A "sense of place" remains in the consciousness of all those who visit the main atrium. The minimalist detailing and the treatment of walls and floors as planes of marble cause people and objects to read strongly as "figures." The visual quality of people in motion is emphasized. The tempered-glass guardrails on the bridges and balconies allow one to see the whole person in motion. Individuals and groups alike are comfortable here, without being self-conscious, because it is a generous space with many subspaces which invite exploration. Moreover, it has no single focal point where one could be the center of attention. It is a theatrical place where everyone has a chance to be an actor in the drama of enjoying this museum.

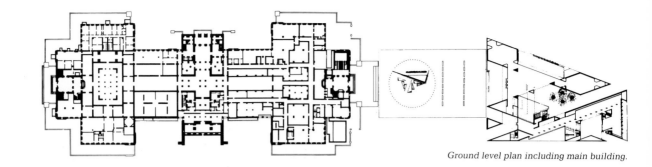

Ground level plan including main building.

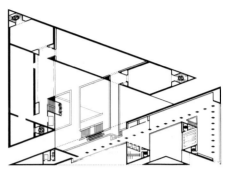

Main gallery level 4 plan.

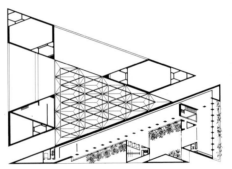

Level 7 plan.

Center for Advanced Study atrium.

HYATT REGENCY SAN FRANCISCO
San Francisco, California

ARCHITECT: *John Portman & Associates*
CONSTRUCTED: *1974*
ATRIUM: *300 feet by 170 feet by 170 feet high
(triangular in plan and section)*

Of all the Portman hotel designs this one makes the strongest urban design statement. It is a building located at a crucial point in the city, where Market Street meets the Bay in front of the Ferry Building. The triangular site at this pivotal point derives from the rotation of street grids on the north side of Market Street. The site can also be considered as the last block in the five-block Embarcadero Center, composed of office towers and low-rise commercial buildings. The focal point of this development is the Justin Herman Plaza, which is unfortunately separated from the Bay by the expressway. (See Figure 2-4.)

The form of the building is a direct response to these site conditions. It is triangular in plan with the main entrance at the corner of Drum and Market streets. The massing also addresses the site in that the line of Market Street is maintained with a seventeen-story vertical facade with no setbacks. The entrance corner is marked and expressed by the elevator core, capped with a revolving restaurant set within a square concrete frame. The Drum Street facade is also a vertical plane, with a continuous colonnade at ground level. The north facade, however, slopes at a 45 degree angle, responding to the open space of the plaza and forming a kind of amphitheater by virtue of the guest room balconies which compose the facade.

The giant interior atrium complements the exterior plaza; together, they represent a focal point for the Embarcadero Center. The four-block sequence of walkways, shops, and miniplazas is directly linked by a bridge to the atrium, which is three levels above the street and which constitutes the datum plane for all of Embarcadero Center. The treatment of the atrium establishes a continuity with these exterior spaces through the use of a concentric pattern of gray pavers on the floor, with fountains, trees, flowers, plants, birds, benches, and sculpture all bathed in daylight. Thus, the exterior plaza and interior atrium are like great outside and inside rooms.

Although this atrium can be thought of as an urban space, its role is also as a hotel lobby. The walls that define the space are formed of galleries, which lead to the guest rooms. The atrium floor is a plaza containing a coffee shop and cocktail lounge (under fabric-covered trellis ceilings) surrounded by other restaurants, bars, and retail shops. (See Figure 5-33.)

Six capsulelike observation cars riding on the outside of an inverted elevator core

John Portman & Associates

Building section.

create constant visual animation for observers. For riders, it is an exhilarating experience as the capsules rapidly rise seventeen stories and arrive at the revolving cocktail lounge. (See Figure 5-5.)

The uniqueness of this atrium is its triangular section formed by the great sloping north wall of galleries. This is a structural tour de force, an A-frame in concept with the structural sloping wall braced against the vertical wall by steel girders. A gap is left between the two walls of guest rooms, forming a continuous, 30-foot-wide, 300-foot-long skylight. The seventeen-story vertical south wall of galleries is lined with planters of ivy which

simultaneously "soften" the atrium space and keep guests from leaning too far over the balconies.

This atrium can be likened to the visions of Piranesi (1720–1778), a great soaring space full of geometric complexity and alive with the constant movement and activities of people. The space is also unusual since the sloping wall seemingly defies gravity. The skylight could have been wider to bring in more daylight, since the space under the sloping wall is somewhat gloomy, even on a sunny day. Nevertheless, this atrium is full of drama, with powerful inclinations derived from the inventive building section.

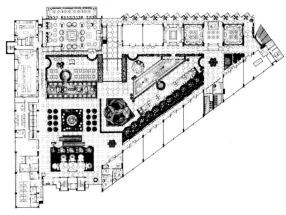

Atrium level floor plan.

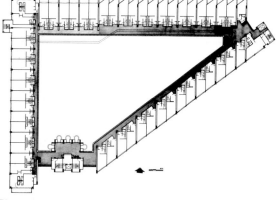

Plan at first guest level.

HYATT REGENCY ATLANTA
Atlanta, Georgia

ARCHITECT: *Edwards & Portman*
CONSTRUCTED: *1967*
ATRIUM: *120 feet by 120 feet by 23 stories*

This building truly revolutionized the design of hotels in the present architectural era. It was John Portman's first realization of the atrium hotel concept based upon the 1888 Brown Palace precedent. The recent history of hotel design has been so influenced by the success of this building that the atrium hotel has become the standard of prestige for all luxury hotels. A great many atrium hotels have been built in the last fifteen years with the Hyatt hotel group leading the way. (See pages 26–28.)

The Hyatt Regency Hotel in Atlanta is the classic prototype for the atrium hotel scheme. All of the 800 guest rooms have a direct and equal relationship to the atrium in their arrangement along single-loaded galleries stacked on twenty-two levels. The base of the building contains two below-grade levels of parking, two below-grade levels of meeting rooms, and the entry-level piazza with its services and amenities. A circular well around the elevator shaft visually relates the lower levels to the main floor with escalators connecting these levels. A revolving restaurant is supported on the elevator shaft, well above the atrium skylight. The atrium itself is well defined and clearly comprehended, being square in plan and rectilinear in section. The top of the space is given definition by a translucent skylight surrounded by a clear glass clerestory which can serve as a smoke reservoir in the event of a fire.

John Portman's design philosophy, expressed as ''an architecture for people and not for things,'' is well realized in this building. Various tenets of his philosophy include:

Order and Variety The spatial order of the well-defined atrium is strong enough to sustain the juxtaposed variety of circular elements.

Movement (An Orchestrated Journey) The processional sequence of entry to elevator and thence to room is explicitly revealed.

Light, Color, and Materials (Humanizing a Building) Abundant natural light, red-carpeted galleries, and white floor pavers in concentric patterns are representative methods for achieving this design concern.

Nature and Water Pots of flowers, balcony planters, a lighted fountain, and birds in cages contribute to the visual and acoustical effects.

People Watching People Places to sit and watch the changing scene are provided.

Shared Space One can occupy two spaces simultaneously; for example, a gallery in the atrium, or the cocktail lounge suspended in the atrium.*

John Portman & Associates

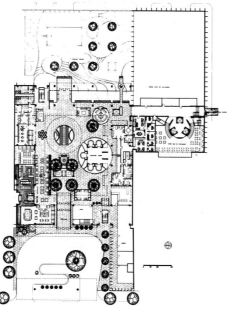

Street level floor plan.

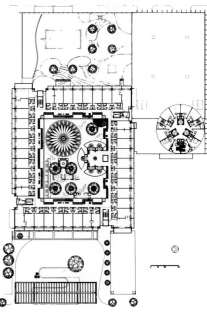
Typical guest room floor plan.

The Hyatt Regency Atlanta is a spatial event which must be experienced to be fully understood. No one can enter its atrium without being captivated by the grandeur of the space. Riding the capsule-like elevators is a kinetic experience not easily forgotten. Each gallery level provides a different vantage point, progressing from the familiarity of a residential balcony to the vertiginous thrill of the atrium summit. As a piazza, the atrium floor has many intimate settings for waiting, drinking, dining, and socializing. Everyone who occupies this space becomes simultaneously a spectator and an actor. It is an atrium building where spatial euphoria can be shared by all.

* J. Portman and J. Barnett, *The Architect as Developer*, McGraw-Hill, New York, 1976. These tenets are the chapter headings for Part II of Portman and Barnett's book.

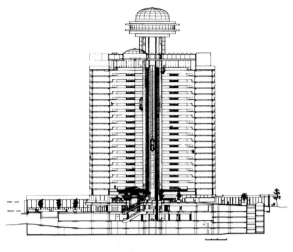

Longitudinal section.

HYATT REGENCY O'HARE
Rosemont, Illinois

ARCHITECT: *John Portman & Associates*
CONSTRUCTED: *1971*
ATRIUM: *153 feet by 155 feet by 115 feet high*

This hotel is conceptualized as a satellite to Chicago's O'Hare Airport, primarily serving business executives for meeting, lodging, and dining. As a satellite it is self-contained, being isolated from downtown Chicago and alienated from the surrounding airport traffic and noise. Thus, the scheme turns inward on itself, focusing on a large ten-story atrium. Here the symbolic role of the atrium as the haven, the protected place at the center, is complete. The space is given over to people and their needs, in contrast to the surrounding context which largely serves the machines of transportation. The building exterior is hard, of concrete and reflective bronze glass. The atrium has been softened by plants, trees, and sculpture, all bathed in sunlight. It is a place of rest and repose where guests become rejuvenated and gain sustenance.

This atrium design truly celebrates the processional movement of people, with a sense of constant animation. The guest enters at the ground-floor convention level and comes up to the atrium floor on an escalator set in a large well space. The elevator core is the focus of attention, being located in the center of the square atrium. The observation cars ride on the outside of the elevator shaft, giving the guest a dynamic view of the space. Bridges connect the elevator lobby to the surrounding galleries leading to the guest rooms. Guest rooms in the four round towers at each corner of the atrium are connected to it via pedestrian bridges. This entire processional sequence is self-evident, with continuous orientation to the atrium giving the guests a sense of security while simultaneously allowing them to experience the grand space. Thus everyone entering and using the hotel participates in this communal space, which lends a sense of social cohesion.

The design of this atrium achieves a considerable level of sophistication. The placement of the elevator core in the center with connecting bridges (changing direction on alternate floors) articulates the atrium into four square quadrants. The awesome scale is thus reduced, since one can relate to a single quadrant space. The spatial scale is further reduced by the placement of eight silk oak trees, each in a pool of light provided by a 1000-watt matalide fixture suspended from the skylight. Two of the quadrants are given special identities, one by a 53-foot hammered copper sculpture and the other by a banner composed of 700 Japanese silk kites arranged in a cylindrical form 16 feet in diameter and 90 feet high. (See Figure 5-37.) The galleries which surround the

John Portman & Associates

Alexandre Georges

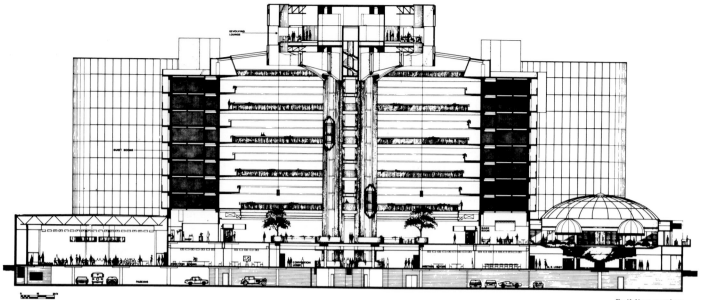

Building section.

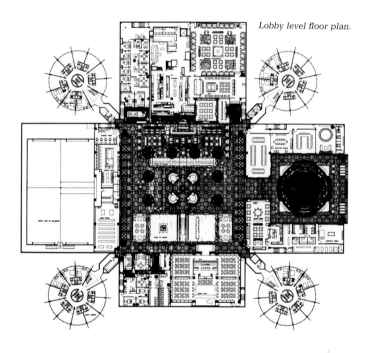

Lobby level floor plan.

atrium on all sides are stepped back in section, relieving the possible visual oppressiveness. They are of board-formed concrete with built-in planters filled with overhanging vines, which soften the effect of these hard surfaces. Suspended over the atrium is a circular revolving restaurant, which is supported by the elevator core and which defines the top of this space. Between the restaurant and roof edge is a continuous skylight supported by steel ribs.

The role of the atrium as social and circulation center is highly appropriate to the functioning of this hotel. It is a fun place to be, the center of action, a place to meet, wait, drink, eat, and relax. If there is a fault with this scheme, it is the large size of the well opening to the lower floor, which removes valuable floor area from the atrium itself.

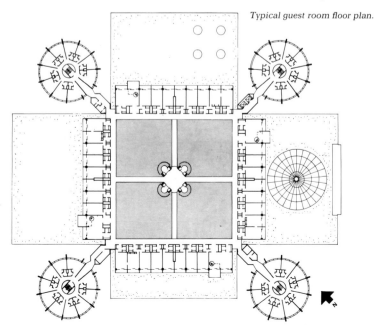

Typical guest room floor plan.

Design Study 29

THE ATRIUM ON THE BAYSHORE
Tampa, Florida

ARCHITECT: *Rowe Holmes Barnett Architects*
CONSTRUCTED: *1982*
ATRIUM: *T-shaped plan, 22 stories high*

This luxury condominium project offers an extra special amenity to its residents in the form of a twenty-two-story atrium. The processional sequence from building lobby, up the glazed-front elevators and around the open galleries to one's apartment entry, greatly heightens the joy of dwelling here. This sequence alternates between the east and west sides of the atrium on alternating floors, allowing the bedrooms and breakfast areas of some apartments to have private balconies overlooking the atrium. The guardrail design alternates between solid stucco and aluminum picket, with curved corners intended to ease the sense of movement. Planter boxes are hung from the picket rail to add ambience and combat the fear of heights.

The U-shaped building plan is symmetrical and stepped in order to give each apartment a corner balcony with views across and either up or down Tampa Bay. Six units per floor on twenty-two floors yields a total of 126 condominiums. The two units nearest the bay are the largest and most expensive, although they have no direct contact with the atrium. In addition, their entrances are along the corridor farthest from the elevators. The ground floor space around the atrium is given over to personal storage, mechanical rooms, and recreation rooms, which open onto the exterior gardens and recreation facilities. A six-story parking garage, with tennis courts on the roof, is directly connected via bridges to the elevator lobby. In 1982, the condominium prices ranged from $134,500 to $249,000 depending upon their floor area (1622 to 1913 square feet including balconies), location relative to the bay, and vertical location within the building.

The atrium has a very definite energy role since it is a naturally ventilated space. Sun coming through the clear Plexiglas, barrel-vaulted skylight heats the air at the top of the atrium creating strong vertical convection currents. (See Figure 4-14.) This hot air escapes through a series of continuous louvers around the base of the skylight, in turn inducing cross circulation through the apartments which face the atrium, since each of them has large windows. Five large (48-inch) direct-drive fans have been added on the roof to exhaust smoke from the atrium in case of fire. They are also used, when needed, to improve apartment ventilation by accelerating the stack effect. Additional grow lighting for plants has been added for use in the winter, when inadequate daylight reaches the bottom of this tall atrium. The architect reports that a tinted Plexiglas

Gordon H. Schenck, Jr.

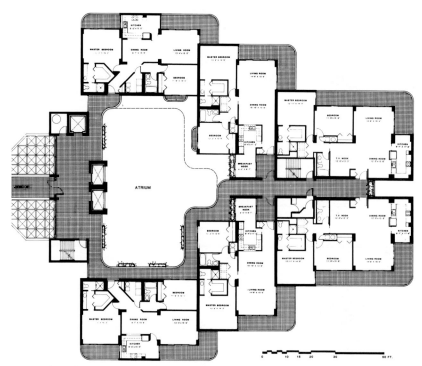

Second floor plan.

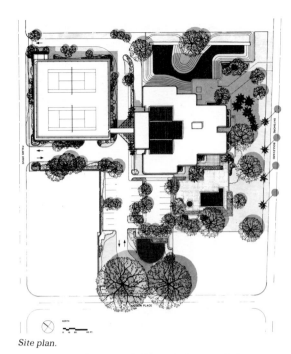

Site plan.

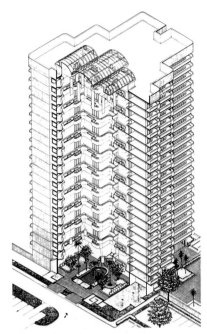

Isometric section.

skylight would have helped to reduce the overheating (now corrected by the fans) and high brightness at the top of the space.

This building demonstrates the design validity of a large-scale atrium in an apartment building. All residents share the indoor garden and its lush plantings and fountain, which harmonize with the bayside location and subtropical landscape. The strong sense of orientation, security, and joy of life in this scheme encourages the development of a sense of community.

Gordon H. Schenck, Jr.

Design Study 30

HYATT REGENCY WEST HOUSTON
Houston, Texas

ARCHITECT: *Lockwood, Andrews & Newnam*
CONSTRUCTED: *1983*
ATRIUM: *L-shaped, 134 feet by 172 feet by 62 feet high*

This is one of the new generation of atrium hotels by Hyatt in which the guest rooms no longer surround and so define the grand space. In this scheme, the 400 guest rooms are contained in six separate wings connected to the atrium and each other by bridges and galleries. Four of the wings are double-loaded for plan efficiency. These rooms offer long sweeping views facing exterior courtyards or overlooking the atrium itself. The latter is L-shaped, 16,000 square feet in area and five stories high, divided by a series of bridges leading to three observation elevators. The ground floor accommodates 20,000 square feet of meeting rooms, a 9800 square foot ballroom, two restaurants, two bars, and an entertainment lounge, in addition to the necessary administrative and hotel support functions.

The most outstanding feature of this design scheme is the 3-acre artificial lake which surrounds the front of the building and flows through the atrium. The entry drive crosses the lake, arriving at a space frame canopy. The lake itself contains 1½ million gallons of water with a maximum 12-foot depth, two cascading waterfalls, and a 30-foot fountain. Only the glass wall of the atrium interrupts the water surface. The atrium interior has lush plantings and trees around and within the water. Pedestrian walkways, seating areas, and restaurant tables are adjacent to the water and only slightly above it. There are few intervening guardrails, making the water a very tangible experience. (See Figure 5-39.)

The architectural treatment is in many ways a response to the hot, humid Houston climate. The building exterior is sheathed entirely in reflective glass, tempered for the spandrel bands, and float glass above. Where facade planes penetrate to the interior, the same fenestration is continued. Tinted float glass is used for atrium walls which separate exterior from interior with a minimum of mullions and steel trusses for bracing. The roof is a solid plane except for a somewhat random pattern of individual bubble skylights which bring in shafts of sunlight. The general strategy is to reduce solar heat gain by restricting overhead sun penetration and to create shaded spaces with views through tinted glass.

The overall impression of this atrium is of an elegant oasis. Interior architectural surfaces are white, including the ceiling and its space trusses, to serve as a neutral background for the subtly colored furnishings and to receive the reflected sunlight.

Lockwood Andrews & Newnam

Lockwood Andrews & Newnam

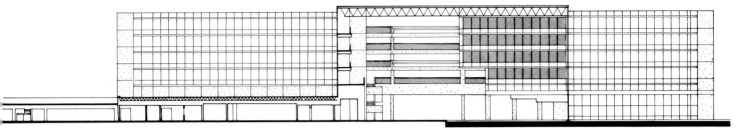

Building section.

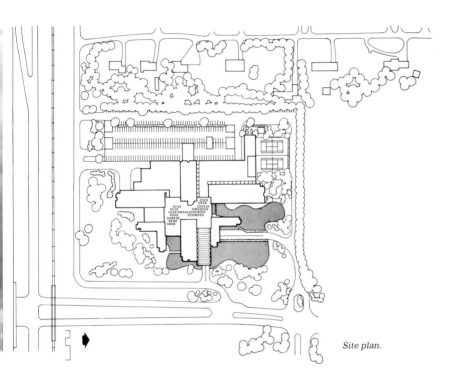

Site plan.

Guardrails are a combination of tempered glass with metal handrail, solid plastered plane with metal guardrail, or low plastered plane with a separate linear planter. The interior design firm Hirsch/Bender Associates selected upholstered seating of solid subdued colors, which enriches the spaces without being visually distracting. A light lavender plush carpet with a subtle geometric pattern is used on all floors for circulation areas and on the ground floor in seating and dining areas, providing needed visual continuity. Granite and paving stone are used for other ground-floor public areas. In this building, dappled sunlight, the sound of water, interesting reflections, distant views, and lush landscaping have been integrated into a cohesive atrium design. It is a place which projects the rest and refreshment which befit a luxury hotel.

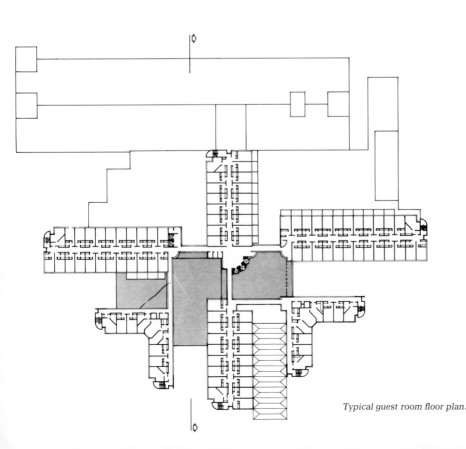

Typical guest room floor plan.

Design Study 31

HYATT REGENCY DALLAS
Dallas, Texas

ARCHITECT: *Welton Becket Associates*
CONSTRUCTED: *1978*
ATRIUM: *irregular plan, 16 stories high*

The Reunion area of Dallas is a redevelopment zone on the western edge of the downtown commercial district, between the Stemmons Freeway and the old railroad tracks. This 1000-room luxury convention hotel is the most prominent structure in the area, with its highly articulated massing rising to thirty stories, all surfaced in uniform reflective glass. To the east, the 1916 Union Station has been restored and connected to the hotel via a passage under the railroad tracks. South of the hotel is a new multipurpose arena seating 20,000 spectators. Between the two is a 10-acre development of parks and plazas containing the fifty-story Reunion Tower. This tower, supported on four slender concrete shafts, has become a Dallas landmark, with its geodesic sphere enclosing a revolving restaurant, cocktail lounge, and observation deck.

The plan form of the Hyatt Regency Dallas is basically an unsymmetrical, stepped U-shape, opening to the south and facing the Reunion Tower. The guest rooms are arranged around the atrium, which opens up to dramatic views, with a six-story wall of glass and a sloping skylight up to the sixteenth floor. This sloping skylight is interrupted by special suites with gallery access on the seventh, eighth, eleventh, and twelfth floors. At the northern end of the atrium, three observation elevators (and additional enclosed elevators) travel the thirty-story height — sixteen stories inside the atrium and fourteen stories along the building exterior. This could actually be termed a partial atrium since not all hotel rooms face the atrium. Some hotel rooms are in the tower above the atrium and others are in the double-loaded corridor wing north of the elevator bank.

In its sectional aspects the atrium is well defined as a space. The galleries, which step in plan along the sides, but not in section, contrast with the stepped section of the southern wall. The solid guardrails, with an occasional semicircular balcony, give coherence to the space. The galleries which encircle the atrium on four floors tend to contain the space on the southern side. Yet the space *seems* very open, as it widens toward the mostly glazed south facade. (See Figure 5-25.)

The ground floor of the atrium, however, is confused in its geometry and furnishings. Entry is from below via an escalator set at an angle, up to a circular plaza with a "crystal ball" at its center. The circular plan motif continues with various stepped areas for seating, drinking, and eating. A cascading fountain drops as a waterfall to the lower level. The planting and furniture

arrangements are "spotty" and uncoordinated with the architectural spaces. The entire effect is somewhat chaotic; only the continuity of the floor pavers holds it together.

The atrium as a space stands in stark contrast to the building exterior. It has a sense of human scale and activity, with

warmth of colors, trendy details, and enticing features (elevators, fountain, landscaping). The exterior is scaleless and forbidding, with no indication of habitation or purpose. The massing addresses the expressway in a provocative manner, with the element of interior surprise reserved for those who enter its confines.

Welton Becket Associates

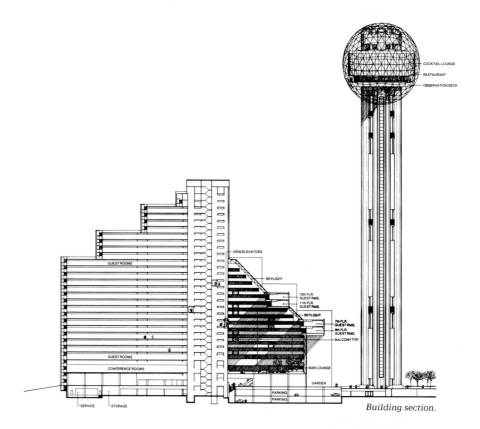

Building section.

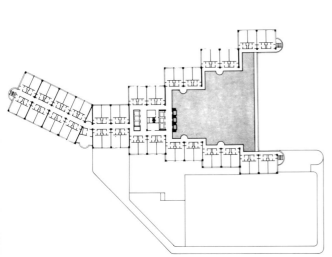

Typical guest room floor plan.

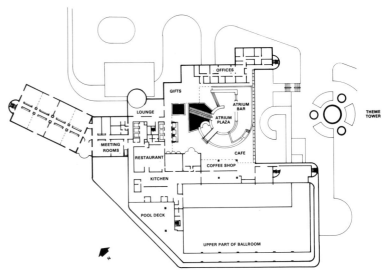

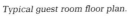

Second floor, atrium level plan.

Michael Bednar

Design Study 32

VISTA INTERNATIONAL HOTEL
Washington, D.C.

ARCHITECT: *Holle & Graff Architects (with Smith & Williams Group)*
CONSTRUCTED: *1982*
ATRIUM: *80 feet by 84 feet, 14 stories high*

The only way to accommodate this hotel program on this site was to create an inward-oriented atrium scheme. The mid-block site on M Street at Thomas Circle had buildings to the height limit on both sides and a narrow alley in the back. Since each hotel floor had to have a source of light and air, and there was only one street frontage, additional frontage was created around the atrium. This scheme is unlike those of most hotels with atria, since the single-loaded corridors are at the building periphery with the rooms facing the atrium — except along M Street, where the rooms face out.

This is a luxury hotel with 413 rooms, six suites, a health club, a ballroom, meeting rooms, two underground parking levels, and five bar-restaurants. These functions are zoned vertically with the ballroom and health club below grade, meeting rooms and restaurants on the first two levels, and hotel rooms above. A vehicular drop-off with parking garage entry occupies the entire M Street frontage, causing conflicts with the axial pedestrian entrance.

This is the only known atrium building in which the spaces surrounding the atrium have no exterior source of daylight and ventilation; that is, they rely exclusively upon the atrium. Special exemptions to the building code were sought and obtained. Natural ventilation in greater quantity than required if used only as make-up air is provided through the ductwork. Increased window sizes facing the atrium were necessary to compensate for daylight losses through the skylight. These windows were sized based upon the worst condition at the bottom of the atrium, with the tinted-glass windows being even greater in size.

The atrium is conceived as an enclosed urban square formed by three interior facades. The fourth side is a fourteen-story, north-facing, glass wall which visually links the grand space to the street. Hotel rooms either have bay windows with clear glass or sliding doors with tinted glass opening onto balconies. Brick paving, potted trees, street lamps, and a sculptural clock tower complete the urban appointments. Abundant daylight floods the space from the square-domed skylight covering the entire atrium. The Victorian richness and variety of materials, colors, and textures lends an atmosphere of tasteful lavishness to the space. The octagonal residential seating arrangement with carpeted floors seems out of place in this urbane setting. Otherwise, the splayed geometries, projecting balconies, bridges,

Bob Bennett

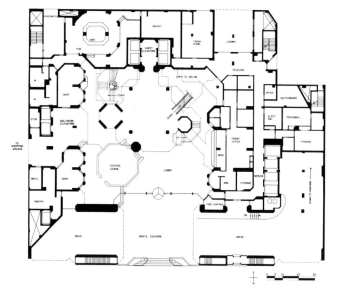

Lobby level plan.

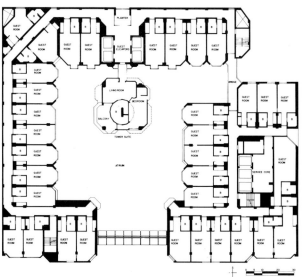

Typical guest room level plan.

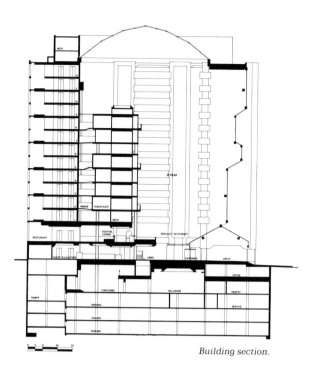

Building section.

and stairs create visual variety and intimate scale.

The crowning feature is the Givenchy tower, an eight-story freestanding sculptural tower within the atrium. Each floor has an executive suite with black reflective-glass facades and landscaped balconies, all designed by French couturier Hubert de Givenchy. The tower is open for circulation at the atrium floor, with a lounge on the second level. This tower within a tower serves as a focal point for the atrium while functioning as a working part of the hotel. It engages the space of the atrium through its balconies while shaping the space around it by its figural nature. The Givenchy tower adds a further touch of elegance and excitement to an already intriguing place.

Design Study 33

HYATT REGENCY CAMBRIDGE
Cambridge, Massachusetts

ARCHITECT: *Graham Gund Associates*
CONSTRUCTED: *1977*
ATRIUM: *5-sided plan, 15 stories high*

In this Hyatt hotel, the atrium has been designed not so much as a space to surprise and awe, but as a space to invite and welcome. Graham Gund has designed a large atrium which establishes orientation; within it, he created many spaces of smaller scale to address the need for intimacy. Primary access is from the back, through a series of restricted spaces and an allée of trees to the registration desk. Restaurants on the next two levels project into the atrium, with a second-level terrace overlooking the Charles River. One does not become fully aware of the vertically expansive atrium until ascending in the four elevator observation cars. Projecting balconies and a special cantilevered overlook at the third level aid in reducing the scale and sustaining visual interest.

The site affords spectacular views across the Charles and downriver to Boston. To arrive at the building form, architects sheared the linear plan, offset the two wings, and inserted an atrium at the center, with its 100-foot-high great window canted toward downtown Boston. The ends of the hotel have been stepped to form seventy rooftop terraces with long views up and down the river. The parking garage and vehicular drop-off are at the rear of the site, leaving the front of the hotel uncluttered and allowing it to be situated close to the river's edge.

The hotel design concept of collective residency establishes a strong design direction for detailing and furnishing. Gallery guardrails change frequently from brick to concrete to iron railings, with groups of planters containing grape ivy interspersed to soften, visually, their hard edges. A sand-molded, soft rose-colored brick was chosen for selected interior surfaces and also was used for exterior facades. Other touches which bring warmth are light oak wood trim, bronze hardware, incandescent lights, and beige colors. Furnishings are residential in scale and character, favoring comfort over appearance. The pool at the base of the elevators adds a refreshing sparkle. The most intriguing feature is the trompe l'oeil painting by Richard Haas which is high on a wall adjoining the great window. The four-story painting of a Venetian pallazzo facade reinforces the implied association between this place and a lavish residence.

The design scheme for this 500-room hotel is a remarkable achievement, for it takes the usual elements of a large hotel and composes them in a way which is at once comprehensible and comfortable. In design expression, it exhibits an attitude sympathetic to the building's users. It is no wonder that this hotel has become one of Hyatt's most successful.

View from Charles River.

Steve Rosenthal

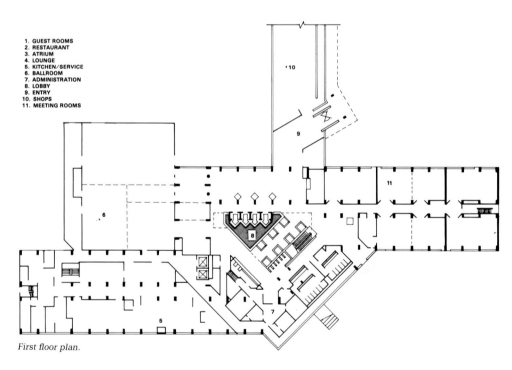

1. GUEST ROOMS
2. RESTAURANT
3. ATRIUM
4. LOUNGE
5. KITCHEN/SERVICE
6. BALLROOM
7. ADMINISTRATION
8. LOBBY
9. ENTRY
10. SHOPS
11. MEETING ROOMS

First floor plan.

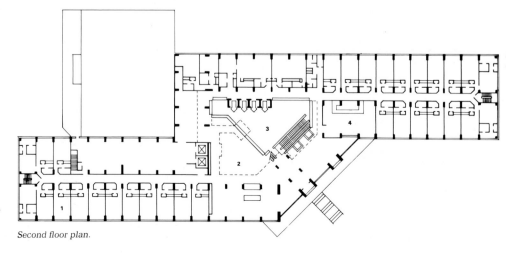

Second floor plan.

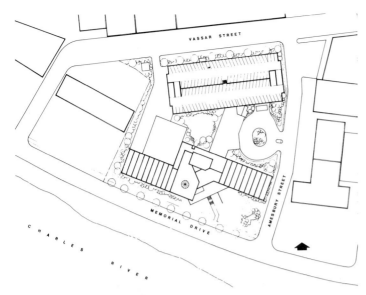

Site plan.

Steve Rosenthal

205

HYATT REGENCY SAN ANTONIO
San Antonio, Texas

ARCHITECT: *Thompson, Ventulett, Stainback & Associates with Ford Powell & Carson*
CONSTRUCTED: *1981*
ATRIUM: *irregular plan, 14 stories high*

The Paseo del Rio (river walk) in San Antonio, Texas, is a pedestrian walkway alongside a loop in the San Antonio River, which winds through the commercial district one level below street grade. At the eastern end of this loop a piece of the river walk has been extended to the city's primary historic attraction, the Alamo. San Antonio's new 640-room luxury Hyatt hotel sits astride this extension, with the water flowing through the building one level below the street-level lobby entrance. This new water feature begins across the street from the Alamo and through a series of cascades, pools, falls, and rapids reaches its natural counterpart. The pedestrian ways along its sides pass by retail areas in the hotel. (See Figure 2-3.) The hotel functions begin at street level, with a one-story public elevator providing access to the Paseo. Thus, in a brilliant piece of urban design, this building enriches the existing pedestrian system. (See Figure 5-38.)

The form of the building also springs from this urban design strategy with the fourteen-story atrium positioned over the river walk. The U-shaped building plan's two primary blocks of guest rooms are along double-loaded corridors, with the northern block having its own garden terrace. The five observation cars of the elevators are positioned next to the river walk. The public functions on the first three hotel levels are treated as terraces which project into the atrium and overhang the pedestrian way.

The all-glass western facade of the atrium serves to establish a visual connection between the hotel and the city. Guest rooms and public spaces have spectacular views of the city; the river walk offers similarly interesting views into the hotel. Since this is a western facade in a very hot climate, deep translucent sunshades have been fixed to the outside of this glass wall above the first two levels. Although necessary, they do fragment the views. This facade is also the primary source of natural light. The roof of the atrium is opaque, but raised, to provide clerestories all around, giving balance to the daylighting.

The design execution enhances the atrium space, which is still this building's main feature. The consistent expression of an exposed concrete frame visually articulates the space. Yet there is enough geometric variation at the public levels to create special places and programmatic events. Low planting has been consistently used at balcony edges and higher planting

R. Greg Hursley

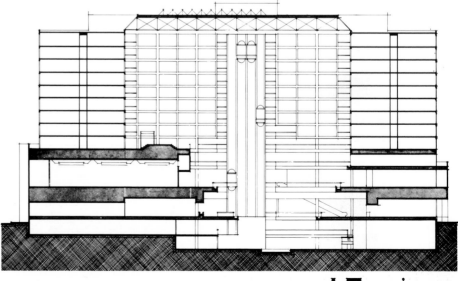

Building section looking west.

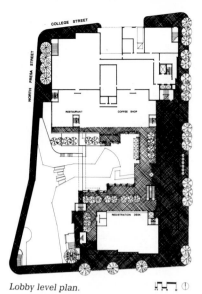

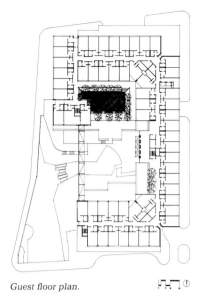

Lobby level plan.

Guest floor plan.

R. Greg Hursley

has been used at the river walk and terrace spaces. Colors, furnishings, and details are all well coordinated and subdued so as to establish presence without distraction.

This atrium is very successful because it functions at many spatial levels simultaneously. It is first and foremost an urban event to be experienced by all. As a public space it serves as a node along the river walk. The northern garden terrace is a place of repose surrounded by guest rooms. The various terraces on the public levels of the hotel are special spaces oriented to the larger atrium. The balconies at the elevator lobby on each floor and the elevator cars continue this design strategy of articulation and orientation at the smallest scale. Thus it is a scheme of many spaces, all related to the atrium, which in turn is related to the city. The skill with which these spatial relationships have been established is a joy to behold.

MERCANTILE WHARF BUILDING
Boston, Massachusetts

ARCHITECT: *John Sharratt Associates*
CONSTRUCTED: *1976*
ATRIUM: *36 feet wide by 225 feet long by 84 feet high*

This is an excellent example of the role an atrium can play in the adaptive reuse of a handsome old building. This six-story granite and brick warehouse, orginally designed by Gridley James Fox in 1856, had a 100-foot depth, with thick masonry cross walls 25 feet apart. Its only realistic reuse was for housing, but the building depth was excessive. The winning design competition solution proposed carving out the unneeded space in the center to form a 25-foot-wide atrium (36 feet wide including the galleries) which would provide well-organized circulation and a ground-floor user amenity.

The redesigned building contains shops on the ground floor and 121 apartments on five upper floors. Since the masonry cross walls were a structural limitation, apartments larger than one bedroom were organized vertically with their own staircases. The most spatially interesting units—which have skylights and loft spaces—are located at the top of the building under the sloping roof. These upper units also feature portions of exposed wood roof trusses and granite exterior walls. Not only is there architectural variety but also social variety, since forty-two units are moderate in price, forty-three units are low in price, and thirty-six units are for the open rental market. Apartments are reached via the residents' lobby off of Atlantic Avenue, which leads to two elevators positioned in the center of the atrium, and thus to galleries which surround the space. Resident lounges are located on each floor at both atrium ends.

The ground floor has a public character which is somewhat unusual for an apartment building. The periphery is lined with shops which have recessed entrances facing the surrounding streets and secondary entrances facing the atrium. Additional entries are located at the building ends. The original building was much longer, but expressway construction removed its southern end. A relationship between the atrium floor level and the large adjacent park is established through the use of landscaping in raised brick planters and dark red quarry tiles. Thus this space becomes a meeting ground and amenity for residents and the community alike.

Steve Rosenthal

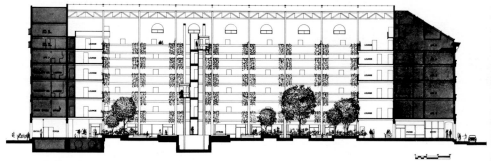

Longitudinal section.

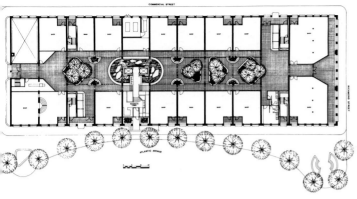

Ground floor plan.

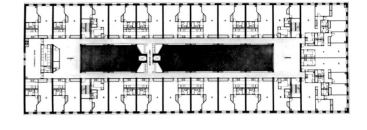

Typical floor plan.

Site plan.

N

Architecturally, the atrium is given an unadorned character in keeping with the original warehouse structure. The original brick cross walls are exposed as the dominant vertical element. Gallery guardrails and atrium walls are white plaster with wood trim. The latter have built-in overhead lights and planters. The new skylight is of clear insulated plastic, almost flat in configuration, with a steel structure. Two hydraulic elevators are freestanding, with glazed observation cars which seemingly descend into pools of water. Being yellow and blue-green, they are perhaps the only incongruous element in an otherwise beautifully executed project.

CONSTITUTION QUARTERS
Charlestown, Massachusetts

ARCHITECT: *Anderson Notter Finegold*
CONSTRUCTED: *1981*
ATRIA: *Two linear atria 230 feet long, one linear atrium 475 feet long; all 30 feet wide and 60 feet to 75 feet high.*

Steve Rosenthal

When the Charlestown Navy Yard was phased out, many substantial buildings in an interesting waterfront location were left behind. This particular group of five buildings (listed in the National Register of Historic Places) has been rehabilitated into a rental apartment complex fronting on a marina and adjacent to a new city park. Spanning nearly a century, from the 1850s to the 1940s, the buildings range from handsome neo-Georgian to stripped-down modern industrial. Their orthogonal relationships coherently define the landscaped exterior spaces, which open onto the water. One of the buildings has been converted to a parking structure; another has been stripped to its steel skeleton as a reminder of the industrial past.

Three of these structures were three-story linear-atrium industrial buildings and have been converted to six-story, linear-atrium apartment buildings by inserting new floors. Open galleries for apartment access line both sides of the atria with the ground floor being treated as an interior residential street, complete with entry stoops, landscaping, and quarry tile paving. The very long atria (one pair being 705 feet) were divided into bays with elevators and foot bridges to achieve a residential scale. Entrances are at the ends, except for a major side entrance opposite the park. The total of 367 apartments includes one-, two-, and three-floor types with slight variations due to existing building circumstances. Units at the top enjoy high sloped ceilings with skylights.

Atrium interiors are treated with a directness befitting their industrial heritage. Steel roof trusses are exposed and painted orange. Additional strips of skylight were added to the roof of the neo-Georgian building, which had an existing clerestory monitor. The other old building had been previously modified with north-facing, saw-toothed monitors. All of these were saved, along with the same north-facing, saw-toothed monitors on the newer building. The interiors have all been done in planes of white-painted drywall, including atrium walls, guard-rails, monitor ceilings, and gallery ceilings. Although this treatment is useful for distributing daylight, articulating the overwhelming linearity would have improved the scale and sense of interior facade. Interesting sculptures and murals,

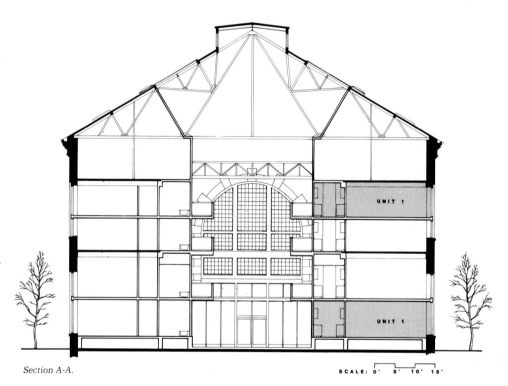

Section A-A.

SCALE: 0' 5' 10' 15'

including an intriguing spatial banner of many elements by Mario Kon, add visual enrichment. All in all, this is an excellent example of rehabilitation which respects the integrity of the historic structures while converting them to a new use.

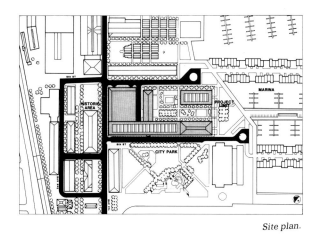

Site plan.

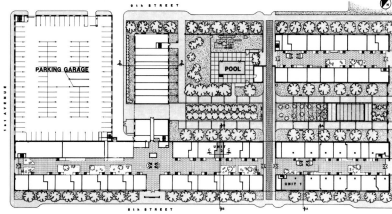

Ground level plan.

Steve Rosenthal

Design Study 37

LOEWS ANATOLE DALLAS HOTEL
Dallas, Texas

ARCHITECT: *Beran & Shelmire Architects*
CONSTRUCTED: *1979*
ATRIA: *Atrium I 130 feet by 130 feet by 177 feet
high; Atrium II 240 feet by 130 feet by 140 feet high*

This is real estate entrepreneur Trammell
Crow's ultimate development of the
atrium hotel. It was Trammell Crow, as
codeveloper of the Hyatt Regency Atlanta,
who first supported the atrium hotel
concept. He introduced the atrium into his
Dallas Trade Mart and World Trade Center
across the Stemmons Freeway from this
hotel. (See page 219.) His intention has
always been to humanize large buildings
by giving them spirit and scale. The
atrium accomplishes this by providing
large public spaces which support the dy-
namics of living.

The Loews Anatole Dallas is a 900-room
luxury convention hotel completely based
upon the atrium concept. The initial
scheme, with all of the guest rooms surrounding one giant atrium, was discarded
in favor of the twin atria. They are positioned at 90 degree angles to each other
with a grand lobby in between. The
elevator core joins the two atrium corners,
thus serving both spaces with four conventional and four observation cars, the latter
facing Atrium I. Galleries lined with grape
ivy provide access to all guest rooms.
Atrium I is square in plan and thirteen
stories high, providing direct access to a
1000-seat auditorium, the swimming pool,
an elegant restaurant, and a coffee shop.
Atrium II is rectangular in plan and ten
stories high, providing direct access to the
ballrooms, a discotheque, a Chinese
restaurant, a Mexican restaurant, and
several retail shops. Meeting rooms are on
the mezzanine level.

The twin atria have been designed as
gracious public rooms rather than as
interior parks or plazas. Plantings and
trees have been used judiciously to define
spaces for eating and drinking. The floor is
paved in light-colored marble with an
inlaid brick geometric pattern. Atrium I
features a sunken octagonal lounge with a
lucite sculpture rising from the centrally
located fountain. Atrium II features a
piano bar under modular canvas canopies,
a snack shop topped by a curious 66-foot-
high aluminum sculpture, and a triangular
brick clock tower with a fire stair inside.
Hanging from the ceiling are five enormous batik banners from Ceylon, ranging
in length from 88 to 136 feet. These
artifacts, along with numerous other valuable art objects (some from Trammell
Crow's personal collection), create a
sophisticated eclectic atmosphere, one
which should make people feel comfortable and at home.

The soaring, truncated pyramidal
skylights are the dominating architectural
feature of both atria. The one over Atrium

Atrium I view.

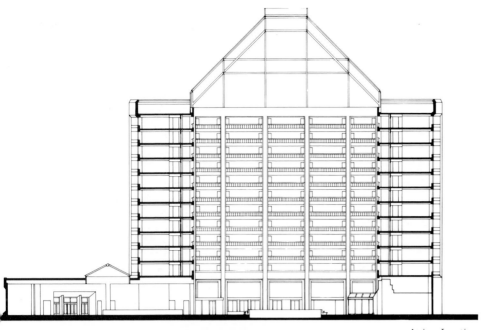

Atrium I section.

II is actually a double pyramid with an opaque saddle element in the center. (See Figure 5-16.) These skylights are supported by black-painted steel trusses and purlins, forming an interesting tracery against the sky. Reflecting glass reduces some of the heat gain, but the atria are flooded with abundant daylight. Since the skylights soar six stories above the roof line, they give this building its unique exterior profile.

This atrium hotel is certainly awe-inspiring in scale, which befits its Texas location. The eclectic assemblage of artifacts and furnishings becomes absorbed by this scale, except for the batik banners, which are visually obtrusive because of their size and placement. However, the proposition that these are gracious public rooms rather than interior parks or plazas is uncertain. The large-scale pyramidal skylights which depict the skydome, and features such as street lamps and the clock tower, make these atria seem like outdoor spaces. At best, the balance between outdoor and indoor has been evenly construed, resulting in two provocative atrium spaces.

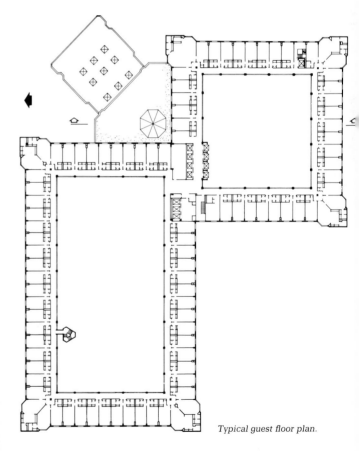

Typical guest floor plan.

Atrium II view.

Design Study 38

ANTOINE GRAVES HOMES
Atlanta, Georgia

ARCHITECT: *Edwards & Portman (with Henry Norris)*
CONSTRUCTED: *1965*
ATRIA: *twin atria, one 72 feet by 90 feet by 7 stories, the other 72 feet by 90 feet by 8 stories*

Alexandre Georges

It is indeed auspicious that John Portman's first atrium building would be this public housing project in which he used the atrium concept to solve a difficult design problem. The site was too restrictive for the usual walk-up apartment buildings. Moreover, Portman wanted a socially cohesive scheme for the elderly residents. Finally, it had to satisfy the restrictive public housing budget.

Portman's solution was to arrange the 210 small apartments to form a courtyard. By placing the service core in the center, he subdivided the courtyard while equalizing travel distances to each unit with direct gallery access. He then covered the twin courts with a rain roof to create communal social spaces. The entry sequence to each unit thus offers a communal experience as well as shelter from the climate, lending orientation and security to the elderly residents. The identical efficiency apartments are not unlike large hotel rooms, with windows on the gallery and a private covered balcony facing the exterior.

The fire code required that, as covered exterior courts, the atria be left open to natural ventilation. This was achieved by leaving the ends of the skylights unglazed and providing an open screen at the entrance. No sprinklers were required and the open galleries could be used as exit ways to the centrally located fire stairs, which exit across the atrium floor.

The architectural execution of this building is also quite interesting. Prestressed concrete Y beams span the atria and support linear plastic skylights. Panels used for gallery guardrails are a different color on each floor. Apartments have sliding windows facing the atria to allow cross ventilation in each unit. Since the site is sloped, one atrium floor is 15 feet lower than the other. The main entrance is at this lower level, which includes community rooms, support spaces, and administrative offices. Two terraces project over this lower atrium floor at the level of the second, more private, atrium.

Thus this building serves as a precursor for the atrium hotels which were soon to follow. It was born of a social motivation to create a sense of community. It also stands as an ideal design example of public housing for the elderly.

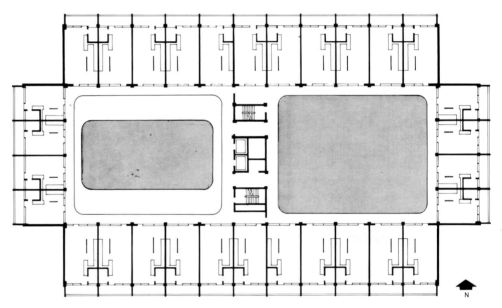

Typical floor plan.

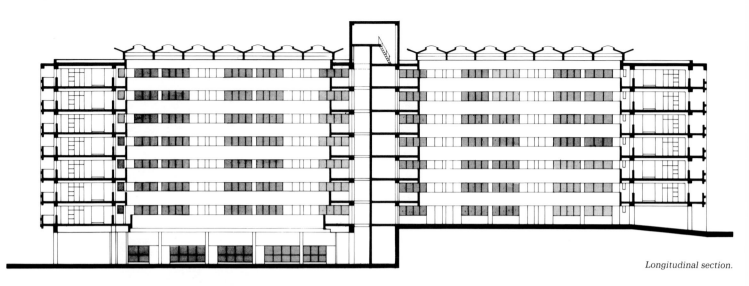

Longitudinal section.

Bill Barnes

Michael Bednar

OLD POST OFFICE BUILDING
Washington, D.C.

ARCHITECT: *Arthur Cotton Moore/Associates;*
McGaughy, Marshall & McMillan; Associated Space
Design; Stewart Daniel Hoban
CONSTRUCTED: *1983*
ATRIUM: *96 feet by 180 feet by 164 feet high*

This classical atrium building was designed for the Post Office in 1899 by U. S. Treasury Department Supervising Architect W. J. Edbrooke. Its nine-story cortile was enclosed at the first floor with a steel and glass structure for use as a mail sorting room. In 1929, the architects of the Federal Triangle recommended its demolition since its Romanesque exterior was not compatible with their classical revival design. The depression stayed its destruction until the 1960s, when planners again recommended its removal. Preservation groups and spirited individuals saved the day, leading to the building's adaptive reuse.

This is the first building to be completed under the Public Building's Cooperative Use Act of 1976 allowing private enterprise ventures in public buildings. The fifty small shops and restaurants on the lower floors — named The Pavilion — represent a $10 million investment by developer Charles Evans, who also pays a small rental fee to the General Services Administration. The upper eight floors accommodate the National Endowment for the Arts, the National Endowment for the Humanities, and the Institute of Museum Services.

This renovation has been accomplished with only a few minor alterations. The old skylight was removed, leaving the steel frame, and a new steel truss and purlin structure was built at the top of the cortile. The main floor has been cut away, opening up the basement level, which is accessed by sweeping axial stairs. A small mezzanine has been installed to create a third retail level. In the northwest corner of the atrium, a new elevator takes visitors to the observation deck of the clock tower, the second highest point in Washington.

The design execution is somewhat dichotomous since there were two architects, two clients, and two vastly different functions. Arthur Cotton Moore's restoration of the building and preparation of the retail space has been handled with considerable sensitivity to the existing fabric, revealing the beauty of the atrium and its highly articulated galleried facades. The main entry from Pennsylvania Avenue lacks orientation to the atrium, but the side entries work well. Benjamin Thompson's designs for the storefronts and interiors tend to be busy and cluttered, detracting from the space itself and competing with the varied activities. The black-and-white checkerboard floor is visually obtrusive and the plantings are too dispersed.

The premises underlying this project are so sensible they defy any alternatives. An

Michael Bednar

Maxwell MacKenzie

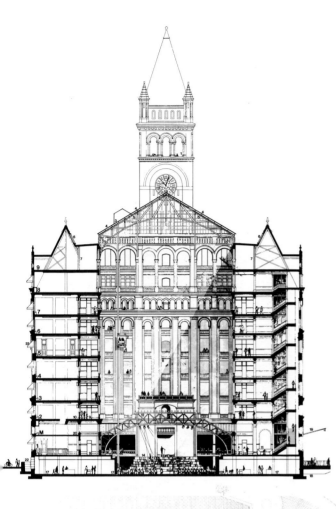

KEY:
1 Observation Deck
2 Observation Elevator
3 Roof-Top Elevator Transfer
4 Glass Roof
5 Thermal Louvers
6 Clerestory Windows
7 Studio Office Space
8 Cortile
9 Circulation Corridor
10 Office Space
11 Elevator Lobby Control Station
12 Old Mailing Room Trusses with Glass Roof Removed
13 Relocated Ornamental Iron-Work Balustrade
14 Stepped Tower Foundation
15 Stage
16 Public Shopping Arcade
17 Commercial Space
18 11th St. Ground Level Entrance
19 Glass Canopy
20 Mezzanine Level Office Space
21 Original Elevator Cages
22 Light Wells
23 Awnings

architecturally distinguished building has been saved and put to good use. A place has been created that has the potential to bring together in a congenial atmosphere 115,000 office workers, 11 million tourists, and numerous local residents. Prior to this time, there were virtually no shops or restaurants along this stretch of Pennsylvania Avenue; and there were none along the Mall, one-half block away. This grand democratic room is appropriate to the public spirit of this part of Washington. Being able to stroll here, have lunch, buy a drink, and listen to the live entertainment makes one thankful for the effort which brought this project to fruition.

Transverse section.

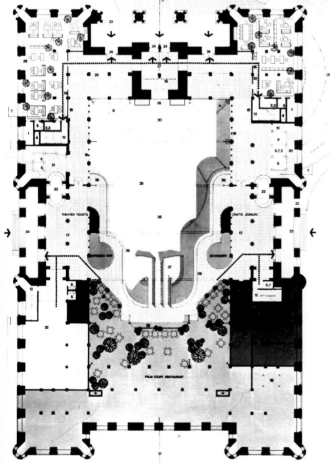

KEY:

SPACE USES
Federal Use
Out-lease Space
Circulation Space
Emergency Egress
Cortile Circulation

UTILITY AND EQUIPMENT SPACES
1 Mechanical Equipment
2 Electrical Equipment
3 Telephone Equipment
4 Duct Shafts
5 Toilet Facilities
6 Passenger Elevator
7 Service Elevator
8 Express Elevator to Tower
9 Elevator Equipment Room
10 Janitor's Closet
11 Women's Retiring Rooms

FIRE-SAFETY IMPROVEMENTS
12 Smokeproof Stair Tower with 2 hr Rated Enclosure
13 Smoke Partition
14 Emergency Elevator
15 Wall-Mounted Sprinkler
16 Ceiling Mounted Sprinkler

SPECIAL FEATURES
17 Marble Floors
18 Marble Wainscot
19 Wood Screens
20 Existing Open Stairs
21 Existing Elevator Enclosure
22 Security Guard Station
23 Ramped Entrance for Handicapped
24 Restored Wood Entrance Doors
25 Mail Room Trusses
26 Wood Flooring
27 Pennsylvania Avenue Entrance Lobby
28 Stepped Tower Foundation
29 Line of Mezzanine Floor Above
30 Stage Below
31 Glass Canopy
32 NCPC Public Hearing Room
33 11th Street Entrance Lobby
34 12th Street Entrance Lobby
35 Cortile Open to Below
36 Box Balcony
37 Escalator and Main Public Stairs
38 Relocated Ornamental Iron-Work Balustrade
39 Decorative Lighting
40 Brick Paving

First floor plan.

Design Study 40

WORLD TRADE CENTER
Dallas, Texas

ARCHITECT: *Beran & Shelmire Architects*
CONSTRUCTED: *1979*
ATRIUM: *175 feet by 140 feet by 208 feet high*

Jess Alford

This building is the international trade component of developer Trammell Crow's atrium-oriented wholesale merchandising mart, which also includes the Dallas Trade Mart, the Home Furnishings Mart, the Market Hall, and the Apparel Mart. Info Mart, the sixth component, is now being built along Stemmons Freeway near the Home Furnishings Mart. This 1.4 million square foot building contains over 600 showrooms for jewelry, gifts, floor coverings, furniture, leisure goods, and gourmet foods. Only the ground floor is open to the public; it includes trade offices, consulates, travel agencies, eateries, and money exchanges.

The design concept for the Dallas World Trade Center was to create an inward-looking building that focused on a community plaza called The Hall of Nations. The fifteen-story atrium is surrounded by galleries, which offer the glazed-front showrooms contact with daylight and view, since the building exterior is without fenestration. Four observation cars ride the freestanding elevator tower, which is on axis with the entry and porte cochere. A pair of escalators on the same axis provide easy interfloor transportation. The whole circulation scheme is designed to maximize access and marketing exposure for all tenants.

The atrium plan is a four-by-five-bay square grid (35 feet by 35 feet), which is expressed in the beam structure supporting the pyramidal skylights. (See Figure 5-15.) On the ground floor, trees are located at each grid point. A colonnade surrounds the space on three sides, with a sidewalk cafe along the fourth side. A circular reflecting pool in the center captures the overhead visual activity. Brick gallery guardrails are interrupted at the corners by planters with an iron balustrade. Two vertical cylindrical banners, composed of hundreds of national flags, are suspended from the skylight and provide additional spots of color. On the whole, the architectural treatment is subdued in order to feature the vitality of the showrooms and buyers. This grand vertical space does indeed capture the spirit of an international marketplace.

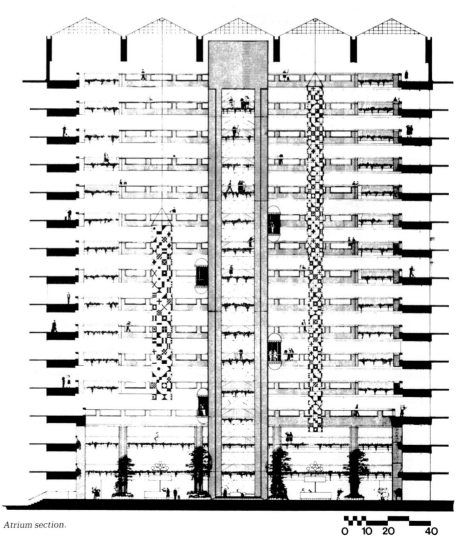

Atrium section.

0 10 20   40

218

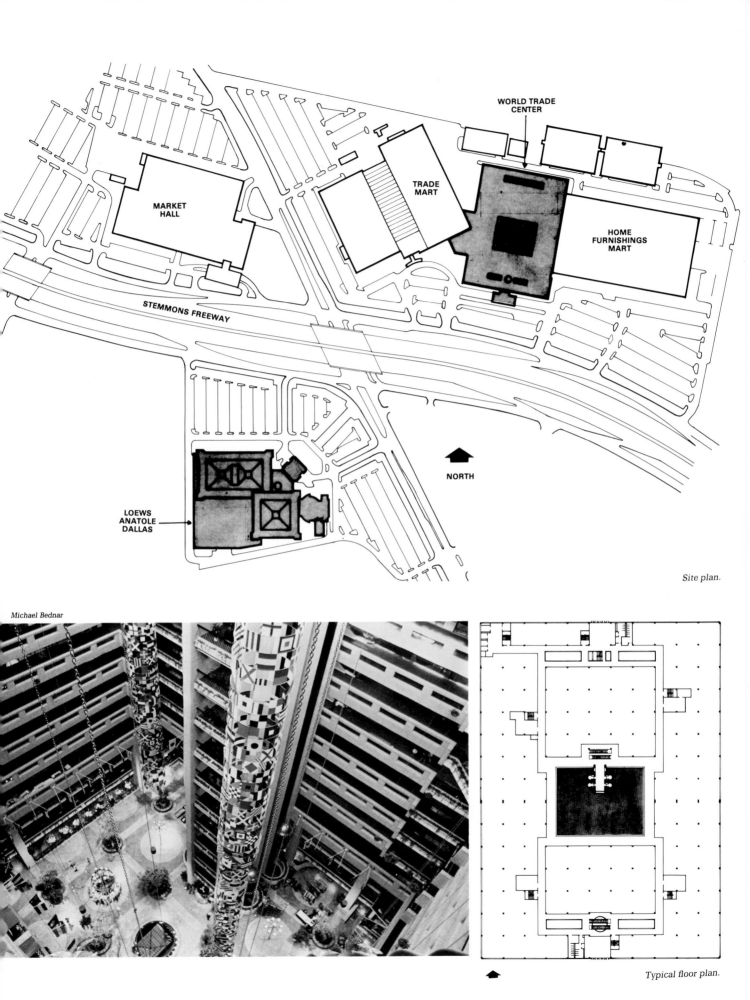

WORLD TRADE CENTER

TRADE MART

MARKET HALL

HOME FURNISHINGS MART

STEMMONS FREEWAY

LOEWS ANATOLE DALLAS

NORTH

Site plan.

Michael Bednar

Typical floor plan.

Design Study 41

ATLANTA APPAREL MART
Atlanta, Georgia

ARCHITECT: *John Portman & Associates*
CONSTRUCTED: *1979*
ATRIUM: *semicircular, 90 degree quadrant with 6-story stepped section*

This unusual and interesting building lends further support to the proposition that the atrium design concept is both highly adaptable and completely viable. This central space serves the dual role of providing orientation within the mammoth 1.2 million square foot apparel mart and of accommodating a 2000-seat fashion theater. The tiered balconies which surround the atrium expand the viewing capacity to 5000 persons. The atrium has the curved form of an amphitheater, which focuses attention on the stage at the atrium floor. The fashion events lend an air of glamour and excitement to the merchandising activity.

This building is another element within John Portman's grand scheme for Peachtree Center, occupying an entire 400-foot by 400-foot block. A diagonal bridge connects the Atlanta Merchandise Mart with the Apparel Mart at a second-level entry and vertical circulation core which includes observation elevators, escalators, and open circular stairs. There is also a street-level vehicular drop-off and entry leading directly to the 120,000 square foot exhibition hall. Below are two levels of parking for 500 cars. Above are six floors of showrooms for 1000 tenants, with both internal corridors and galleries facing the atrium. Guardrails are generally solid planes of concrete, except those facing the stage, which are a low, wide concrete grid supporting planters.

A couple of unusual technical problems were encountered during planning and construction. In terms of the fire code this building is a mixed use of merchandising and assembly requiring a full sprinkler system and special smoke exhaust capabilities. Emergency egress is via circular stair towers at each building corner, which are open to the air and exit to the street. These also allow fire fighters direct access onto each floor. The atrium skylight is supported by radially placed, deep concrete beams which in turn support acrylic skylights arranged in strips of uniform width with slivers of opaque roof panels in between. The resulting low, flat profile was difficult to drain.

From the outside this building appears as a hermetically sealed structure with uniform concrete walls which are without fenestration except at the ground floor. Inside, it is full of daylight and life, with plants and crowds of people. The glazed showroom walls reveal their colorful contents. This atrium — surrounded by showrooms — and the fashion show as focal event suit each other admirably, coalescing space and time into place and occasion.

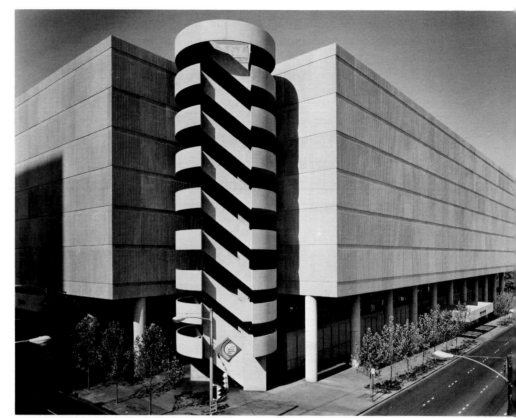

Paul G. Bestwick

John Portman & Associates

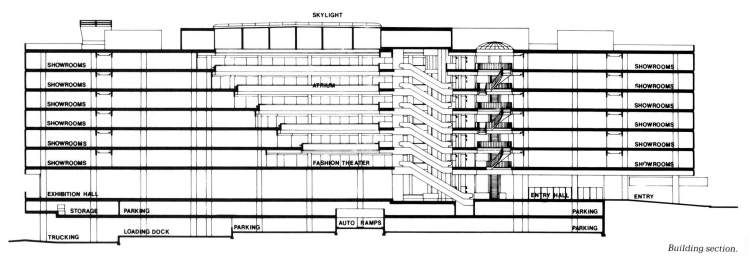

SKYLIGHT

SHOWROOMS | SHOWROOMS
SHOWROOMS | ATRIUM | SHOWROOMS
SHOWROOMS | SHOWROOMS
SHOWROOMS | SHOWROOMS
SHOWROOMS | SHOWROOMS
SHOWROOMS | FASHION THEATER | SHOWROOMS

EXHIBITION HALL | ENTRY HALL | ENTRY

STORAGE | PARKING | PARKING
TRUCKING | LOADING DOCK | PARKING | AUTO RAMPS | PARKING

Building section.

Michael Bednar

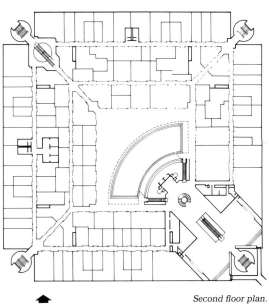

N

Second floor plan.

Design Study 42

THE PHILADELPHIA BOURSE
Philadelphia, Pennsylvania

ARCHITECT: *H2L2 Architects/Planners*
CONSTRUCTED: *1981*
ATRIUM: *40 feet and 60 feet wide by 240 feet long by 9 stories*

Michael Bednar

In 1895, the Philadelphia Bourse was constructed as designed by George Hewitt, a former partner of Frank Furness. It housed the stock exchange with its two-story trading floor covered by a sky-light. The upper six floors were offices facing a light court. It was one of the first steel-framed buildings in the city, a fact not evident from the heavy masonry exterior. The building's form had evolved from the site, with narrow frontages on 4th and 5th streets and narrow alleys on either side. Vertical masonry blocks faced the two principal streets, with central entrances leading to the linear skylit atrium which joined them. The Bourse functioned as a center of trade and commerce until the great depression, after which it became dormant for forty years.

In 1979 the transformation of the Bourse into a mixed-use retail and office building took place:

- An additional mezzanine was built around the trading floor to complement the existing one.

- Three wells were inserted into the main floor in order to develop the basement level as commercial space.

- Escalators were installed at the ends of the atrium to connect the four retail levels.

- The original skylight was removed and a new acrylic domed skylight was built at the roof level.

- The masonry wall surrounding the light court was removed and a new glass curtain wall installed.

While the transformation was taking place, complex structural and reconstruction problems were being resolved. The original steel frame had to be reinforced in various places where the new mezzanine was built; new floor openings had to be created and new stairs and escalators installed. The roof had to be reinforced to accept the new skylight load. The partially load-bearing masonry wall facing the light court had to be removed and the structure reinforced in gradual stages.

The retail section of this scheme has been executed with considerable finesse, creating an inviting and pleasurable place. Victorian details have been faithfully restored and new elements, such as etched-glass guardrails, have been designed to harmonize. Cast-iron fire stairs were relocated from the office blocks to serve as striking, freestanding elements. Theatrical incandescent lighting along the galleries and transverse beams lends the place an air of festivity. Colors and floor tile patterns are warm and mellow.

Signage and furnishings have been carefully controlled to enhance the ambience. This rich interior stands in high contrast to the subdued exterior which could not be altered due to the rehabilitation requirements of the 1976 Tax Reform Act.

The revitalized Bourse building has six floors of contemporary office space (190,000 square feet) above a four-level retail shopping mall (110,000 square feet), with both elements sharing a nine-story atrium. However, there is a dramatic difference between the lower retail section and the upper office section of the atrium. At the retail levels the atrium is approximately 60 feet wide (to the columns); it is surrounded by galleries; and it is richly ornate in Victorian details, colors, and materials. At the upper levels, the atrium is only 40 feet wide, with a flush aluminum and glass curtain wall on the long sides and flat-surfaced ends containing one six-story arched window. A series of glazed bridges cross the upper atrium at midpoint, dividing it into two sections. The heavy, ornate beams which supported the original skylight remain in place, further subdividing the atrium vertically. This contrast between the lower and upper sections of the atrium, although necessary in this two-part building, is too great, compromising the atrium's role as a unifying building space.

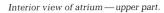
Interior view of atrium — upper part.

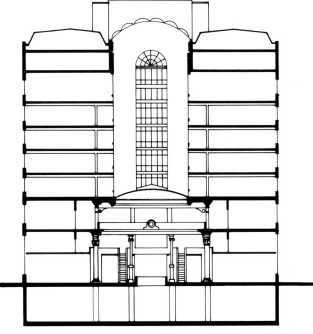

Transverse building section.

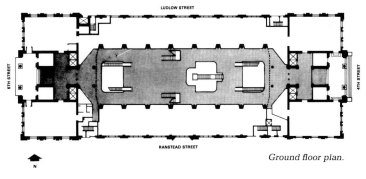

Ground floor plan.

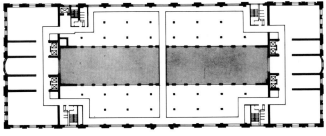

Typical floor plan.

Interior view of atrium — lower part.

Design Study 43

GALLERIA II
Houston, Texas

ARCHITECT: *Hellmuth, Obata & Kassabaum*
CONSTRUCTED: *1977*
ATRIUM: *340 feet by 100 feet by 12 stories*

Galleria II is the second phase of the well-known multiuse complex built in 1968 along the West Loop expressway in Houston. In form, Galleria I is essentially a linear, three-level shopping mall enclosed with a barrel-vaulted skylight. Galleria II is much more interesting as an atrium because it fosters a relationship between a major department store, a hotel, a shopping mall, twin office towers, and parking garages. Galleria II is located at the western end of Galleria I, with the axes of the two atria perpendicular to each other at the point where they join.

The spatial integration of the many functions at Galleria II is achieved through the sophisticated development of the building section. Two levels of parking are placed below grade with two levels of shops (330,000 square feet) at grade and above, followed by two additional parking decks on top of the shops. Two office towers, on opposite sides of the atrium, rest on top of this base building providing 227,000 square feet of office space on six levels. Two short, three-level shopping malls at either end of this central atrium join a major department store and a 500-room hotel to it. The elevator core is placed where the axes of Galleria I and Galleria II cross, with bridges to the opposite sides. Pedestrian stairs and escalators provide ready access between the parking and shopping levels. Circulation is well organized and comprehensible, a necessary feature of this complex design scheme.

The design treatment of the atrium is disciplined and controlled; the complexity of the space is given prominence over the elements which comprise it. All structural surfaces are treated as planes and painted a uniform off-white. All bridges, balconies, and stairs have guardrails made of thin steel elements which are visually unobtrusive. High-traffic floors are paved with square, cream-colored tiles. The braced-truss north and south walls are fully glazed with reflective glass. A strip of skylights along each atrium side provides overhead daylight. Furnishings are sparse; signage is controlled; and plantings are carefully placed. The half-round, cantilevered balconies along the office facades are the strongest visual feature, creating an interesting repetitive pattern. (See Figure 5-30.) This design integrity is a notable achievement; in many other mixed-use centers, ''design gymnastics'' tend to overpower the place. Here the movement of people and their activities are featured, along with the ever-changing patterns of daylight.

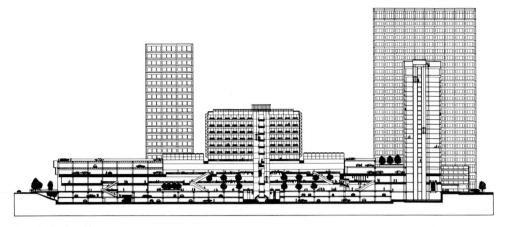

Longitudinal section.

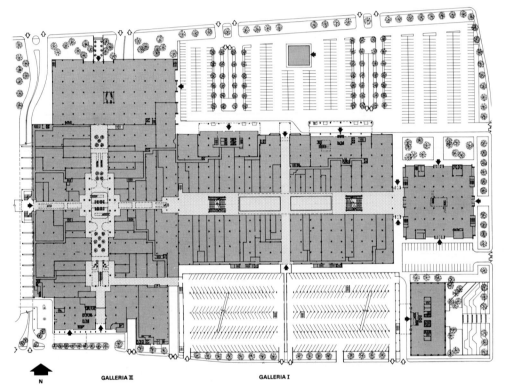

GALLERIA II   GALLERIA I

N

Level 1 plan, Galleria I and II.

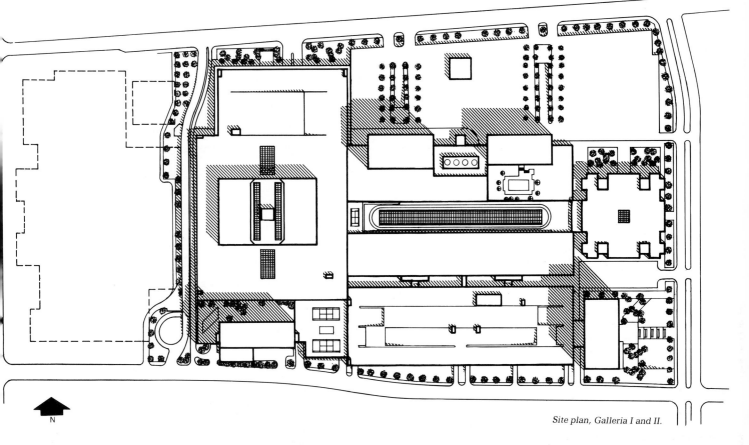

Site plan, Galleria I and II.

Atrium view looking north.

Atrium view looking south.

Design Study 44

THE PARK IN HOUSTON CENTER
Houston, Texas

ARCHITECT: *Morris/Aubry Architects*
CONSTRUCTED: *1983*
ATRIUM: *55 feet wide by 400 feet long by 65 feet high*

Phase I of the mammoth thirty-three block Houston Center Project consists of nine center city blocks with four office towers, a hotel, two parking garages and a retail mall called the Park. The latter is actually part of a two-block multiuse project which includes a three-level parking garage on one block, a twelve-story office slab bridging Caroline Street, and the 190,000 square foot shopping center which linearly unites the other elements. Four glazed bridges provide direct pedestrian connections to project components on four adjacent blocks.

This downtown retail mall primarily serves daytime office workers with its 100 restaurants and shops. The major entry sequence begins at the corner of McKinney Avenue and San Jacinto Street and continues through a street-level commercial passage to an observation elevator or escalators, which arrive at the second-level mall. The mall runs linearly on two levels the length of two blocks crossing Caroline Street. At the Austin Street end there are additional escalators and elevators to the parking garage below, but no street-level entrance. The glazed atrium extends vertically six stories, allowing four office floors to have windows onto this active space. Office floors above the atrium can view the mall through its skylight. The reflective-glass and brick curtain wall facade of the office slab extends unaltered into the atrium.

The main architectural feature of the shopping center is the curved skylight, which spans over 50 feet. It is supported by segmentally curved aluminum girders with secondary purlins and mullions. The glazing is LOF Varitran 708 heat-strengthened, laminated safety glass, 9/16-inch thick. This system survived the onslaught of Hurricane Alicia, which blew roof gravel throughout the area. Some of the outer glass panes were cracked, but water tightness was retained. There are two interior glass-washing rigs which run on rails the length of the skylight. One rig reaches the curved portion while the other is used for the flat upper portion.

Jud Haggard

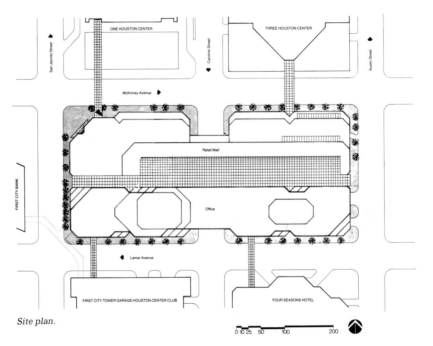

Site plan.

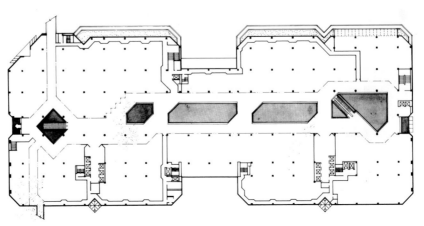

Level 4 plan.

226

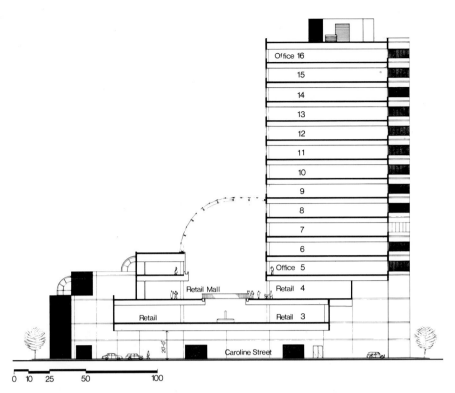

Although the retail mall is termed the Park, the image it projects remains that of a shopping center rather than a landscaped city park. A million dollars worth of landscaping is presently overshadowed by the brightly colored pipe sculptures in each floor well, some of which are used as fountains. The interiors designed by RTKL Associates of Dallas are rather neutral, planar surfaces except for the balustered guardrails. The space is dominated by the magnitude of the skylight, which dramatically opens it to the sky and to views of the surrounding office towers. The repetitive linear pattern of this glazed element grants the project its architectural image from both within and without. (See Figure 2-9.)

Office 16
15
14
13
12
11
10
9
8
7
6
Office 5
Retail Mall   Retail 4
Retail   Retail 3
20'-0"   Caroline Street

0 10 25   50   100

Transverse section.

Jud Haggard

227

BUTLER SQUARE
Minneapolis, Minnesota

ARCHITECT: *Phase I: Miller, Hansen, Westerbeck, Bell; Phase II: Arvid Elness Architects*
CONSTRUCTED: *Phase I: 1974   Phase II: 1980*
ATRIA: *each nominally 64 feet by 90 feet by 9 stories*

Miller, Hansen, Westerbeck, Bell

This double-atrium, adaptive reuse project is basically the result of design ingenuity. The original 1906 registered landmark warehouse building was based upon a 14-foot by 16-foot structural grid of heavy Douglas fir members. The 200-foot by 400-foot floors were unusable for commercial purposes without an atrium to serve as a source of light and air for the center of the building. Since the building was divided in half by a fire wall, two atria were designed to be built in two phases. The atria were formed by eroding the interior of the building and taking apart the timber frame structure. The resulting atria are stepped in plan and section according to the structural grid, being wider at the top on the south side and wider at the bottom on the north side. Some beams and columns in the atria have been left in place, without floors or ceilings, to suggest this means of creative demolition.

This building, two blocks from the Nicollet Mall, was vacant for ten years before developer Charles Coyers decided to build a multiuse center. Each phase has two floors of retail shops with seven floors of offices above. The atrium also helped to reduce the 20,000 square foot floor area to a more manageable rental size.

The basic design strategy was to preserve the strong integrity of this landmark building. The exterior received only minor alterations. Inside, brick walls, structure, and wood ceilings were sandblasted and left exposed. New mechanical systems were run in a raised floor. However, the Phase II mechanical system was significantly altered to make it twice as efficient as the Phase I system. (See Figure 4-16.) Sliding glass doors with cantilevered planters were installed to form the atrium facades. Materials salvaged from the demolition that formed the atrium were used to form spandrel and guardrail details. A new ridge-and-furrow skylight covers both atrium spaces.

The atria have a highly constructivist character, looking like a giant Tinkertoy project with the potential for continuous change. The rhythm of the structural frame flows throughout, granting a discipline surrounded by a great deal of spatial variety. The beam-to-column connections are celebrated with black iron connectors. The color of the old Douglas fir lends a glow of warmth, enhancing the nineteenth-century ambience. Natural light is not reflected well and the atrium section gets wider at the bottom, creating darker spaces under the overhanging bays. Visual associations across the atrium convey the sense of being in a village of offices and shops sharing the grand space.

View of Atrium I.

Phillip MacMillan James

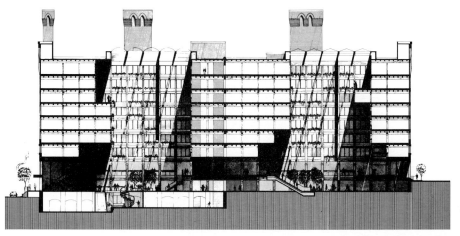

Longitudinal building section.

Second floor plan.

View of Atrium II.

Arvid Elness Architects

229

Design Study 46

CITICORP CENTER
New York, New York

ARCHITECT: *Hugh Stubbins and Associates*
CONSTRUCTED: *1978*
ATRIUM: *65 feet by 60 feet by 7 stories (nominal dimensions due to varied section)*

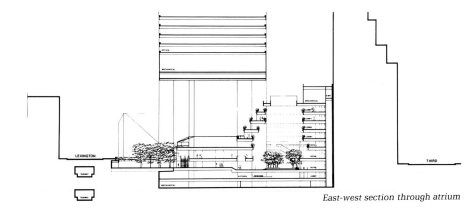

East-west section through atrium

Citicorp Center on Lexington Avenue in Manhattan is composed of three primary elements: a fifty-nine-story office tower, St. Peter's Church, and a seven-story commercial center. (See Figure 2-8.) These elements, along with an existing office building, together occupy an entire urban block. However, they are intertwined (except for the existing building) at the street and concourse levels in a complex system of circulation, access, and common spaces. Although the church and office tower are architecturally intriguing, only the commercial center will be presented here, since it contains the atrium.

The commercial center is organized around a seven-story atrium which gives it focus and orientation. It does not depend upon street frontage except for pedestrian access to the interior of the block. Thus, it is clearly an inward-oriented scheme. The bulk of the commercial center is actually located behind the office tower core, up against the party wall of the existing office building. Its primary access is via a sunken plaza (which also gives access to the subway) at the corner of 53rd Street

and Lexington Avenue. The passage then leads around the office tower core to the atrium, where escalators and an elevator bank provide vertical access to its many levels. Secondary entrances are provided from each side street via stairs. The approximately square atrium, stepped in section, is surrounded by galleries, with stores and restaurants on two sides. This sectional development of the commercial center is largely made possible by the daring scheme by which the office tower is raised eight stories above street level on four large piloti.

The atrium possesses the same clean elegance as the exterior of the complex. All planar surfaces are sheathed in natural-colored aluminum with minimalist

detailing. Guardrails are of tempered glass. The brick floor is surrounded by trees and other flora in raised planters. An abundance of daylight enters the ridge-and-furrow skylight. Artificial lights are prominent in rows of suspended can fixtures in the atrium and theatrical incandescent lights lining each gallery edge.

The result is an indoor version of the Rockefeller Center public spaces without the ice skating rink. The sunken exterior plaza is not very spacious because of the trees, which hinder circulation, and the large number of angled stairs. However, the atrium is a veritable oasis, available to the public for free use. It is a bright and cheerful space to be sought out as a refuge from the frantic cityscape. (See Figure 5-31.)

Hugh Stubbins & Associates

Norman McGrath

Design Study 47

TRUMP TOWER
New York, New York

ARCHITECT: *Swanke Hayden Connell Architects*
CONSTRUCTED: *1983*
ATRIUM: *nominally 68 feet by 68 feet to storefronts,*
6 stories

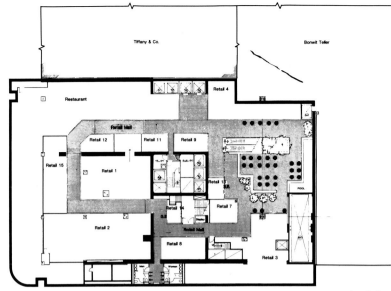

Garden concourse level plan.

The Trump Tower atrium was the first development of this kind built in response to the Special Fifth Avenue Zoning District enacted in 1971. Intended to enhance the retail activity along the world-famous avenue, this project includes fifty prestigious shops with direct ties on four levels to the Bonwit Teller department store located on 57th Street. A 20 percent floor area bonus was granted for this public pedestrian amenity, allowing the tower above the six-story atrium to include thirteen floors of offices and thirty-six floors of apartments. The residential lobby is entered from 56th Street whereas the office lobby is along the pedestrian concourse running from the main Fifth Avenue entrance to the IBM Court. (See Figure 2-10.) The atrium, located at the back of the site, opens onto the pedestrian concourse with paired escalators providing vertical connections. These pedestrian spaces are open from 9:00 a.m. to midnight for a variety of activities.

This is a partial atrium extending six floors from one level below the street to a landscaped roof terrace surrounding a sloped space-frame skylight. Nominally square in plan, with a few projecting corners, the atrium is surrounded by shops

varying in size from 160 to 3500 square feet (totalling 100,000 square feet), maximizing leasing flexibility. The majority of shops are along a pedestrian loop around the building core, away from the atrium. The dominant feature is a water wall which defines the atrium's east side, with water flowing down a six-story marble surface. On the garden level a restaurant is located next to the pool at the base of the water wall. (See Figure 5-40.)

Images of opulence and intensity pervade this place. Opulence is projected by the richly colored breccia perniche marble walls and floors, the pink-mirrored escalator sides and gallery spandrels, and the polished bronze handrails and store-

front frames. Intensity is both spatial and visual. Escalators along one side of the space afford dramatic and dynamic viewing opportunities. Both escalator and gallery guardrails are of tempered glass, increasing the sense of spatial excitement. A rich visual experience is created by the combination of rose–peach-colored marble with glistening water, highly textured landscaping, and bronze trim, all bathed in daylight. In addition to this, the multiple reflections and transparent surfaces result in a visual intensity which defies description. The glamour and excitement of the Trump Tower atrium are befitting to a setting on Fifth Avenue in the center of Manhattan.

Building section.

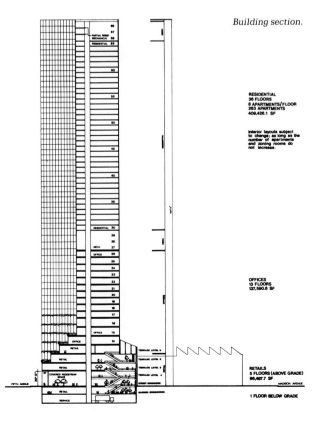

Index

Page numbers in *italic* refer to design studies of individual buildings.

About the Author

Michael J. Bednar is Associate Professor of Architecture at the University of Virginia School of Architecture where he formerly served as co-chairman of the Division of Architecture. He holds a Bachelor of Architecture degree from the University of Michigan and a Master of Architecture degree from the University of Pennsylvania. He is a practicing architect in Charlottesville, Virginia, a member of the American Institute of Architects, and chairman of the Charlottesville Planning Commission.

His previous affiliations include the practice of architecture with I. M. Pei & Partners in New York and with Geddes, Brecher, Qualls & Cunningham in Philadelphia and research at the School of Architecture at Rensselaer Polytechnic Institute. He has authored, coauthored, edited, or contributed to a number of architectural books and studies, particularly in the areas of architectural planning for special education and design for the handicapped and elderly.